GHOSTS
I'VE MET

Hans Holzer

BARNES
& NOBLE
BOOKS

NEW YORK

Book design by Lundquist Design, New York

ISBN-13: 978-0-7607-6631-6
ISBN-10: 0-7607-6631-2

Printed and bound in the United States of America

15 14 13 12 11 10 9 8 7 6 5 4 3

CONTENTS

THE GHOST HUNTER
RETURNS

WHEN MY FIRST BOOK, *Ghost Hunter,* was published, I helped sell it by appearing as a guest on numerous television and radio programs, sometimes with photographs taken by me at various haunted locations.

At first I was invited only by local interview programs which thought of the Ghost Hunter as a nice change of diet from their usual club women, product pushers, movie stars in town to publicize a new picture, and other such inexpensive entertainment. To their amazement, the audience liked me, and I was frequently asked to repeat. Naturally, nobody paid me.

In America, TV interview programs do not pay, on the theory that one hand washes the other. There were exceptions. In Pittsburgh, for instance, John Reed King and Westinghouse always made me feel like a king myself. They spotted me in the best part of the program, paid all my expenses, and in general understood the word "guest" in its original sense.

As the book picked up readers, letters started to pour in. Some were from people with questions on their mind—questions my book had reopened for them. Despite a disdainful husband or wife, many came forward to write to me of their own psychic adventures and ask for an explanation.

I always tried to answer these letters, and I frequently went to the writers' homes to talk to them. Now and then I found a genuine haunting and followed through on it. Sometimes I found self-deception or illness. I always tried to be helpful, but honest. My telephone started to ring at odd hours, and foreign mail mixed with the domestic correspondence.

Between October of 1963 and the summer of 1964, thousands of copies of *Ghost Hunter* were sold. As a result, psychic investigations and ghosts were no longer a matter for the lunatic fringe to talk about, or something people just don't mention in polite society. To the contrary, my career as a lecturer started to boom. I spoke before learned societies, colleges, women's clubs, even churches. Some of my audiences, to be sure, came to laugh or out of curiosity, but very few walked out unimpressed with the subject. Not with me.

Syndicated columnists like Earl Wilson wrote reams of material about my work of investigating and freeing ghosts (and people from ghosts). Wilson did it tongue-in-cheek, but he was sincere in his own way.

Local television eventually begat national television, and it was not long before people like Mike Douglas, Steve Allen, Art Linkletter, and Johnny Carson asked me to appear before their cameras. Steve Allen in particular played it straight and the results were a hushed audience as picture after picture of hauntings and ghosts was shown and explained. I played it straight, too, and the result was unusually good. Art Linkletter played it cautiously, asserting that he did not believe in ghosts *a priori,* but then he had a lot of impressionable sponsors. Linkletter's audiences wrote me letters for five months after my first appearance on the show, running into many hundreds, and clamoring for information, help in distress, and more of me on television.

On one occasion, Johnny Carson had one of the Gabor sisters as a fellow guest. We discussed witchcraft and she wanted to know if she wasn't a witch because of certain uncanny happenings in her life. I assured her that, to the best of my knowledge, she was not a w-i-t-c-h, spelled *that* way, and hoped fondly she would stop interrupting. By prearrangement with Carson's producers, I invited him to accompany me to a haunted house in Rye, New York, and assist in my investigation, which would then be telecast on his program. He quickly accepted the challenge, and I prepared the people living in the house for the coming of the great man.

Unfortunately, the event never materialized, for Carson's producers decided against the project.

After a hundred or so television and radio appearances I realized that I could best serve the cause of psychic knowledge by having a series of my own, and I committed myself to this goal.

Meanwhile, back at the office, the mail kept piling up. Many, many letters were from people literally beleaguered by the Unseen Forces. My help was not a matter of sometime curiosity, but of immediate do-or-die concern. Whenever the house in question was near New York, I went and helped. I arranged for a trip to California, paying my own expenses, to help a lady in distress who could no longer bear living in the haunted house she once called home. I had to turn down or delay investigating dozens of good cases for each case I could get involved in right away.

This book deals with some of my adventures as the Ghost Hunter after my first book was published. My life as a writer and researcher underwent considerable changes during this time. I was no longer an unknown who had to explain himself. People didn't always remember my name or my correct nickname, but whether they call me "the ghost man," "the ghost chaser," or "the fellow who talks to ghosts"—they could always place the face.

Then, too, I acquired an army of supporters. To be sure, they are not as tangible as the ones who sometimes stop me in the street and ask, "Haven't I seen you on TV?"—but they are the ones who really appreciate me more than anyone else. The ghosts I managed to pry loose from their erstwhile emotional prisons, with the help of Mrs. Ethel Johnson Meyers and other good mediums, attached themselves to me in a grand gesture of gratitude, and now and again they "come through" at séances or meetings held at various times and in many parts of the world.

Truly, *Some of my best Ghosts are Friends.*

GHOSTS
I'VE MET

THE TRANCE
LINGERS ON

T IS RATHER REMARKABLE, I think, that I have not received a single derogatory letter from anyone who read my first book, *Ghost Hunter*. On the other hand, cases kept pouring in, and in some instances, people who lived in haunted houses described by me write or call to tell me of their own uncanny experiences in these places.

One of my favorite cases was the Clinton Court case, in the very heart of New York's theatrical district. Old Moor, the sailor, and the little girl ghost who fell to her death on the winding stairs of Governor Clinton's old carriage house had a charm all their own.

Consequently I was rather pleased when I picked up the telephone on a cold morning in January of 1964, and heard a pleasant female voice telling me that its possessor had been a friend and frequent visitor of the people who rented the upstairs apartment at Clinton Court. I asked the lady, whose name was Alyce Montreuil, to put her experience in writing. A week or two later she obliged:

> The people who lived there from 1959 to 1963 are
> Danny Brown and Frank [Doc] Benner. Also Mr. Benner's

mother, who is a lady of eighty-six years. Several times when Mrs. Benner would go out on the porch, the front door would close, locking her out of the house. As you know, this porch is above the stone steps. The porch is sheltered on three sides, so there is no possibility of a draft blowing the door shut. Also, the door was never locked, but when she tried to open it, it always was. I have two dogs, a toy poodle and a Yorkshire terrier. These dogs have traveled all over the country, and visit everyone that I do. They are not nervous or frightened by anything. When I would go to visit at the Governor Clinton house, I always took the leashes off at the sidewalk, and they would run to the back. Mrs. Benner has a poodle, and my dogs were always anxious to play with her. When they got to the bottom of the steps, it was as though they had brakes. No matter who was at the top of the steps, they would not go up those stairs. I had to carry them. When it was time to go, they dreaded to go out on the porch, because they knew they had to go down those stairs. I would go to the bottom, walk away, call them, and they would start down. Half-way down they turned and ran back up and into the house. This might not seem like much, but if you knew these dogs—all they live for is to go for a walk. When I can't plead with them to go out, something is mighty strange. Once when Mr. Benner was ill, I stayed overnight. That front door I mentioned earlier, I locked myself. In the morning not only was it unlocked, the door was standing open. *I know* I locked it, because I slept on a couch downstairs, and I didn't want to sleep in a strange bed with the door unlocked. (You saw that neighborhood!) I took a lot of ribbing about that door. If "Mom" had been locked out once or twice, we would think nothing of it, but this happened to her every time she stepped out on the porch. Mrs. Benner is now living in Ohio with relatives, but her son and Mr. Brown live in New York.

Ghost Hunter, or, for that matter, this book, could not have been written were it not for invaluable aid given me by Ethel Johnson Meyers and others like her. Mrs. Meyers assisted me whenever I asked, and accompanied me to many of the haunted houses mentioned in this volume. It wasn't always possible for her to be with me, partly because the distance from New York is too great and I have no Foundation paying our expenses; and partly because the original witnesses to a haunting are sometimes mediumistic themselves and may very well create conditions similar to those under which their experience took place, thus making it at least probable that the uncanny event may again happen in my presence. In other cases I had the help of psychics who lived in the locality of the haunting, but nobody works quite the way Ethel Meyers does.

Although she had a busy career as a voice teacher, she gave in to demands for private sittings with recommended individuals, just as all great mediums have done from time to time. Once in a while I asked for her services outside of hauntings, when I thought that a group of important people should be acquainted with her unusual powers. Such was the case on March 5, 1964, when we assembled at the elegant home of public-relations expert Tam Noyes. Present were also Ann Steinert of the *New York Journal-American,* Ben Caruthers of Hilton-International Hotels, Gail Benedict, then Public Relations Director of the Savoy-Hilton Hotel in New York, a lady identified only as Bea A., whom I had never met or heard of before, and an equally unknown man named Tony.

Needless to say, Ethel Meyers had never met Mrs. Noyes or any of the others, except Miss Benedict, my wife and myself; there was no opportunity to exchange much conversation or probe for clues to the identity of those present. The newcomers were carefully kept from even giving their names in the presence of Mrs. Meyers.

In deep trance, Mrs. Meyers' control Albert took over, as he had done so many times in the past. We were prepared for some familiar greetings from loved ones, as often happens in these "open sittings." To my surprise, Albert proceeded to say that he had someone with him on the Other Side who wished to address a Bea. The lady whose second name I did not know sat up attentively. Presently, a faint but clearly audible voice came from Mrs. Meyers' entranced lips, and said, "Marion . . . Marion."

Bea A. seemed visibly shaken, but did not reply at first. "Marion" then proceeded to say that Margaret was with her, and that the baby was also present.

After the séance, I asked the lady about these names. She readily confirmed that Margaret and the baby were indeed part of her immediate family, who had passed on, one only recently. The medium could not possibly have known this, of course.

As the sitting continued, another discarnate personality spoke through the medium. It was obvious that someone else was speaking, for the voice, tonal quality and even facial expressions were completely dissimilar to "Marion's." "This is Mother," the visitor said, and Ben Caruthers bent forward eagerly to catch every word. Evidently he had recognized the caller.

A conversation ensued between them, and the visitor mentioned that "brother George" was with her.

Later Mr. Caruthers confirmed that he had had a brother named George, who had passed on some time before. He was quite sure it was the voice of his mother he had heard. Again, Mrs. Meyers had never met Mr. Caruthers before, nor had she any knowledge of his late brother George.

Finally, Albert returned and took over the "instrument," as he usually calls the medium. "You'll get some action regarding a television adaptation of your book," he said in a jolly tone.

Nothing would please me more, but up to then nothing had transpired that would have given me the slightest inkling of such a project. Nevertheless, the following morning I received a telephone call from a man interested in just such an idea. True, it has not materialized, but then Albert did not say it would.

One of my close friends was the late *New York Daily News* columnist Danton Walker, whose haunted house in Rockland County I had helped "de-ghost." It came as a shock to me when I heard of his untimely passing in the summer of 1960, while attending a revival of a play he wrote years ago, in Provincetown, Massachusetts. As soon as I could, I arranged for a séance to see if my late friend had not left some unresolved problems in the material world. Knowing that his family had been fairly estranged, and that his "family" in the later years of his life consisted of his assistant, Connie Soloyannis, and his "man," Johnny T., I was naturally very surprised to hear that Johnny had not been left the house in Rockland County, or anything else of substance.

The séance was an attempt to find out if Danton was pleased with the state of things, and I told Mrs. Meyers nothing further than that a sitting would take place on September 7, 1960.

We went to the apartment belonging to Johnny T., next door to Danton's old apartment, on East Forty-sixth Street, in New York.

As she sat in a soft chair, Ethel Meyers received a first clairvoyant impression of a presence. "Craybill . . . or something like it . . ." she muttered. I found out later that Danton's childhood home was called Carabell.

I handed her a watch given by Danton Walker to Johnny. As soon as Mrs. Meyers touched the metal, she started to cough violently.

"What's the matter with my eyes now? Feels like someone struck me in the eye."

"Danton could hardly see the last couple of years," Johnny said. Mrs. Meyers looked around the circle. Present, in addition to Johnny T., were Connie Soloyannis; Anita B., a publicist, and Gordon V., both friends of the late Danton Walker. But Mrs. Meyers moved her head in Mr. Soloyannis' direction.

"Connie . . . checks."

Later, Connie Soloyannis confirmed that Walker had been too weak to sign some checks in his last hours, and had been concerned over it. Now Mrs. Meyers drifted into trance. There was silence for a moment, and we could hear each other breathe as we waited for the appearance of someone we all knew well. That way, identification would be possible on the spot.

Ethel Meyers seemed to find it difficult to speak. Her face assumed a squinting expression, and suddenly I realized that it strongly resembled the facial characteristics of my late friend Danton.

"Tsk, tsk. . . ."

It sounded very much like a peculiar sound Walker liked to make, when addressing someone.

"I can't make it . . . pain's gone . . . why did they turn off the light?! I wasn't gone yet. Why did they have to turn off the light. I want to know! I wasn't dead when I got over here. I gotta know. Everything is going backwards. It hurts still. I don't like to look. It's funny . . . very droll." I remembered that "droll," an unusual word, was one of Danton's favorite expressions.

The entranced medium was now fully under the control of my late friend.

"My friends are like glass, the fish in bowl lives in a glass house."

I asked if he had any unfinished business he wanted us to know about. "Duplicate will . . . changed five years ago . . ."

Suddenly the entity became very agitated. Expressing his

unhappiness with certain arrangements made, he slipped away before we could question him further.

On December 1, we attempted to make contact once more. Again Danton talked about papers and wills, but the details were of such private nature that I cannot disclose them here.

Again, on December 9, Danton communicated through Ethel Meyers, and complained about his eye and difficulty in speaking. I remembered, of course, that he had died of a stroke and had, indeed, had difficulties of speech before his passing. What seemed to bother him was that his two trusted friends had not received a share of the estate.

Later, I found out that Johnny had made his peace with the heirs, and I haven't heard anything further since except for one little detail. A pewter jar, on which the late Danton Walker's house ghost had impressed his heavy ghostly thumb, had been in England to be psychometrized. This happened in 1952. Years later, I finally managed to see my good friend Michael Bentine again, and he returned the jar to my custody, where it is now. I don't know whether Danton wanted Johnny T. or me to have it, but for want of a better claim, I shall preserve it just as I have preserved the memory of a good and generous friend, Danton Walker.

Just as talented in a psychic sense as Ethel Meyers, but different in that she is a clairvoyant medium rather than a direct-trance medium, was Betty Ritter, of New York City. Over the years I "sat" with her time and again, and also had her along on some haunted-house expeditions as well. She appeared on television and radio with me, and was, beyond the shadow of a doubt, a very good medium.

From the wealth of material confirming her abilities and at the same time throwing light on the World Beyond, I have been able to select only a small amount.

On May 10, 1963, in the presence of my wife, Catherine, and

myself, Betty went into her special brand of "walking trance," in which she obtains and gives messages purporting to come from Beyond the Veil. Although she knew nothing whatever about Catherine's family, she managed to mention Fedor (my wife's brother), Maria (her grandmother), a man with the initial A (her father, Alexander), Rose (her only sister), and Anatol (her half brother).

She also mentioned a Mr. Zimmerman. Derk Zimmerman is a Pittsburgh television producer with whom I have had frequent dealings.

But I was not the only one who found Betty's messages and predictions fascinating. Many things she had predicted to me over the years have already happened. But they are of a private nature, sometimes not very spectacular, yet to me they were indications of her clairvoyant talents.

Like other good psychics, Betty eventually had to go professional in order to make ends meet. She saw only those who have been recommended to her by friends or researchers like myself, and she charged them a very modest fee for her time. Various research societies also made use of her services.

Mrs. Walter Hanley, of Jackson Heights, New York, was one of the members of a group belonging to the American Society for Psychic Research which sat with Betty under the sponsorship of Allen McRoberts, one of the leaders of the Society.

Here is her statement:

During the winter of 1952 a group of eight or ten of us met each week with Mrs. Ritter [then Betty Rogers]. One evening in early spring, Mrs. Ritter, after coming out of a deep trance, said she had been told that she would hold a winning ticket in the forthcoming Sweepstakes. A month or two later we were not surprised to hear that she held a winning ticket and her forecast had come true.

At another meeting, as told to me by a scientist attending the meeting, the following incident occurred. He had purchased a package months before, had placed it on a closet shelf at his home and practically forgotten it. Remembering it this particular evening, he brought it to the meeting unopened and asked Mrs. Ritter to go into trance and then describe its contents. As he hadn't opened the box since its purchase he only remembered its contents vaguely.

Coming out of trance, Mrs. Ritter sat up and in amazement said she had just been in Egypt. She described catacombs—a large place with mummies all around the walls. She then saw two men coming towards her carrying a small box. She wondered at this and thought it silly that it took two men to carry this small box. They kept repeating, "Remember the box. Remember the box."

Inside she saw a small mummy in two colors, which she described; she also saw the letters of the mummy's name, and, on the bottom, the name of the man who had carved it.

The box was then opened and all of Mrs. Ritter's descriptions were found to be correct.

Incidentally, the name of the winning horse in the Sweepstakes was "High Spirits"!

On still another occasion, Betty Ritter conducted a private sitting with Mr. and Mrs. Harry C. Bricker, two cautious students of psychical research.

Here is the report of this séance:

Extracts from a sitting held with Betty Ritter on January 24, 1951, at 8:30, Mr. and Mrs. Harry C. Bricker.

While she was making a prayer, Mrs. Ritter printed a W. and an E., and between them she doodled a little tree. She also wrote the word Frank and the letter L. After the prayer was finished, she said:

"When things come to me during my prayer, I have to write them down so I don't forget them. [To H.C.B.] I saw you sitting at a table making plans. Who are W. and E.? Frank and L.?"

For some time before this sitting, I had spent much time making planting plans for our summer place in Connecticut—plans involving principally the planting of many trees. Note the automatic doodling of a tree. Frank and AL (Mrs. Rogers got the latter as L)—are the two men who are going to help us do the planting. "It seems very silly, but I keep seeing a horse's head."

My brother-in-law, who died about a year ago, brought with him, when he came from the West to live with us, an engraving of the head of a race-horse, of which he was very proud. He mentioned it frequently and made many jokes about it. He hung it up in his room the very day he arrived, and it is still hanging on the wall.

"I see a man, very strong and broad-shouldered. I feel my own shoulders broadening. He is not tall, rather short. He must have been very strong, I get the feeling. [Suddenly] I still am! That's him saying it, not me! . . . He is holding up Masonic symbols. . . . He is holding up two fingers, like this [holding up her hand with the index and middle fingers held up and separated]. I see the number 2. He keeps smiling all the time, and he keeps calling, 'Harry! Harry!' "

My brother-in-law was short and broad. He was very strong and proud of it. He was a Mason, a Shriner, and proud of it. He was fond of fun, and always smiling. My name is Harry. The number 2 and the two fingers may signify that he is together with our son, who died a month before he did.

Mrs. Bricker: "How is he connected with us?"

Betty Ritter: "He says, '*Schwester.*' Was he your brother? [To my wife]"

He was my wife's brother.

"I see the letter A lying down. That's a bad condition. I feel a pain here [holding her stomach]. No good news for her. She's a child? I see the number three."

Mrs. Bricker: "Will she ever get well?"

Betty Hitter: "No, she never will. It's better that she should pass on."

Alice is our niece, a child of three. Only after the sitting did we learn that for the last five weeks she had had diarrhea. The doctors say she is hopelessly ill of a nerve ailment and that she will never be normal.

"That strong man I talked about—beside him, I see a heart."

My brother-in-law had a bad heart and died of a heart attack.

"Beside him I also see the letter R."

Possibly his sister Rose, also dead.

"I see the letters H and L."

Henry and Leopold—brother and cousin of my wife— died recently within a few weeks of each other. They and my brother-in-law had been rather close in life. Note the significant coupling of these two initials.

"I see the strong man again, and beside him I see a lot of shoes and the letter S. Did this other person make shoes? Was he a shoe salesman?"

The letter S may stand for my wife's uncle Shep, who in life manufactured sports footwear. He died about two years ago. He and my brother-in-law were close cronies.

"I see a very young-looking man, I see him driving about in a car very much to and from New York City."

Mrs. Bricker: "What did he do?"

"I see many books—he studied a great deal."

Mrs. Bricker: "What subject was he studying?"

Betty Ritter: [To the "spirit"]: "Please tell me . . . Please . . . [To us]: Never mind. He will tell me later. If I try too hard, I become tense, and that's no good. I must keep relaxed . . . [Later] He is opening a book to me and showing me a picture. It's the picture of a skeleton. Was he a doctor? . . . And now he is showing me the doctor's symbol—the snakes, you know.. . . . Now I see the number 8."

Our son was very youthful-looking for a doctor. He got his M.D. at twenty-one and died at twenty-four. He was slender and boyish-looking. He drove a great deal between New York City and Connecticut, usually two or three times a week. He died in August, the eighth month.

Submitted,

Harry C. Bricker.

Miss Kay P., whose full name is known to me, and who lived on Long Island, New York, reported to me the remarkable success of an hour spent with Betty Ritter:

In May of 1960 I had a private reading by Betty Ritter; at the time I was very concerned about my son whom I hadn't heard from in over a year and I didn't know of his whereabouts. Mrs. Ritter told me at this time, at this reading, in the early part of May, that I would see him in a few months, that I would run into him and that I would be very shocked when I saw him and that he was in desperate need of my help and would be ashamed to get in touch with me.

A few months later, in August, to be exact, I was contacted indirectly about him and his whereabouts and indeed I was shocked. He had gotten into trouble and I went to see him. At this same reading Mrs. Ritter mentioned a woman, Gertrude G. I told her I knew no one with such a name, but she turned out to be my son's attorney.

I had never heard of this woman and yet the name was exact. Betty Ritter also told me that I would see my son somewhere in the vicinity of McDougal Street or 8th Street, in New York City, and that too proved correct.

She also told me of someone with the initial "A" being ill or in trouble (this initial "A" stood for my employer); and that someone not too old, a man in the spirit world (her husband had departed five years ago and was a man in his very early 50's), was holding up one finger, which indicated that it was a call from the spirit world that this person with the initial "A" was being called in one day, one month, one year, and nearly to one day one year later, in the month of May 1961, this employer of mine passed away.

A friend of mine from South America, who knew very little about the subject of psychic research when I first met her, eventually was so fascinated by what I told her of the work being done, that she decided to test these truths for herself.

Monica R. was in her middle twenties and lived in Jackson Heights, New York. Her personal circumstances were not known to me at the time she went to see Betty Ritter. I had only met her a cou-

ple of times socially and never discussed her family or private life
with her.

After seeing Betty Ritter, she communicated with me on
November 20, 1963:

> As you requested I am writing you about my visit with
> Mrs. Betty Ritter. She started by speaking of an *L* with a
> heart condition, on the Other Side. *L* was my father, who
> indeed passed away due to a heart condition. Then she
> mentioned a separation between myself and a husband *G*.
> My first husband's name began with a *G*. She mentioned
> my grandmother with the letter *S*. Also true. In the begin-
> ning she brought out the letter *J*. I asked for clarification,
> and eventually Mrs. Ritter mentioned *Jose,* a person in this
> life, who is actually my brother-in-law.
>
> Then the real shock was *P*. Actually my second hus-
> band's name was Domingo, but I always called him "Pepe"
> and the nickname stuck and everyone, including his family,
> called him "Pepe." All his letters to me are signed "Pepe."
> The message was:
>
> "Keep your chin up for I'm with you and guiding you."
> Then the letter *M* was shown in connection with *P,* which
> could mean "Modesto," who was the other young man
> with Pepe in the accident.

Nobody was more remarkable in his particular specialty of psychic photography than English-born John Myers. This wealthy
industrialist and philanthropist needed exposure to the barbs of
nonbelievers the way, as Jack Benny once put it, "a stag needs a hat-
rack." Nevertheless, on my urging, he on occasion consented to vol-
unteer his presence and psychic acumen for experiments in psychic

photography under the strictest of test conditions.

In April of 1964 I asked John Myers to conduct another such an experiment for the benefit of a small group of people, including among others Pat Davis, an editor and reporter for the United Press. I asked her to be the actual person to handle the photographic paper during the experiment. Neither John Myers nor I ever touched the paper, developing liquids or anything else connected with the experiment.

When Myers was present in the well-lit room, faces and figures appeared on the papers. When we repeated the experiment with an identical batch of papers a few minutes later, with Myers out of the room, nothing happened. The papers were—and remained—blank. His presence within a few yards is evidently necessary to yield positive results. Jacob Gerstein, attorney-at-law, witnessed the event and here is his statement:

At about 5 P.M. on Saturday, April 25, 1964, I met with Dr. Myers at his apartment in Sutton Place South, at his request. Present on this occasion were Dr. S. A. Bell, a Madison Avenue dentist; a lady friend of his whose name I do not recall, and a Miss Lee Perkins.

Dr. Myers, in the presence of these other persons, told me the following. Dr. Bell and the two ladies had earlier that afternoon purchased at the Willoughby-Peerless photographic shop at Forty-third Street and Lexington Avenue three packets of photographic paper. Dr. Myers added that while he had accompanied the trio to the store, he had not touched the packets, nor had he selected the shop for the purchase. Dr. Bell and the two ladies confirmed these statements. Dr. Bell added that he and the ladies had initialed the packets; that they were unopened and that they had been in his possession since the moment they were purchased.

Dr. Bell stated that he found himself unable to attend the demonstration Dr. Myers had scheduled for that evening and asked me to suggest what should be done with the packets. I asked Dr. Myers if he perchance had a large envelope and a stapling machine. Dr. Myers produced them. I then asked Dr. Bell to place the three packets in the envelope. Before this was done, I examined each of the packets. They bore three sets of initials. Dr. Bell told me that he and the ladies had affixed their initials to the packets when they were purchased. I can vouch for their condition and state that none of the packets had been opened at the time they were placed in the large envelope. I then stapled the envelope and affixed Scotch tape to it. I then had Dr. Bell and the ladies place their initials where the flap meets the envelope.

At about 8 P.M. that evening, I joined about 20 other persons at Dr. Myers' apartment. In the presence of the others, I personally opened the large envelope. I examined it very closely and confirm that it had not been opened or tampered with.

In full view of the guests, this is what occurred. First, the three packets were withdrawn. They were placed on the dining-room table alongside of which were three large, shallow, metal pans filled with liquid. I attended to these details.

Dr. Myers requested one of the guests, a Miss Davis, to come forward. I know of my own knowledge that Miss Davis had never met Dr. Myers before in her life, since we were both introduced to her at the same time by Hans Holzer. I also asked Miss Davis whether she had ever met Dr. Myers and she said she had not, until that evening.

Dr. Myers requested Miss Davis to take her choice of

the three packets and to open it. After she made her selection and before the packet was opened, a number of persons, including me, examined it very closely. It was sealed tight and carried three sets of initials. Miss Perkins, who was present, identified the initials as being hers and also those of Dr. Bell and his friend.

Dr. Myers requested Miss Davis to open the packet that she had selected, to remove the individual sheets therefrom and to submerge them into the first of the three pans. She did so, one by one.

To the astonishment of everyone present, and I again repeat this was in full view of all of the guests, manifestations consisting of photographs of persons and objects appeared on the various sheets. Among them is this photograph which is clearly a likeness of the late Frank Navroth. I know this to be a fact because I knew and had occasion to see Mr. Navroth many times before he passed on.

Another photograph which "came through" was one of a young girl who was identified by one of the guests as being a likeness of his niece who passed on about five or six years ago. A third was a remarkable likeness of the late Congressman Adolph Sabath.

Undoubtedly there are other gifted mediums waiting to be discovered all over the world, and I am most eager to find them. Mediums, incidentally, should be trained in this very difficult work, and the British College of Psychic Science in London is about the only place where this was—and is—being done on a reliable, scientific basis. In America, we have as yet to establish a comparable institution. There was, and is, interesting work done by the American Society of Psychic Research, the Edgar Cayce Foundation, and Parapsychology Foundation, but nothing comparable to the British College.

My own group, the Committee for the Investigation of Paranormal Occurrences, had neither staff nor funds to conduct a program even in the most rudimentary form.

Thankfully, Ethel Meyers, Betty Ritters, John Myers, and others helped us understand the World Beyond the Veil.

WHEN THE GHOST HUNTER MEETS A GHOST

T HE TIME COMES in every researcher's life when he wants to experience personally something with which he has hitherto been involved only through other persons. Mind you, I became convinced that so-called Ghosts are very real many years ago simply by the weight of evidence obtained from what I, and others, consider reliable sources. After all, very few people doubt that Antarctica exists even if they have never been there themselves; others have and have reported this fact.

In science the quality of observation and of the observer are just as important as the observed facts themselves. I get tired of being asked, "Do you believe in ghosts?" Belief has nothing to do with it.

I deal in facts. Opinion is a detriment when observing, an advantage *only after* the facts are in.

As time went on, my own keen but rather detached and critical interest in the Uncanny, the so-called Supernatural, yielded much fascinating material. I learned to sift the false from what seemed to me probably true material, and then went into the corroboration of

this material with the same approach I use when I do purely historical research. Sometimes I tell a librarian that that is all I'm doing,
for checking the veracity of ghostly statements is not always apt to
bring too much co-operation from a stuffy librarian!

Over the years, starting with picking up a technical book on the
subject as a teenager, up to today, I have talked to a great many people who have had Sixth Sense experiences and I have learned to
evaluate their testimony.

When I made my initial survey for the Parapsychology
Foundation back in 1960 and 1961, I used a specially designed
questionnaire which helped me determine the nature of my witnesses, their moods and motivations and other pertinent facts about
the cases.

I still use this "interview in depth" technique in all my investigations, and simple story telling won't do the trick. When I report
someone's experiences, you can be sure I have looked into the person's background and checked other details before accepting the
story.

By the same token, one must not discount a person's testimony
simply because it sounds odd, or does not fit into the accepted
scheme of things. This is a common mistake orthodox scientists
make when dealing with parapsychological material. Unless one has
"been there" when an event happened, or has available some strong
facts that would tend to lessen a person's value as a witness presumably telling the truth, one has no scientific basis for being a "doubting Thomas." If mere doubting were by itself science, the world
would not have radio, television, space flight, and practically every
other unusual sign of progress we now possess, for all of these
accomplishments of mankind were at one time doubted and assailed
as impossible by the more orthodox element among the men of science and learning.

The point I wish to make is that secondhand information can

be just as exact and valid as firsthand experiences and in many branches of accepted science it is the only way one obtains information and knowledge. Historical researchers rely entirely on other people's reports, even other people's opinions; there is hardly a modern doctrine or branch of learning where the testimony and word of accepted authorities is not an important and integral part of the current structure of belief, conviction, view—whatever the "now" of scientific thinking may be called at any given time.

In psychic research, our main body of information is people's observations. This forms the cushion upon which the basic theories are built. Added to this are two types of scientific participation: laboratory experiments and spontaneous phenomena.

Laboratory experiments were for many years conducted by Dr. Joseph Rhine of Duke University and certainly proved the existence of a nonphysical world which Dr. Rhine calls the "World of the Mind." He amply proved the actuality of "psi" factors in determining the "guessing" of sequences in card tests, and the falling of experimental dice has shown that the mind can influence their courses. But the greater human experiences of precognition, premonitions, apparitions, physical manifestations ranging from footsteps to actual materializations of human forms—these cannot successfully be produced at will within the confines of a laboratory simply because they require the presence of an actual, true emergency—an emotional factor not present in a laboratory. It is this point that some orthodox scientists fail to appreciate.

Of course not every valid scientific fact need be capable of duplication at will. Some of the fireworks in the heavens, stars colliding or otherwise behaving in a unique fashion, may not be reproduced in the laboratory; yet, they are nevertheless valid scientific facts of great importance.

The second class of observable phenomena is called spontaneous because they are unplanned and one cannot always know when and where they will occur, or even why they do. Sitting in a haunted house all night long will seldom produce anything more than a stiff back, unless one uses a trance medium the way I have done and am doing.

Yet one may walk into a house with psychic connotations and unexpectedly something does occur that is extraordinary.

As Ghost Hunter I always consider such experiences a bonus, not expecting them, but happy if they do come my way. For years, I had to be content with other people's testimonies, but as time went on, I discovered a subtle change taking place within me. Evidently by associating with psychics so much I had also developed my own latent powers to a point where I might have firsthand experiences in the psychic realms. Mind you, just because I do on occasion hear or see "something" uncanny, I haven't stopped taking others' testimonies seriously. I am not a medium. But I am convinced that within all of us there is a budding psychic sense, born into us completely naturally, which can be developed as time goes on. Some have more of it than others, but to me it seems a lost or suppressed faculty worthy of attention.

As I have told my radio and television audiences time and again, there is really nothing supernatural in the world—there are only some facets of human personality not yet fully understood that should be explored further.

From time to time I have seen whitish outlines in darkened rooms where a medium has assured me she saw a figure. How much of this was mere suggestion and how much of it objective truth is hard to tell.

My first experience with an apparition in good light came when I was quite alone in the room. Years ago, my father and I were living in a two-room penthouse apartment on the nineteenth floor of a building on New York's Riverside Drive. The door between the two rooms was shut, and the entrance door, as well as the door to the terrace, was always kept locked at night. Nobody could come into my room by natural means.

Because I suffer at times from low blood pressure and migraine headaches, I sleep with my head on several pillows. One night, in my sleep my head slid off the pillow and dangled down from the bed. Had I remained in this position for more than a few moments, I would have had an attack of severe migraine and been an invalid for a week.

Suddenly I awoke to find a gentle hand pushing my head back onto the pillow. The room was fairly bright because of the light of the moon pouring through the many windows—practically an entire wall was made of windows. Looking up, I saw next to my bed the white-gowned figure of my late mother, who had passed on years before. It took some moments to rally my senses, and by the time I had fully come to, she had vanished into thin air. But I am sure of what I saw. It was not a dream. Dreams don't cast shadows, and my mother did just that! Evidently she had come to me when there was an emotional need for her to do so.

My first physical contact with a ghost happened in 1962, when my wife and I went ghost hunting in Connecticut. I received more than I bargained for when I accompanied my good friend, psychic Ethel Johnson Meyers, to a 1,700-foot-high mountaintop in the deepest woods of Connecticut.

Not only did I investigate a haunted house, but I was touched by "Grandma Thurston," who passed in the eighteenth century, but is still very much in evidence in the 1754 house atop Mount Riga.

In an almost inaccessible part of New England, this wooden structure was once owned by the Wentworth family, but then belonged to the Sawtelles. They took their ghostly guest in stride.

Time and again steps were heard when there was nobody visible, the door opened of its own volition, the dog was nervous for no reason, and once, when one of the men went to fetch some drinks on a tray, they were all spilled for no accountable reason. Perhaps Grandma Thurston, Puritan that she was, didn't approve of drinks.

At any rate, we arrived at this picturesque, candle-and-kerosene-lighted house (no electricity or telephone up here!) around 10 P.M. The "loom room," the oldest part of the house, was then a guest room. A woman staying there had clearly heard the sound of a loom going at night—even though there was nobody around.

As I walked into the main room of the little house, and stood before the fireplace, I suddenly felt someone tug at my elbow. It was unmistakable, a strong, yet gentle tug. I turned around. Nobody was behind me or near me. I talked to the owner about it.

He nodded. Oh, yes, they all had been tugged at the elbow at various times in that spot. Seems as if Grandma Thurston wanted attention after all these years!

At midnight we drove still farther into the wilderness, to an Indian rock deep in the backwoods. In the still of the mountain night, I could clearly hear the whispering of voices. Eventually I made out a whitish shape above the rock.

Ethel Meyers made contact with the spirit of the Indian, executed, they say, by white settlers, when he tried to regain his lost homestead, back in the eighteenth century when there were still Indians in that part of the country. After a short séance, the white form dissolved, and the voices trailed off, until they were indistinguishable from the faint croaking of a frog in the underbrush.

Ethel Meyers had a glow on her face. The restless one was free, thanks to her good services.

THE TOWN-HOUSE
GHOST

T HE REMARKABLE THING about this case is that it introduced my wife to the realities of physical phenomena, just as Grandma Thurston's restless ghost had brought a firsthand experience to me for the first time.

Of course that is not the most important thing about this case by a long shot—the quality of the persons reporting the ghost was very high and their power of observation keen. By the same token, they were not overanxious for publicity and for that reason I will withhold the actual location of the Town House. But the names and everything else about this case are true.

In November, 1963, I received an urgent telephone call from Mrs. Jan Bryant Bartell, who occupies part of a very old house in New York's Greenwich Village. I asked her to put her experiences into a short report, which arrived the following morning:

> I live with my husband and dog in a converted mansion off lower Fifth Avenue which was the turn-of-the-century Town House of Lillian Nordica, the opera diva. I have heard, too, that at one time or another, the house was

owned and occupied by the Thomas Fortune Ryan family. In addition to its own distinction, the house is flanked by one of the former Mark Twain residences and the erstwhile family home of the poetess, Emma Lazarus. I live on the very top floor, which in the era of Mauve Decade elegance had been the servants' quarters. From the day I took up abode here, despite the quaint charm of the apartment, I have sensed *something dark and brooding,* something of unrest enveloping the premises.

Now, I no longer merely sense this amorphous, but pervasive quality. I know. Briefly, this knowledge has been built up, during a five-year residence, upon the following:

1. The sound of something having been dropped (often quite loudly) which upon investigation discloses—nothing. And always, always, the sound of footsteps, sometimes tentatively, sometimes furtively, but always audibly and ceasing suddenly to be followed by the *faint rustling* in a room that announces another presence.

2. The appearance one evening at a recently vacated dinner table of a small, dried grape, neatly centered upon a dessert plate whose contents had quite thoroughly been consumed a few moments before.

3. The fright of a cleaning woman upon claiming to have seen a woman in white go quickly through a small room. The woman assumed it was I until she found *me* in another part of the apartment. This same room having a vague sound of activity in it around two-thirty and three o'clock in the morning and too often for my shredded nerves; the sense of a tangible presence having come to *stand beside my bed* to jerk me fearfully awake from a pre-sleep state.

4. The agitated actions of a dog whom we lost a year

and a half ago, who would stare into apparently empty space and then, cautiously stalk something, or someone, out of the room.

5. A new dog is strongly reacting to things my material vision cannot penetrate. Two weeks ago, this highly sensitive and intelligent puppy was drawn in the small hours of the morning to an empty (?) chair at which she sniffed violently, raised her head, laid back her ears and quickly retreated.

6. A few evenings ago, my husband and I were having a quiet conversation when, suddenly, a wild weird sound came from the puppy who was lying facing the disturbed and disturbing small room. We looked in amazement to see her mouth opened wide, with the half-wail, half-moan sounds coming from her throat, all the while she quite plainly followed the progress of someone (or something).

When we rose to investigate, she entered the room gingerly, sniffed hard at the pillows upon my bed—and retreated.

There have been other things which I shan't attempt to catalogue here—little things and yet they loom large in creating the over-all motif in psychic tapestry.

By profession, I am an actress and writer—and an ardent amateur archaeologist. I seem to have a rather peculiar magnetism which prompts people to stare at me unabashedly and which often draws quite perfect strangers to me with unsolicited confidences. For some time, I have become increasingly aware that I am endowed with the psychic gift for precognition and for evoking a potpourri of odd little occurrences which more mundane personalities are content to label "coincidences" and dismiss at that.

My husband and I are trying to find other quarters, but until they materialize, we need help.

My wife and I went to the Bartell home in November 1963, and found it a charming, moody Victorian apartment, furnished with impeccable taste and embued with a timelessness that belied its disturbed state.

We received a most cordial welcome from Contessa, the large, brown "puppy." She was a most exuberant dog and it seemed hard to think that she could lie on the floor frozen stiff with fear of the Unknown.

Mr. Bartell, who was present, was the manager of a large chain of restaurants. He was not as emotional as his wife, but he too had been impressed with the strange atmosphere of the house.

"Is there anything else you haven't told me in your letter?" I asked Mrs. Bartell.

"I have frequently been fingered lightly over my face and arms," she said.

"You mean, lightly touched by someone you could not see?"
She nodded.

"In the larger room—there is a sitting room leading into a large dining room—in the larger room I've smelled scents I never use," Mrs. Bartell added, "and of course there was that shadow of a person I saw, and always those footsteps without explanation."

"Quite," I said, and walked about the apartment. The bedroom was separated from the other two rooms by a wall, and one had to enter it from the common corridor. Evidently the apartment had once been the living quarters of servants, as was the custom with the top-floor apartments of town houses in the nineteenth century. Also, I felt very strongly that structural changes had taken place, and that perhaps the wall had been taken out and doors rearranged. Later, Mrs. Bartell confirmed this.

"Let us sit down and go over your experiences once more," I suggested. "And please start at the beginning."

Mrs. Bartell, a vivacious young lady with dark hair and

sparkling eyes, thought for a moment, as if to put her recollections into proper sequence.

"The beginning was in October five years past, when we moved into the apartment. I had not been living here more than two weeks when it came to my attention that there was a certain book I wanted to own which was being handled by Samuel Weiser, a bookseller who specializes in books on occult phenomena. I called the store and I asked if he had the book and he said no, but that it would take only a few days to get it.

"In a few days he called me and said, 'Can you come in? I have the book you wanted.' It was a day on which I couldn't make that particular visit and he offered to send a delivery boy over with it. I opened the door to a wildly disheveled, pale, quaking little fellow who stood outside with my book. Without saying hello, he said, 'Lady, is this house haunted?' I looked at him in amazement and said, 'Why do you ask?' 'Because *somebody* followed me up the stairs!'

"This was after I had been here two weeks, and I had already heard footsteps. Constantly. I had told my husband and was accused of having great imagination. It was quite a shock to have a perfect stranger confirm all this.

"During the entire time I've lived here, there have been the sounds of footsteps. They come down the hall and appear to stop at the little door of that small room. I usually sleep in that room, since my husband snores a little and it makes me nervous.

"I stay up reading quite late. At 2:30 or 3:00 A.M. every morning, there is constant movement behind the couch, and the hair in back of my neck stands up. Sometimes I say 'For God's sake, God bless you, please I'm exhausted, I want to get some sleep,' and it stops; it always stops."

"Always at the same time?" I asked.

"Yes, between 2:30 and 3:00 A.M. Also I became very ill the first week we moved in here, and I have been ill on and off more than I have ever been in my life since we came to this apartment. I have almost never quite been well in this place.

"We were here about two weeks and we had no curtains at the windows, we hadn't yet had a chance to have them made, and it was a very bright moonlit night. I was lying on the divan just ready to fall asleep. There were no lights whatsoever in the apartment, and I was ready to turn over on my left side, that would be facing the wall. Just as I turned over and was ready to sink into sleep, *a huge black shadow* went right across that wall and I screamed. My dog almost jumped up to the ceiling, my husband came running out of his room and I was sitting there, a shaking wreck. My husband insisted I'd seen the reflection of the trees outside, but the trees stop at the third floor and it could not very well have been a tree.

"Then there are sounds as though things have been crashed to their destruction in this apartment. I look about and think that I am going to find one of my pieces of Wedgwood shattered, a perfume bottle or something, yet nothing has been touched, nothing has been disturbed, nothing is broken."

"Do you ever feel a human presence?" I asked.

"Mainly in this small room. There have been any number of occasions when I have just been ready to fall asleep. Times without number I have lain there and felt, and sensed, and heard all at once this sudden *presence,* which kept me awake and, of course, there is nothing to be seen.

"After this has gone on long enough I sleep with all the lights on."

"Anything else?"

"Many times I would be in the kitchen and I would turn around very quickly because I felt somebody behind me. Of course there wasn't. I discussed this with a friend of mine who is a highly intuitive person. She got very pale, and said, 'Well, I wasn't going to frighten you, Jan, but now I'm going to tell you.

" 'You recall when I came up to visit you. We had been talking and you were going to show me something and had left the room, but I wasn't aware that you had gone. I was standing there reading something when I thought I heard you directly behind me and I turned around to say, "Jan, this is very interesting." Of course you were in the bedroom at the time.' "

"Who was the person?" I asked.

"A very close friend of mine, Mrs. Mary Dietch; she lives on the East Side in the Mid-fifties. She said this has happened several times in the apartment, when I leave the room and she'll be busy with something and think that I have returned and start to speak, and of course there is nobody there."

I pointed at the kitchen door. "What about the time your maid saw a whitish form?"

"The cleaning woman comes in the afternoon. She is a very charming woman. We became very friendly and very fond of each other and we chattered all the time; we got more chatter then cleaning done on some days.

"Well, one afternoon I was in this small kitchenette, she was in the bathroom, and we were talking back and forth, when Dorothy came out of the bathroom and started to go into that room to tell me something, but in the midst of talking she suddenly just stopped. I poked my head out of the kitchen and said, 'Well, what were you going to say?' She turned with a look of complete shock on her face and said, 'Mrs. Bartell, did you just leave that room?' I said, 'No, I did not.' She said, 'You've been in the kitchen all the time?' I said, 'Yes, yes.'

"She shook her head. 'I saw a woman in white just come through there!' I was wearing a white blouse, it was summertime, so she thought it was me."

"Did your husband ever hear anything?" I asked.

"He just hears footsteps. The footsteps go on at all hours, early morning, early afternoon, late afternoon, early evening—I'm forever running into that long hall and saying, 'Who is it?' and of course there is nobody there."

"Are they the footsteps of a man or a woman?"

"I'm not able to tell you that, they are tentative, very tentative and very light, walking very slowly.

"There was this very strange Sunday evening. We had an early supper and then we went into the bedroom to watch a television program. Later I remembered I had the dishes on the table and I came in to do them. We had eaten a particularly delicious dessert in which we practically licked the plates clear, there just wasn't anything left on them. Yet, there right in the center of *my* plate, very precisely centered, was a small dried grape. We had no grapes in the house."

"When was the last time you saw anything or heard anything unusual?" I asked.

"Well, the most recent occurrences took place last week and about a week or so before that. I'll take you back to the earlier one. I was asleep and was awakened out of a sound sleep for no reason I'm aware of. I sat bolt upright in bed and looked around and felt very nervous. I got out of bed and came into the kitchen for a glass of water. Contessa, my dog, followed me in. I put the light on in the kitchen—it was about 3:30 or 4:00 in the morning—and was looking around, *when I heard this movement.* There was Contessa at this blue chair, she sat bolt upright at the side and sniffed and peered at the seat, and then backed away."

"You mean, as if she had seen someone?"

"As if she had seen a figure sitting in that chair. I hurried back to bed. When I lay down in my bed, my pillows and my sheets were cold as ice."

"The footsteps were heard at one particular location at night, near the bed?"

"Footsteps are heard mainly during the day and in the hall, and I have gone to great trouble to ascertain that nobody was home, because it's an old building and the partitions are thin and many times you can hear footsteps from the apartment downstairs. But at these times there was nobody home next door, there was nobody home downstairs in either apartment."

"When you heard the footsteps and your husband heard the footsteps, did they both seem to come from the same direction?"

"Yes, they appear to come from this area, down the hall."

"Mrs. Bartell, one more question," I said. "In your earlier years did you ever have any psychic experiences before you moved to this house?"

"When I was a little girl of nine, I lived in Washington, D.C. One day I went with my parents to Mount Vernon; it was our first trip there. Mother and Dad had not seen the tomb of Martha and George Washington. It began to rain and we took refuge in the 'cook house,' thereby getting hopelessly lost in the vast grounds.

"The rain stopped and we set out from the wharf to the tombs and in those days there were no markers to the grave. We became hopelessly lost when I suddenly heard myself say, 'I know where it is, just follow me.' And of course, I was laughed at; most children are when they make statements like this.

"Well, I did lead them directly to the tomb, and I'd never been there in this life at all."

When we left that evening, I was hopeful that I had calmed the house. I had turned towards the empty room and quietly spoken to the Unseen Visitor, telling her to leave the living alone and that her world was no longer the world of the flesh. Sometimes this will do it, sometimes not.

A day later, Mrs. Bartell was on the telephone again. The footsteps were continuing. Could I come again? This time I decided to bring my favorite medium, Ethel Johnson Meyers.

On November 27, we ascended the by-now-familiar old stairs to the top floor of the old town house.

On arriving, Mrs. Meyers, who had no idea of our plans for that evening, remarked that she felt the apartment full of great activity. It was at this moment, when we were all quietly seated around the darkened room—the Bartells, Ethel, my wife and I, and a Mr. Rockefeller, a friend of the Bartells—it was at this moment that a small table next to my wife's chair jumped. It did not jump high or far, but she had her eyes on it at the time, and she said it moved of its own volition as if some unseen hand had touched it.

Mrs. Meyers observed a feeling of jealousy in the atmosphere and added, "I was touched; there is someone sitting on the settee between us."

She felt a woman's presence almost at once. "She wants to go somewhere, there is urgency. But the apartment has been changed," she added, "and now the woman can't go."

"I have a feeling the piano area is the center of activities here."

"Correct," Mrs. Bartell nodded.

"I feel a very young person, and an aborted child, whose remains have been here at one time."

I thought of the nineteenth-century servant woman and the rigid code of that time, and the many affairs quietly perpetrated in the fashionable town houses of that day.

Ethel Meyers was now in a state halfway between clairvoyance and trance.

"Mallison," she murmured, "Renée, or Reney. The third person is the child. There is a pungent odor here."

Fred Bartell also noticed the scent, and my wife confirmed it, too. I did not sense it myself.

"A pretty young blonde, with large blue eyes and a tiny nose . . . Renée . . ."

The trance became more noticeable now.

"He put it on my finger . . . the ring . . . Mrs. John J. Mallison. I was born here . . . twenty-nine years. . . . March sixteenth, eighteen forty-eight. . . . Where is my husband?"

"What is his name?" I asked softly.

"Henry . . . Henry McDermott," the entranced medium replied.

"Is he here now?"

"No, no . . . saw him last two years, now no more."

"What about a child?"

"No, NO!"

I decided to try and see if she knew in what year her tragedy occurred.

"Who is President of the United States?"

"They killed him."

"Whom?"

"Abraham."

"Who is now President?"

"Andrew Johnson."

Suddenly, the entity started to speak of the other man.

"John comes to play with me now, I can't go to him."

I firmly insisted she tell me about this John.

"He went, but he never came back. I lied to you, there was a child, but she died. I like it very much here. I can play with the little one. I lost a little one."

"What did your husband do for a living?"

"He made jewelry. He made my ring."

"Where was his shop?"

"Twenty-three . . . Twenty-three . . . Twenty-three . . ." She seemed hopelessly lost for the moment.

"What did your father do?"

"Supply restaurant . . ."

"Why are you here?"

"Papa did not know. . . . he's at the window, with blood . . . I lied, I'm nineteen not twenty-nine . . . married with ring now . . . Papa did not believe me . . . John has gone . . . they took him, Abraham took him, they killed him. . . ."

The emotions overcame the entranced medium at this point, and the entity slipped out, leaving the medium momentarily lifeless. Within a moment, though, control Albert took over and in his usual crisp voice announced that all was well.

"There was a miscarriage previous to the marriage," he explained, "and the father did not approve of the match. But they were married.

"The little girl died. She did abort the first child; there were two children; mother and child died together in childbirth. The husband was killed in battle. Reeny is really Irene, but the name Mallison is correct. Irene's mother also died in childbirth; there were four older girls and three boys."

"What about the name McDermott?"

"It is not quite correct."

With that, he bade us release "the instrument" as it was half past ten and she seemed visibly tired.

The next day, November 28, I received a phone call from Mrs. Bartell.

Somehow she was impressed with the correct name. Not McDermott, but McDevitt, she felt. But she was not sure.

On November 29, she called again, to report some chills, but she remembered my farewell speech to the ghost the previous time, and asked her gently to go away. The chills passed quickly.

As I always do, I tried to corroborate some of the material obtained in this manner. The Civil War period is particularly difficult as many of the records no longer exist. I could not find Mr. Mallison in the few sources available to me, namely Trow's city directories and commercial listings. But I did find a Henry McDermott who lived nearby, at 203? West Nineteenth Street, in the year 1868.

I checked in with Mrs. Bartell several times later, but things were always well in hand. Once in a while, Contessa would sniff at something only she could see or sense, but nobody saw any lady in white, and the town house settled into a period of calm.

Quite possibly the young servant girl found peace with both her men in a world where these things aren't taken so literally.

THE GHOSTS OF STAMFORD HILL

"MR. HOLZER," THE VOICE on the phone said pleasantly, "I've read your books and that's why I'm calling. We've got a ghost in our house."

Far from astonished, I took paper and pencil and, not unlike a grocery-store clerk taking down a telephone order, started to put down the details of the report.

Robert Cowan was a gentleman with a very balanced approach to life. He was an artist who worked for one of the leading advertising agencies in New York City and his interests ranged widely—from art to music, theater, history and what have you. But not to ghosts, at least not until he and his actress-wife, Dorothy, moved into the 1780 House in Stamford Hill. The house was thus named for the simplest of all reasons: it was built in that year.

Mr. Cowan explained that he thought I'd be glad to have a look at his house, although the Cowans were not unduly worried about the presence of a non-rent-paying guest at their house. It was a bit disconcerting at times, but more than that, curiosity as to what the ghost wanted, and who the specter was, had prompted Bob Cowan to make a call to the Ghost Hunter.

I said, "Mr. Cowan, would you mind putting your experiences in writing, so I can have them for my files?"

I like to have written reports (in the first person, if possible) so that later I can refer back to them if similar cases should pop up, as they often do.

"Not at all," Bob Cowan said, "I'll be glad to write it down for you."

The next morning I received his report, along with a brief history of the 1780 House.

Here is a brief account of the experiences my wife and I have had while living in this house during the past nine and a half years. I'll start with myself because my experiences are quite simple.

From time to time (once a week or so) during most of the time we've lived here I have noticed unidentifiable movements out of the corner of my eye . . . day or night. Most often, I've noticed this while sitting in our parlor and what I see moving seems to be in the living room. At other times, and only late at night when I am the only one awake, I hear beautiful but unidentified music seemingly played by a full orchestra, as though a radio were on in another part of the house.

The only place I recall hearing this is in an upstairs bedroom and just after I'd gone to bed. Once I actually got up, opened the bedroom door to ascertain if it was perhaps music from a radio accidently left on, but it wasn't.

Finally, quite often I've heard a variety of knocks and crashes that do not have any logical source within the structural setup of the house. A very loud smash occurred two weeks ago. You'd have thought a door had fallen off its hinges upstairs but, as usual, there was nothing out of order.

My wife, Dorothy, had two very vivid experiences about five years ago. One was in the kitchen, or rather outside of a kitchen window. She was standing at the sink in the evening and happened to glance out the window when she saw a face glaring in at her. It was a dark face, but not a black person, perhaps an Indian; it was very hateful and fierce.

At first she thought it was a distorted reflection in the glass but in looking closer, it was a face glaring directly at her. All she could make out was a face only and as she recalls it, *it seemed translucent.* It didn't disappear, *she did!*

On a summer afternoon my wife was taking a nap in a back bedroom and was between being awake and being asleep when she heard the sounds of men's voices and the sound of working on the grounds—rakes, and garden tools—right outside of the window. She tried to arouse herself to see who they could be, but she couldn't get up.

At that time, and up to that time we had only hired a single man to come in and work on the lawn and flower beds. It wasn't until at least a year later that we hired a crew that came in and worked once a week and we've often wondered if this was an experience of precognition. My wife has always had an uneasy feeling about the outside of the back of the house and still sometimes hears men's voices outside and will look out all windows without seeing anyone.

She also has shared my experiences of seeing "things" out of the corner of her eye and also hearing quite lovely music at night. She hasn't paid attention to household noises because a long time ago I told her "all old houses have odd structural noises" . . . which is true enough.

Prior to our living here the house was lived in for about 25 years by the Clayton Rich family, a family of five. Mr.

Rich died towards the end of their stay here. By the time we bought it, the three children were all married and had moved away.

For perhaps one year prior to that a Mrs. David Cowles lived here. She's responsible for most of the restoration along with a Mr. Fredrick Kinble.

Up until 1927 or 1928, the house was in the Weed family ever since 1780. The last of the line were two sisters who hated each other and only communicated with each other through the husband of one of the sisters. They had divided the house and used two different doors, one used the regular front door into the stair hall and the other used the "coffin door" into the parlor.

Mr. Cowan added that they were selling the house—not because of ghosts, but because they wanted to move back to the city. I assured him that we'd be coming up as soon as possible.

Before we could make arrangements to do so, I had another note from the Cowans. On February 9, 1964, Bob Cowan wrote that they heard a singing voice quite clearly downstairs, and music again.

It wasn't until the following week, however, that my wife and I went to Stamford Hill. The Cowans offered to have supper ready for us that Sunday evening, and to pick us up at the station, since nobody could find the house at night who did not know the way.

It was around six in the evening when our New Haven train pulled in. Bob Cowan wore the Scottish beret he had said he would wear in order to be recognized by us at once. The house stood at the end of a winding road which ran for about ten minutes through woodland and past shady lanes. An American eagle over the door, and the date 1780 stood out quite clearly despite the dusk which had started to settle on the land. The house has three levels, and the Cowans used for their dining room the large room next to the kitchen in what might be called the cellar or ground level.

They had adorned it with eighteenth-century American antiques in a most winning manner, and the fireplace added a warmth to the room that seemed miles removed from bustling New York.

On the next level were the living room and next to that a kind of sitting room. The fireplace in each of these rooms was connected one to the other. Beyond the corridor there was the master bedroom and Bob's rather colorful den. Upstairs were two guest rooms, and there was a small attic accessible only through a hole in the ceiling and by ladder. Built during the American Revolution, the house stands on a wooded slope, which is responsible for its original name of Woodpecker Ridge Farm.

Many years ago, after the restoration of the house was completed, Harold Donaldson Eberlin, an English furniture and garden expert, wrote about it:

> With its rock-ribbed ridges, its boulder-strewn pastures and its sharply broken contours like the choppy surface of a wind-blown sea, the topographical conditions have inevitably affected the domestic architecture. To mention only two particulars, the dwellings of the region have had to accommodate themselves to many an abrupt hillside site and the employment of some of the omnipresent granite boulders. Part of the individuality of the house at Woodpecker Ridge Farm lies in the way it satisfies these conditions without being a type house.
>
> Before communal existence, the country all there-abouts bore the pleasantly descriptive name of Woodpecker Ridge, and Woodpecker Ridge Farm was so called in order to keep alive the memory of this early name. Tradition says that the acres now comprised within the

boundaries of Woodpecker Ridge Farm once formed part of the private hunting ground of *the old Indian chief Ponus.*

Old Ponus may, perhaps, appear a trifle mythical and shadowy, as such long-gone chieftains are wont to be. Very substantial and real, however, was Augustus Weed, who built the house in 1780. And the said Augustus was something of a personage.

War clouds were still hanging thick over the face of the land when he had the foundation laid and the structure framed. Nevertheless, confident and forward-looking, he not only reared a staunch and tidy abode, indicative of the spirit of the countryside, but he seems to have put into it some of his own robust and independent personality as well.

It is said that Augustus was such a notable farmer and took such justifiable pride in the condition of his fields that he was not afraid to make a standing offer of one dollar reward for every daisy that anyone could find in his hay.

About 1825 the house experienced a measure of remodeling in accordance with the notions prevalent at the time. Nothing very extensive or ostentatious was attempted, but visible traces of the work then undertaken remain in the neo-Greek details that occur both outside and indoors.

It is not at all unlikely that the "lie-on-your-stomach" windows of the attic story date from this time and point to either a raising of the original roof or else some alteration of its pitch. These "lie-on-your-stomach" windows—so called because they were low down in the wall and had their sills very near the level of the floor so that you had almost to lie on your stomach to look out of them—were a favorite device of the *néo-Grec* era for lighting attic rooms. And it is remarkable how much light they actually do give, and what a pleasant light it is.

The recent remodeling that brought Woodpecker Farmhouse to its present state of comeliness and comfort impaired none of the individual character the place had acquired through the generations that had passed since hardy Augustus Weed first took up his abode there. It needs no searching scrutiny to discern the eighteenth-century features impressed on the structure at the beginning—the stout timbers of the framing, the sturdy beams and joists, the wide floor boards, and the generous fireplaces. Neither is close examination required to discover the marks of the 1825 rejuvenation.

The fashions of columns, pilasters, mantelpieces and other features speak plainly and proclaim their origin.

The aspect of the garden, too, discloses the same sympathetic understanding of the environment peculiarly suitable to the sort of house for which it affords the natural setting. The ancient well cover, the lilac bushes, the sweetbriers, the August lilies and the other denizens of an old farmhouse dooryard have been allowed to keep their long-accustomed places.

In return for this recognition of their prescriptive rights, they lend no small part to the air of self-possessed assurance and mellow contentment that pervades the whole place.

After a most pleasant dinner downstairs, Catherine and I joined the Cowans in the large living room upstairs. We sat down quietly and hoped we would hear something along musical lines.

As the quietness of the countryside slowly settled over us, I could indeed distinguish faraway, indistinct musical sounds, as if someone were playing a radio underwater or at great distance. A check revealed no nearby house or parked car whose radio could be responsible for this.

After a while we got up and looked about the room itself. We were standing about quietly admiring the furniture, when both my wife and I, and of course the Cowans, clearly heard footsteps overhead.

They were firm and strong and could not be mistaken for anything else, such as a squirrel in the attic or other innocuous noise. Nor was it an old house settling.

"Did you hear that?" I said, almost superfluously.

"We all heard it," my wife said and looked at me.

"What am I waiting for?" I replied, and faster than you can say Ghost Hunter, I was up the stairs and into the room above our heads, where the steps had been heard. The room lay in total darkness. I turned the switch. There was no one about. Nobody else was in the house at the time, and all windows were closed. We decided to assemble upstairs in the smaller room next to the one in which I had heard the steps. The reason was that Mrs. Cowan had experienced a most unusual phenomenon in that particular room.

"It was like lightning," she said, "a bright light suddenly come and gone."

I looked the room over carefully. The windows were arranged in such a manner that a reflection from passing cars was out of the question. Both windows, far apart and on different walls, opened into the dark countryside away from the only road.

Catherine and I sat down on the couch, and the Cowans took chairs. We sat quietly for perhaps twenty minutes, without lights except a small amount of light filtering in from the stairwell. It was very dark, certainly dark enough for sleep and there was not light enough to write by.

As I was gazing towards the back wall of the little room and wondered about the footsteps I had just heard so clearly, I saw a blinding flash of light, white light, in the corner facing me. It came on and disappeared very quickly, so quickly in fact that my wife, whose head had been turned in another direction at the moment, missed it. But Dorothy Cowan saw it and exclaimed, "There it is again. Exactly as I saw it."

Despite its brevity I was able to observe that the light cast a shadow on the opposite wall, so it could not very well have been a hallucination.

I decided it would be best to bring Mrs. Meyers to the house, and we went back to New York soon after. While we were preparing our return visit with Mrs. Meyers as our medium, I received an urgent call from Bob Cowan.

"Since seeing you and Cathy at our house, we've had some additional activity that you'll be interested in. Dottie and I have both heard knocking about the house but none of it in direct answer to questions that we've tried to ask. On Saturday, the twenty-ninth of February, I was taking a nap back in my studio when I was awakened by the sound of footsteps in the room above me . . . the same room we all sat in on the previous Sunday.

"The most interesting event was on the evening of Thursday, February 27. I was driving home from the railroad station alone. Dottie was still in New York. As I approached the house, I noticed that there was a light on in the main floor bedroom and also a light on up in the sewing room on the top floor, a room Dottie also uses for rehearsal. I thought Dottie had left the lights on. I drove past the house and down to the garage, put the car away and then walked back to the house and noticed that the light in the top floor was now off.

"I entered the house and noticed that the dogs were calm (wild enough at seeing me, but in no way indicating that there was anyone else in the house). I went upstairs and found that the light in the bedroom was also off. I checked the entire house and there was absolutely no sign that anyone had just been there . . . and there hadn't been, I'm sure."

On Sunday, March 15, we arrived at the 1780 House, again at dusk. A delicious meal awaited us in the downstairs room, then we repaired to the upstairs part of the house.

We seated ourselves in the large living room where the music had been heard, and where we had been standing at the time we heard the uncanny footsteps overhead.

"I sense a woman in a white dress," Ethel said suddenly. "She's got dark hair and a high forehead. Rather a small woman."

"I was rummaging through the attic earlier," Bob Cowan said thoughtfully, "and look what I found—a waistcoat that would fit a rather smallish woman or girl."

The piece of clothing he showed us seemed rather musty. There were a number of articles up there in the attic that must have belonged to an earlier owner of the house—much earlier.

A moment later, Ethel Meyers showed the characteristic signs of onsetting trance. We doused the lights until only one back light was on.

At first, only inarticulate sounds came from the medium's lips. "You can speak," I said, to encourage her, "you're among friends." The sounds now turned into crying.

"What is your name?" I asked, as I always do on such occasions. There was laughter—whether girlish or mad was hard to tell.

Suddenly, she started to sing in a high-pitched voice.

"You can speak, you can speak," I kept assuring the entity. Finally she seemed to have settled down somewhat in control of the medium.

"Happy to speak with you," she mumbled faintly.

"What is your name?"

I had to ask it several times before I could catch the answer clearly.

"Lucy."

"Tell me, Lucy, do you live here?"

"God be with you."

"Do you live in this house?"

"My house."

"What year is this?"

The entity hesitated a moment, then turned towards Dorothy and said, "I like you."

I continued to question her.

"How old are you?"

"Old lady."

"How old?"

"God be with you."

The conversation had been friendly, but when I asked her, "What is your husband's name?" the ghost drew back as if I had spoken a horrible word.

"What did you say?" she almost shouted, her voice trembling with emotion. "I have no husband—God bless you—what were you saying?" she repeated, then started to cry again. "Husband, husband," she kept saying as if it was a thought she could not bear.

"You did not have a husband, then?"

"Yes, I did."

"Your name again?"

"Lucy . . . fair day . . . where is he? The fair day . . . the pretty one, he said to me look in the pool and you will see my face."

"Who is he?" I repeated.

But the ghost paid no heed to me. She was evidently caught up in her own memories.

"I heard a voice, Lucy, Lucy—fair one—alack—they took him out—they laid him cold in the ground . . ."

"What year was that?" I wanted to know.

"Year, year?" she repeated. "Now, *now!*"

"Who rules this country now?"

"Why, he who seized it."

"Who rules?"

"They carried him out. . . . The savior of our country. General Washington."

"When did he die?"

"Just now."

I tried to question her further, but she returned to her thoughts of her husband.

"I want to stay here—I wait at the pool—look, he is there!" She was growing excited again.

"I want to stay here now, always, forever—rest in peace—he is there always with me."

"How long ago did you die?" I asked, almost casually. The reaction was somewhat hostile.

"I have not died—never—All Saints!"

I asked her to join her loved one by calling for him and thus be set free of this house. But the ghost would have none of it.

"Gainsay what I have spoke—"

"How did you come to this house?" I now asked.

"Father—I am born here."

"Was it your father's house?"

"Yes."

"What was his name?" I asked, but the restless spirit of Lucy was slipping away now, and Albert, the medium's control, took over. His crisp, clear voice told us that the time had come to release Ethel.

"What about this woman, Lucy?" I inquired. Sometimes the control will give additional details.

"He was not her husband . . . he was killed before she married him," Albert said.

No wonder my question about a husband threw Lucy into an uproar of emotions.

In a little while, Ethel Meyers was back to her old self, and as usual, did not remember anything of what had come through her entranced lips.

Shortly after this my wife and I went to Europe.

As soon as we returned, I called Bob Cowan. How were things up in Stamford Hill? Quiet? Not very.

"In June," Bob recalled, "Dottie and I were at home with a friend, a lady hair dresser, who happens to be psychic. We were playing around with the ouija board, more in amusement than seriously. Suddenly, the Sunday afternoon quiet was disrupted by heavy footsteps coming up the steps outside the house. Quickly, we hid the ouija board, for we did not want a potential buyer of the house to see us in this unusual pursuit. We were sure someone was coming up to see the house. But the steps stopped abruptly when they reached the front door. I opened, and there was no one outside."

"Hard to sell a house that way," I commented. "Anything else?"

"Yes, in July we had a house guest, a very balanced person, not given to imagining things. There was a sudden crash upstairs, and when I rushed up the stairs to the sewing room, there was this bolt of material that had been standing in a corner, lying in the middle of the room as if thrown there by unseen hands! Margaret, our house guest, also heard someone humming a tune in the bathroom, although there was no one in there at the time. Then in November, when just the two of us were in the house, someone knocked at the door downstairs. Again we looked, but there was nobody outside. One evening when I was in the 'ship' room and Dottie in the bedroom, we heard footfalls coming down the staircase.

"Since neither of us was causing them and the door was closed, only a ghost could have been walking down those stairs."

"But the most frightening experience of all," Dorothy Cowan broke in, "was when I was sleeping downstairs and, waking up, wanted to go to the bathroom without turning on the lights, so as not to wake Bob. Groping my way back to bed, I suddenly found myself up on the next floor in the blue room, which is pretty tricky walking in the dark. I had the feeling someone was forcing me to follow them into that particular room."

I had heard enough, and on December 15, we took Ethel Johnson Meyers to the house for another go at the restless ones within its confines. Soon we were all seated in the ship room on the first floor, and Ethel started to drift into trance.

"There is a baby's coffin here," she murmured. "Like a newborn infant's."

The old grandfather clock in back of us kept ticking away loudly.

"I hear someone call Maggie," Ethel said, "Margaret."

"Do you see anyone?"

"A woman, about five foot two, in a long dress, with a big bustle in the back. Hair down, parted in the middle, and braided on both sides. There is another young woman . . . Laurie . . . very pretty face, but so sad . . . She's looking at you, Hans . . ."

"What is it she wants?" I asked quietly.

"A youngish man with brown hair, curly, wearing a white blouse, taken in at the wrists, and over it a tan waistcoat, but no coat over it . . ."

I asked what he wanted and why he was here. This seemed to agitate the medium somewhat.

"Bottom of the well," she mumbled, "stones at bottom of the well."

Bob Cowan changed seats, moving away from the coffin door to the opposite side of the room. He complained of feeling cold at the former spot, although neither door nor window was open to cause such a sensation.

"Somebody had a stick over his shoulder," the medium said now, "older man wearing dark trousers, heavy stockings. His hair is gray and kind of longish; he's got that stick."

I asked her to find out why.

"Take him away," Ethel replied. "He says, 'Take him away!'

"But he was innocent, he went to the well. Who is down in the well? Him who I drove into the well, him . . . I mistook . . ."

Ethel was now fully entranced and the old man seemed to be speaking through her.

"What is your name?" I asked.

"She was agrievin'," the voice replied, "she were grievin' I did that."

"What is your name?"

"Ain't no business to you."

"How can I help you?"

"They're all here . . . accusin' me . . . I see her always by the well."

"Did someone die in this well?" Outside, barely twenty yards away, was the well, now cold and silent in the night air.

"Him who I mistook. I find peace, I find him, I put him together again."

"What year was that?"

"No matter to you now . . . I do not forgive myself . . . I wronged, I wronged . . . I see always her face look on me."

"Are you in this house now?" I asked.

"Where else can I be and talk with thee?" the ghost shot back.

"This isn't your house any more," I said quietly.

"Oh, yes it is," the ghost replied firmly. "The young man stays here only to look upon me and mock me. It will not be other than mine. I care only for that flesh that I could put again on the bone and I will restore him to the bloom of life and the rich love of her who suffered through my own misdemeanor."

"Is your daughter buried here?" I asked, to change the subject. Quietly, the ghostly voice said "Yes."

But he refused to say where he himself was laid to final—or not so final—rest.

At this point the ghost realized that he was not in his own body, and as I explained the procedure to him, he gradually became calmer. At first, he thought he was in his own body and could use it to restore to life the one he had slain. I kept asking who he was. Finally, in a soft whisper, came the reply, "Samuel."

"And Laurie?"

"My daughter . . . oh, he is here, the man I wronged . . . Margaret, Margaret!" He seemed greatly agitated with fear now.

The big clock started to strike. The ghost somehow felt it meant him.

"The judgment, the judgment . . . Laurie. . . . they smile at me. I have killed. He has taken my hand! He whom I have hurt."

But the excitement proved too much for Samuel. Suddenly, he was gone, and after a brief interval, an entirely different personality inhabited Ethel's body. It was Laurie.

"Please forgive him," she pleaded, "I have forgiven him."

The voice was sweet and girlish.

"Who is Samuel?"

"My grandfather."

"What is your family name?"

"Laurie Ho-Ho- . . . if I could only get that name."

But she couldn't.

Neither could she give me the name of her beloved, killed by her grandfather. It was a name she was not allowed to mention around the house, so she had difficulty remembering now, she explained.

"What is your mother's name?" I asked.

"Margaret."

"What year were you born?"

Hesitatingly, the voice said, "Seven-teen-fifty-six."

"What year is this now?"

"Seventeen seventy-four. We laid him to rest in seventeen seventy-four."

"In the church?"

"No, Grandfather could not bear it. We laid him to rest on the hill to the north. We dug with our fingers all night.

"Don't tell Grandpa where we put it."

"How far from here is it?"

"No more than a straight fly of the lark."

"Is the grave marked?"

"Oh, no."

"What happened to your father?"

"No longer home, gone."

I explained to Laurie that the house would soon change hands, and that she must not interfere with this. The Cowans had the feeling that their ghosts were somehow keeping all buyers away, fantastic though this may be at first thought. But then all of psychic research is pretty unusual, so who is to say what cannot be?

Laurie promised not to interfere and to accept a new owner of "their" house. She left, asking again that her grandfather be forgiven his sins.

I then asked Albert, Ethel's control, to take over the medium. That done, I queried him regarding the whole matter.

"The father is buried far from here, but most of the others are buried around here," he said, "during the year seventeen seventy-seven . . . grandfather was not brought here until later when there was forgiveness. The body was removed and put in Christian burial."

"Where is the tombstone?" I asked.

"Lying to the west of a white structure," Albert replied in his precise, slightly accented speech, "on these grounds. The tombstone is broken off, close to the earth. The top has been mishandled by vandals. The old man is gone, the young man has taken him by the hand."

"What was the young man's name?"

"She called him Benjamin."

"He was killed in the well?"

"That is right. He has no grave except on the hill."

"Is the old man the one who disturbs this house?"

"He is the main one who brings in his rabble, looking for the young man."

"Who is Lucy?" I asked, referring back to the girl who had spoken to us at the last séance in the late spring.

"That is the girl you were talking about, Laurie. Her name is really Lucy. One and the same person."

"She was not actually married to the young man?"

"In her own way, she was. But they would not recognize it. There were differences in religious ideas . . . But we had better release the medium for now."

I nodded, and within a moment or two, Ethel was back to herself, very much bewildered as to what went on while she was in trance.

"How do you reconcile these dates with the tradition that this house was built in seventeen eighty?" I asked Bob Cowan.

He shook his head.

"It is only a tradition. We have no proof of the actual date."

We went to the upstairs sewing room where the latest manifestations had taken place, and grouped ourselves around the heavy wooden table. Ethel almost immediately fell into trance again. She rarely does twice in one sitting.

The voice reverberating in the near-darkness now was clearly that of a man, and a very dominating voice it was.

"Who are you?" I demanded.

"Sergeant-major. . . ." No name followed. I asked why was he here in this house.

"One has pleasant memories."

"Your name?"

"Sergeant-major Harm."

"First name?"

Instead of giving it, he explained that he once owned the house and was "friend, not foe." I looked at Bob Cowan, who knows all the owners of the property in the old records, and Bob shook his head. No Harm.

"When I please, I come. I do not disturb willingly. But I will go," the new visitor offered, "I will take him with me; you will see him no more. I am at peace with him now. He is at peace with me."

"How did you pass over?" I inquired.

"On the field of battle. On the banks of the Potomac . . . seventeen seventy-six."

"What regiment were you in?" I continued.

"York. . . . Eight. . . . I was foot soldier . . . eighteenth regiment . . ."

"What Army?"

"Wayne . . . Wayne . . ."

"Who was your commanding general?"

"Broderick."

"Who was the Colonel of your regiment?"

"Wayne, Wayne."

"You were a Sergeant-major?"

"Sergeant-major, eighteenth regiment, foot infantry."

"Where were you stationed?"

"New York."

"Where in New York?"

"Champlain."

"Your regimental commander again?"

"Broderick." Then he added, not without emotion, "I died under fire, first battle of Potomac."

"Where are you buried?"

"Fort Ticonderoga, New York."

I wondered how a soldier fighting on the banks of the Potomac could be buried in upstate New York. But I must confess that the word "Potomac" had come so softly that I could have been mistaken.

"The date of your death?"

"Seventeen seventy-six."

Then he added, as the voice became more and more indistinct, "I will leave now, but I will protect you from those who . . . who are hungry to . . . " The voice trailed off into silence.

A few moments later, Ethel emerged from the trance with a slight headache, but otherwise her old self. As usual, she did not recall anything that had come through her entranced lips.

We returned to New York soon after, hoping that all would remain quiet in the Cowan house, and, more importantly, that there would soon be a new laird of the manor at the 1780 House.

I, too, heard the ghostly music, although I am sure it does not connect with the Colonial ghosts we were able to evoke. The music I heard sounded like a far-off radio, which it wasn't, since there are no houses near enough to be heard from. What I heard for a few moments in the living room sounded like a full symphony orchestra playing the music popular around the turn of this century.

Old houses impregnated with layers upon layers of people's emotions frequently also absorb music and other sounds as part of the atmosphere.

What about the Sergeant-major?

I checked the regimental records. No soldier named Harm, but a number of officers (and men) named Harmon. I rechecked my tapes. The name "Harm" had been given by the ghost very quietly. He could have said Harmon. Or perhaps he was disguising his identity as they sometimes will.

But then I discovered something very interesting. In the Connecticut state papers there is mention of a certain Benjamin Harmon, Jr. Lt., who was with a local regiment in 1776. The murdered young man had been identified as "Benjamin." Suddenly we have another ghost named Harm or Harmon, evidently an older personality. Was he the father of the murdered young man?

The 1780 House is, of course, recorded as dating back to 1780 only. But could not another building have occupied the same spot? Was the 1780 House an adaptation of a smaller dwelling of which there is no written record?

We can neither prove nor disprove this.

It is true, however, that General "Mad" Anthony Wayne was in charge of the Revolutionary troops in the New York area at the time under discussion.

At any rate, all this is knowledge not usually possessed by a lady voice teacher, which was what Ethel Meyers was when not being a medium.

CALL OF THE
MIDWEST

T O SOME PEOPLE, THE IDEA OF GHOSTS and haunted
houses in the prosaic Middle West does not quite fit. Ghosts,
one thinks, belong in English castles and, at best, New England
mansions. But the Midwest—really!

Nevertheless, there was and is a steady stream of letters, phone
calls, even visitors, from the golden wheat belt known as the heart of
the country.

Corn has nothing to do with it, either. People who have psychic
experiences in Dubuque and Oshkosh are not necessarily what New
Yorkers so ungallantly refer to as "hicks." Possessors of some of the
finest and most perceptive minds were born and raised in the middle portions of our country.

After my Art Linkletter appearance, a veritable avalanche of
reports reached me. People wanted my book, and many others who
just wanted to tell me of *their* ghosts.

A woman named Joyce Soule wrote me from Jackson,
Michigan, that she frequently felt an unseen presence and heard
strange noises; a lady by the name of Mrs. Josephine Younker once
lived in a haunted house in Salt Lake City where she saw the appari-

tion of a man who had been killed in the very room she was in; Mrs. Sandra Stover of Wichita, Kansas, told me of her mother whose ghost she had encountered on more than one occasion; some of the letters are genuinely moving and have about them the touch of sincerity and genuineness. Naturally, I investigate each case thoroughly before coming to any final conclusions.

There were also letters of little value, or cases of troubled souls more in need of a good psychiatrist than a parapsychologist. But these were surprisingly few. Then, too, there were letters of almost comical simplicity.

Anthony Klimas of Chicago, Illinois, complained that he had "rapping in my house and pounding at ceiling, knocking at door, calling by name."

Perhaps most typical of most of the letters I received was the almost subdued way in which Mrs. Mathilda Alter, of Decatur, Illinois, wrote of *her* haunted house:

> When I was a child, my mother and five of us children moved to Missouri, just nine miles from Lamar, Missouri, President Truman's home town. Right in Lamar there was a house where no one could lock the doors shut to stay or windows closed. People were afraid of this house and nobody would even move in it.
>
> The house we moved into was claimed to be a haunted house. One evening we were all sitting in the kitchen by the fire of our coal-range, at twilight and no lamps lighted to give any light other than twilight. A "window" came on the wall on the same side of the house as at the front, where it could not be anyone walking by with a lantern.
>
> This shadow went around and appeared on all the four walls of our kitchen. Our big brothers went outside to see

what it was and there was nothing to see. Then we slept upstairs and many nights there would be a rustling noise of heatherbloom petticoats go by our beds from the boys' room through our room to the head of the stairways and then the noise would fade away.

Never did know what that was all about. Then one afternoon my older sister and my mother were in the kitchen sewing and some great big noise hit the floor of the boys' room over the kitchen and sounded like something fell over like a dresser or wardrobe. My mother and sister hurried upstairs to see what the noise could be and everything was in place. Nothing out of the way.

Then one night my oldest brother went up to bed early in the evening and after he had been in bed around an hour, a sound came through to the kitchen from the floor of his bedroom, sounding like someone scooting a kitchen chair back and forth across the bedroom floor. Well, there was no chair in his room, and there also was a carpet from wall to wall on the floor, so we knew it wasn't my brother up in his sleep, but mother checked by going up to see if she could see anything.

Nothing to be seen.

Then when school began my youngest brother and I used to study at the kitchen table and my mother and sister went to the corn crib to shell corn for the chickens' next morning breakfast. While they were down there, my brother and I heard a noise in the stairway like someone coming downstairs using a cane to help him walk.

I picked up the lamp and my brother and I went to the turn in the stairs and there stood the image of an old long-whiskered man with a cane in his hand which very muchly scared us, for I was eight and my brother was eleven years old, and the old man looking at us!

We hurriedly ran back down our few steps and ran to the corn crib to tell Mom and my sister, screaming as we went. My mother hurried to the house to see what the old man looked like, but he had vanished away.

Mother told our neighbor who had told us to expect these things and they told mother and my older brothers that an old peddler had been murdered in the room that my older brothers slept in and his body was put in the attic and his peddler pack was found by the creek that was back of our place, and some of his clothes, too.

We lived there two years but we finally gave up and moved away from there shortly after the last episode.

P.S. I meant to tell you also that a large blood stain was on the floor of the bedroom that was as much as three feet in diameter either way, which was the spot where the murder was performed. We never did find out what happened to the people who did the thing, that lived in this house, but we put a rag carpet down wall to wall on the floor to cover the stain and *that is* where these strange noises started from all the time.

I hope I have not bored you with my story but I am telling you the truth of things that happened there.

No, she had not bored me at all. Giving precise and unemotional testimony, she had told a story which has many parallels in many parts of the world.

Mrs. Harold Schulte of Elkader, Iowa, wrote:

I have had several experiences of this nature. I saw the apparition of a woman as I drove up to a junction stop sign on a pitch-black night at 3:00 o'clock in the morning. She was walking along the highway shoulder directly opposite a country cemetery, and I knew at once what it was.

I drove on to another junction about 200 feet and turned my car around and drove back and she still walked on, not seeing me at all. I saw her twice in the full glare of the headlights of my car. This was the most striking experience I've had, although I have had others. All of which makes me wonder if I could be psychic, too, as some others are.

Mrs. Schulte need not wonder. Only a mediumistic person could have seen a ghost. Although, contrary to popular superstition, cemeteries are usually bare of ghosts, there is always the possibility that a person confused by death might find herself in a grave for which she had not been ready, and her first and strongest thought would be to "walk away" from it immediately.

The interest in things psychic is deeply rooted in the American population, far more deeply than one might suspect on the surface. However, since *Ghost Hunter* came upon the scene, people do come forward and talk about their experiences.

From Independence, Missouri, came this cheerful note:

We have decided to write to you. There are three of us. We started with a meditation group. One day while sitting at the table, two of us saw a spirit of a man; we saw enough to know it was the full form of a man, about 6 feet tall. We could distinguish some features but not all of them.

At another time we saw the spirit of a woman about 5 feet tall. We could distinguish her features also. Both times these spirits vanished without speaking. We have felt cool breezes and smelled strange odors. We have seen streaks of silver light in a darkened room.

We are three housewives and know very little about this. Mrs. Donna Johnson, Mrs. Edith Tate, Mrs. Marie Worth.

Thanks to Gene Lundholm of California, a student of the occult, I heard of a haunted house in Superior, Wisconsin. The witness was a professional nurse of high standing in the community. Here is her statement:

We moved into this house in the year 1909. We were renting from the church, which had used it as a parsonage. We noticed that upstairs, in the back storeroom, there was a peculiar odor. Dad took up the floor thinking there might be dead mice or rats under the floor. My sister had scrubbed the floor with hylex, etc., thinking something might have been spilled.

We found nothing and could never explain the phenomena.

One night, when Mother was in bed in the room next to it, a man entered and stood at the foot of the bed staring at her. She was very frightened. The minister's wife had told Mama that it was a "bad house," but did not tell why. Mother never told us about this until we were grown. A man named William Penn had once lived in it. His daughter was supposed to have looked exactly like me. Mother said that the apparition had just disappeared into thin air after a while.

One night when we kids were sitting at the kitchen table, we heard someone coming down the stairs, slowly. The doorknob turned and the door started to open. We ran out of the house and down the street and met the folks who had been at church.

Later on, after we moved, the house was sold to the hospital for a nurse's training home. I happened to tell one of the girls who trained there that we had lived there. She said she had been expelled from the school of nursing because the authorities said she had been drunk when she reported having seen a man in this particular room when she came home.

Frequently we heard footsteps on all the stairways: from upstairs down and down the basement. Tappings on the windows were explained by Mother as being branches blowing against the window. However, the trees were not close enough to touch the house.

Hildur Lundholm.

Mrs. Charles E. Wofford, of St. Louis, Missouri, had a great deal of American Indian blood.

My grandmother (who raised me) was Cherokee Indian and Irish, and she used to call it "Second Sight." I loved her, but must admit she was a bit overwhelming to live with. We'd had a silly quarrel. She died and I'd not had a chance to make my apology. The night after the funeral I was awakened to see her standing at the foot of my bed. I said "Mama, what are you doing here?—you are dead!" She smiled. I wept. "Oh, I am so sorry. I didn't mean what I said. I loved you so much."

"I know you did, honey, now don't grieve about it any longer. I loved you, too." And with that, she was gone. To this day I believe I truly saw her, but who can prove it was no more than an unusually clear and vivid dream? I think a part of her still remains in that house. Now and then one could hear sounds of footsteps going back and forth upstairs and the sound of furniture being moved about. But no one ever heard it but my mother, me, and mother's two dogs who would simply have fits about it.

Mrs. Wofford had many bouts with the psychic, ranging all the way from apparitions to premonitions. On nine separate occasions, she foretold when someone was about to die or had died.

I did know that my stepfather was going to die in an accident. I was talking to his wife on the phone. The thought went through my head, "Pop is going to die in an accident." I glanced at the clock. It was 5:15 P.M. At 5:20 P.M., my phone went completely haywire and was out of service until 9:00 P.M. It rang at nine—it was one of Pop's friends . . .

"I have bad news for you, Dot."

"Pop was killed in an accident at five fifteen, wasn't he?"

"Yes! How in the name of God did you know?"

"I don't know how I knew. . . . I just did."

"Did someone tell you?"

"No. The thought came to me at that time. I'd been sitting here all evening waiting for your call."

The people who wrote to me of their psychic experiences were by no means spinsters and old people vaguely remembering bygone days. Candy Bosselmann of Fort Wayne, Indiana, was only seventeen. She wrote:

I have a natural gift, but it's not completely developed yet. Our family has always had this. My mother is very psychic and hears knocks on the door or tapping at the window as if done by nails before someone's death. I received a premonition when my grandmother passed away. I heard her scream when she was halfway across town, and smelled flowers in the house three days after she was buried. Every once in a while, someone follows me downstairs . . .

Clifford Steele of Indianapolis, Indiana, was even younger. Then sixteen years of age, this bright, almost precocious youngster came to see me with his mother on my last visit to Indianapolis.

"I knew of my father's death at the time it happened some five miles away in our family car," he said by way of introduction. "Mrs. Ruby Wann, who was present, can attest to this."

Evidently, young Clifford has various forms of psychic abilities. "When President Kennedy was elected to office," he said quietly, "I told mother he'd be assassinated in office." Mrs. Steele nodded agreement. This was in 1960, she added, and horrified her no end. When Clifford was only four years old, he complained of seeing a "white shape" no one else was able to observe.

In 1962, the family lived at Belmont, Ohio, in a house that had been the property and home of one John Frawley for many years. Against the oldster's will, he was removed from his Third Street house by his family and placed in a nursing home, where he eventually died. That he was most unhappy there can be seen from the fact that despite his advanced age and poor condition he once walked away from the home.

Soon after Mrs. Steele and her young son had moved into the house, they noticed a "presence." Bric-a-brac was found crushed when no one was in the house who could have done it, and doors opened at night from the inside. Mr. Frawley had never really left, it would appear.

At another house the Steeles occupied after that, in Indianapolis proper, footsteps coming down the hall were clearly heard by them. They once found the door blocked from the inside and had to crawl in through the basement, although there was nobody in the house at the time who could have done this. The elevator shaft was blocked off, and footsteps always stopped short at the shaft. Clifford thinks the former owner of the house fell into the shaft and died there.

Mrs. Edith O'Brien of Akron, Ohio, had her own brush with the Unknown, which of course wasn't quite so unknown to me after hearing of it thousands of times in more or less the same pattern. She wrote:

> Several years ago, I had rooms in the home of an old family friend who was almost blind. Every night, I made a habit of reading a chapter from the Bible to Mr. Henry before he went to bed. This particular evening as we were sitting in the living room and I was reading the usual chapter, heavy footsteps started from the kitchen door and stopped just at the living-room door.
>
> Needless to say, I was terrified for I had securely locked all the doors hours before, and there was no one in the house but me and Mr. Henry.
>
> I couldn't speak, but Mr. Henry looked at me and said, "Edith, I thought we were alone in the house." I called the police who came and examined the house carefully, but found nothing disturbed and no one but us in the house—no door that had not been locked. The very next night, a heavy oak table which was in Mr. Henry's room was lying across his bed when he went to retire. Since Mr. Henry was nearly blind, I always opened his bed for him before he went to his room and everything had been in order—the heavy table in its usual place. After this happened, Mr. Henry said, "It won't be long until something happens in this house. These same footsteps were heard walking in the same way, and a mirror shattered from top to bottom just before Mother died." Within a few days, Mr. Henry was dead.

Mildred Eastman lived in Willoughby, Ohio, a far cry from gloomy British castles where ghosts are supposed to abound. Apparitions of the dead or dying were nothing new to her.

I have had what might be called "visitations" from the other world since I was eighteen years old. I was playing the piano in a sitting room back of the old parlor, when my attention was drawn to the wide-open doorway. I continued to play, but looked around and saw a short woman standing there with a bouffant dress, hands crossed on the fullness of the gown, her dark hair parted in the middle.

I then noticed that I could see the Christmas tree through her, and I became concerned, and the vision vanished. Three days later my aunt was found dead, and in her possessions was an old daguerreotype and it was the little lady in every respect that I had seen in my vision. She was my aunt's mother.

Again, when my mother was very ill at the hospital, I awoke at 7:30 A.M., sat up in bed, and was amazed to see a milk-white oblong coming onto the bedroom door which was closed. In it, my mother appeared. She had on clothes that I remembered; she pulled her skirt out and touched her hat as much as to say I am on my way, I am leaving. I watched this for some time, then I said out loud, "Yes, Mother, you have left this earth, I am sure, and want to tell me so."

They called me an hour later to tell me that this was the time she actually passed on.

Mrs. H. J. Weidmann lived in Duquesne, Pennsylvania. Her family had "ESP" all their lives and they took it as completely normal and part of their daily lives.

One night Dad and I were up late, when we saw the figure of Bill Schmidt, a friend of ours, at 4:00 A.M., against the kitchen door. Dad said, "Bill Schmidt just died," and at exactly 4:00 A.M., Bill died in a hospital about two miles away from our home. We knew then something was "different" with us. Dad died a year ago, but he has visited our home many times since then. Our lamps go on and off, doors open and close; our dog, who loved Dad, will suddenly sit up and wag his tail as he used to do when Dad would come into the house. My sons, Thad and Christie, and a neighbor boy, Mike, have been here when all of this happened.

Dad took such an interest in all our boys that we feel he's still doing so.

Ghosts are part of the everyday scene to some people who take their supernatural gifts without panic or worry. Of course, they are careful about the persons to whom they tell their experiences. Too many people like to scoff at that which they fail to understand, or don't wish to accept as true under any circumstances if their philosophy of life involves a firm disbelief in any form of a "hereafter."

Jane Dempsey of Pittsburgh, Pennsylvania, wrote that she had lived with the psychic world all her life.

In 1947 I had a very serious operation. Before my operation, my aunt, who was dead for several years, appeared to me and said, "Jane, you're going to have a very serious operation. I am going to be with you for a while, while they are operating, but I can't stay too long. You are going to suffer terribly, and all the doctors will think you're dying, but you won't die." The operation lasted nine hours. It happened just as she said it would.

In 1953 my father appeared to me. In October, 1963, my brother-in-law appeared to me when my sister was laid out, and said he came to get my sister, who was his wife.

Several years ago I had a feeling I should get in touch with a girl friend I had not seen for years. Since I am deaf, I had my daughter call her. She died a few days later. I knew she had books that I wanted. I had my daughter get in touch with the people who were disposing of her things. My daughter said to the woman we had never met, "I would like to buy Mrs. Ralston's books." The woman said, "I'm sorry, but I can't do anything with her books. I have to find a person by the name of Jane Bednards." My daughter said, "That is my mother's maiden name." The woman said, "Take all these books, because Mrs. Ralston has appeared to me and does not want anyone else to have them."

Thus Mrs. Dempsey got her books, and another case entered into the bulging annals of psychic research.

From West Elizabeth, Pennsylvania, came a note from Mrs. Helen Tosi, who, as she says, had "a problem" about a ghost.

We have all seen him in the house, several years ago, a man who lived in the house and who met with an accident in the mines. My two sisters were in bed one night when they woke up and saw him sitting on the cedar chest, and all of a sudden, he disappeared into the hall, and vanished. We have been hearing loud noises in the basement at night and in the kitchen, when we are in bed. I don't know what will happen next.

The man was killed some forty years ago, right after he went to work. His name was Mr. Friday. I still hear foot-steps even now.

And so it goes. English manor houses may be more historical than Pennsylvania coal mines, but the ghosts walk on. In the nether world all boundaries are hazy.

But the Call of the Midwest has other aspects, too. There is a vigorous interest in psychic matters in some quarters where it matters. People like John J. Strader, for instance, whose ancestors helped found the city of Cincinnati and who was one of the leading and most solid citizens of that river city. Jack Strader gladly discussed his interest in Sixth Sense phenomena with anyone intelligent who will listen.

He was not ashamed of it as so many people of substance still are. I remember the time my wife and I were in Cincinnati as the guests of the Straders. At a dinner party the president of the local university engaged me in a bit of scrutinizing conversation. Mr. Strader, of course, had maneuvered him across the table from me, and for an hour and a half we talked of nothing else but the scientific evidence for survival. I cannot for the life of me tell you what I had for dessert that evening, but I do remember that Dr. Langsam was impressed.

Our first meeting with the Straders was under the most unusual conditions. I had been asked to appear on the Ruth Lyons television show on the Crosley Broadcasting stations. I had just returned from California, where I had appeared at length on the Art Linkletter and Steve Allen programs, among many others. I was shocked, however, to receive a letter from Ruth Lyons on January 17, in which the astute TV personality reneged on our meeting:

> I sincerely regret that I do not believe that I can do an interview on your book *Ghost Hunter*, without inviting a great deal of controversy. I am certain that you are entirely sincere in what you believe, but I am afraid I would receive a great deal of mail, both pro and con on the subject of

"parapsychology" which would be very difficult for many of our viewers to understand.

I must confess I wrote Miss Lyons a rather tart letter in which I told her, among many other things, not to underestimate the intelligence of her audience.

When Jack Strader heard of the Lyons incident, he was so incensed that he personally arranged for a visit to Cincinnati for my wife and myself, with full television, radio and press coverage far in excess of what I would have had originally.

Moreover, in meeting Jack and Joan Strader, and their daughter, Jackie, we found ourselves in a group of deeply sympathetic but also sensibly critical people who had already demonstrated such psychic talents as automatic writing and psychic photography.

The family homestead of the Straders was not free of the occult. The room upstairs in which Mr. Strader's mother passed her last painful moments in the physical state, had on occasion been the scene of some unexplained noises, such as knocks and footsteps, especially in the early hours of the morning. On one evening in January of 1964, the Straders had been working a modern and improved version of the planchette, with the important addition of direct psychic impressions received by Mrs. Strader, who was mediumistic. Their daughter was out for the evening, and the Straders, as was their wont, were waiting for her return.

At about 12:30, the doorbell rang announcing the fact that our daughter was safely home from a party, along with her escort. I went to answer the summons and just as the two young people closed the door behind them, the fireplace tongs were seen to rise from their normal position and fling themselves upon the floor, some three feet distant from the regular resting spot.

Of course, Jacqueline knew that some psychic force had to be the answer, so with a gleam in her eyes, she approached the next room where we had been gathered and said, "Better slow it down, things are humming tonight!" The young gentleman never got an explanation . . . and he hasn't been back either.

I believe that excess energy . . . is what partly made it possible for the fire tongs to be lifted and tossed through the air. I further believe that the reason for the "show" was a kind of rebellion on the part of our unseen friends at having our excellent contact disturbed, or broken into. It's just my theory however.

I shall have the tongs firmly lashed down for your visit—just in case!

Well, the tongs did not take off for me, but they did appear in a photograph I took of Jack Strader in the next room playing the organ, on which he was an expert. The point is that the tongs and container were several yards away from the organ and could not possibly have been in the picture I took. Yet, they are superimposed on the organ. My camera is completely double-exposure proof. The Unseen Friends were indeed greeting me in style.

THE GHOST
AT THE ALTAR

HAD HEARD RUMORS for some time of a ghost parson in a
church near Pittsburgh, and when I appeared on the John Reed
King show on Station KDKA-TV in the spring of 1963, one of
the crew came up to me after the telecast and told me how much he
enjoyed hearing about ghosts.

"Have you ever visited that haunted church in M——?" he
asked, and my natural curiosity was aroused. A ghost here in
Pittsburgh, and I haven't met him? Can't allow that. But my stay was
over and I had to return to New York.

Still, the ghostly person of M—— was very much on my mind.
When I returned to Pittsburgh in September of 1963, I was determined to have a go at that case.

With the help of Jim Sieger and his roving reporter, John
Stewart, at Station KDKA, we got together a car, a first-class
portable tape recorder, and photographer Jim Stark. Immediately
following my telecast, we set out for Milvale.

Fate must have wanted us to get results, for the attendant of the
first gasoline station we stopped at directed us to the Haunted
Church. Both the name of the church and its current pastor must

remain hidden at their own request, but the story is nevertheless true.

The Haunted Church is an imposing Romanesque building of stone, erected at the turn of the century on a bluff overlooking the Pittsburgh River. It is attached to a school and rectory and gives a clean and efficient impression, nothing haunted or mysterious about it.

When I rang the doorbell of the rectory, a portly, imposing man in sweater and slacks opened the door. I asked to talk to him about the history of the church. Evidently he had more than a share of the Sixth Sense, for he knew immediately what I was after.

"I am a priest," he said firmly, with a strong Slavic accent. I was somewhat taken aback because of his casual clothes, but he explained that even priests are allowed to relax now and then. Father X., as we shall call him, was a well-educated, soft-spoken man of about forty-five or fifty, and he readily admitted he had heard the rumors about "spirits," but there was, of course, nothing to it. Actually, he said, the man to talk to was his superior, Father H.

A few moments later, Father H. was summoned and introduced to me as "the authority" on the subject. When the good Father heard I was a parapsychologist and interested in his ghost, he became agitated. "I have nothing to say," he emphasized, and politely showed us the door. I chose to ignore his move.

Instead, I persisted in requesting either confirmation or denial of the rumors of hauntings in his church. Evidently, Father H. was afraid of the unusual. Many priests are not and discuss freely that which they know exists. But Father H. had once met with another writer, Louis Adamic, and apparently this had soured him on all other writers, like myself.

It seems that Adamic, a fellow Croatian, had mentioned in one of his books the story about the ghost at the altar—and seriously at that—quite a feat for a nonbeliever as Adamic was said to have been. Father H. had nothing to say for publication.

"No, no, no—nothing. I bless you. Good-bye." He bowed ceremoniously and waited for us to depart. Instead, I turned and smiled at Father X., the assistant pastor.

"May we see the church?" I said and waited. They couldn't very well refuse. Father H. realized we weren't going to leave at once and resigned himself to the fact that his assistant pastor would talk to us.

"Very well. But without me!" he finally said, and withdrew. That was all Father X. had needed. The field was clear now. Slowly he lit a cigarette and said, "You know, I've studied parapsychology myself for two years in my native Croatia."

After his initial appearance, nothing about Father X. surprised me. As we walked across the yard to the church, we entered into an animated discussion about the merits of psychic research. Father X. took us in through the altar door, and we saw the gleaming white and gold altar emerging from the semidarkness like a vision in one of Raphael's Renaissance paintings.

There was definitely something very unusual about this church. For one thing, it was a typically European, Slavonically tinged edifice and one had the immediate feel of being among an ethnic group of different origin from one's own. The large nave culminated in a balcony on which an old-fashioned—that is, nonelectric, nonautomatic—organ was placed in a prominent position. No doubt services at this church were imposing and emotionally satisfying experiences.

We stepped closer to the altar, which was flanked on either side by a large, heavy vigil light, the kind Europeans call Eternal Light. "See this painting," Father X. said and pointed at the curving fresco covering the entire inner cupola behind the altar, both behind it and above it. The painting showed natives of Croatia in their costumes, and a group of Croatians presenting a model of their church.

These traditional scenes were depicted with vivid colors and a charming, primitive style not found elsewhere. I inquired about the painter. "Maxim Hvatka," the priest said, and at once I recognized the name as that of a celebrated Yugoslav artist who had passed on a few years ago. The frescos were done in the early part of the century.

As we admired the altar, standing on its steps and getting impressions, Father X. must again have read my mind, for he said without further ado, "Yes, it is this spot where the 'spirits were seen.'"

There was no doubt in my mind that our assistant pastor was quite convinced of the truth of the phenomena.

"What exactly happened?" I asked.

"Well, not so long ago, Father H. and this painter Hvatka, they were here near the altar. Hvatka was painting the altar picture and Father H. was here to watch him. Suddenly, Hvatka grabbed Father's arm and said with great excitement, 'Look, Father—this person—there is someone here in the church, in front of the altar!'

"Father H. knew that the church was locked up tight and that only he and the painter were in the building. There *couldn't* be another person. 'Where? Who?' he said and looked hard. He didn't see anything. Hvatka insisted he had just seen a man walk by the altar and disappear into nothing. They stepped up to the vigil light on the left and experienced a sudden chill. Moreover, *the light was out.*

"Now to extinguish this light with anything less than a powerful blower or fan directly above it is impossible. Glass-enclosed and metal-covered, these powerful wax candles are meant to withstand the wind and certainly ordinary drafts or human breath. Only a supernormal agency could have put out that vigil light, gentlemen."

Father X. paused. I was impressed by his well-told story, and I knew at once why Father H. wanted no part of us. How could he ever admit having been in the presence of a spirit without having seen it? Impossible. We took some photographs and walked slowly towards the exit.

Father X. warmed up to me now and volunteered an experience from his own youth. It seems that when he was studying theology in his native Croatia, he lived among a group of perhaps a dozen young students who did not share his enthusiasm for psychic studies—who, in fact, ridiculed them.

One young man, however, who was his roommate, took the subject seriously, so seriously in fact that they made a pact—whoever died first would let the other know. A short time later, Father X., asleep on a warm afternoon, suddenly woke up. He *knew* his friend had died that instant, for he saw him sitting on a chair near his bed, laughing and waving at him. It was more than a mere dream, a vividly powerful impression. Father X. was no longer asleep at that moment; the impression had actually awakened him.

He looked at his watch; it was just three in the afternoon. Quickly, he made inquiries about his friend. Within a few hours he knew what he had already suspected—his friend had died in an accident at precisely the moment he had seen him in his room, back at the seminary!

"You're psychic then," I said.

Father X. shrugged. "I know many psychic cases," he said obliquely. "There was that nun in Italy, who left her hand prints on the church door to let her superiors know she was now in purgatory."

Father X. spoke softly and with the assurance of a man who knows his subject well. "There are these things, but what can we do? We cannot very well admit them."

A sudden thought came to my mind. Did he have any idea who the ghost at the altar was? Father X. shook his head.

"Tell me," I continued, "did anyone die violently in the church?"

Again, a negative answer.

"That's strange," I said. "Was there another building on this spot before the present church?"

"No," Father X. said nonchalantly.

"That's even stranger," I countered, "for my research indicates there was a priest here in the nineteenth century, and it is his ghost that has been seen."

Father X. swallowed hard.

"As a matter of fact," he said now, "you're right. There was an earlier wooden church here on this very spot. The present stone building only dates back to about nineteen one. Father Ranzinger built the wooden church."

"Was that around eighteen eighty-five?" I inquired. That is how I had it in my notes.

"Probably correct," the priest said, and no longer marveled at my information.

"What happened to the wooden church, Father?" I asked, and here I had a blank, for my research told me nothing further.

"Oh, it burned down. Completely. No, nobody got hurt, but the church, it was a total loss."

Father Ranzinger's beloved wooden church went up in flames, it appears, and the fifteen years he had spent with his flock must have accumulated an emotional backlog of great strength and attachment. Was it not conceivable that Father Ranzinger's attachment to the building was transferred to the stone edifice as soon as it was finished?

Was it his ghost the two men had seen in front of the altar? Until he puts in another appearance, we won't know, but Pittsburgh's Haunted Church is a lovely place in which to rest and pray—ghost or no ghost.

THE CASE OF THE
BURIED MINERS

I N T H E S E C O N D half of August of 1963, every newspaper in the United States was filled with the day-to-day accounts of a mining cave-in at Hazleton, Pennsylvania. Two men, David Fellin and Henry Throne, survived fourteen days at the bottom of a caved-in mine shaft and were finally rescued through a specially drilled funnel.

On August 28, Fellin gave the Associated Press an interview, in which he said:

> Now they're trying to tell me those things were hallucinations, that we imagined it all.
>
> We didn't. Our minds weren't playing tricks on us. I've been a practical, hardheaded coal miner all my life. My mind was clear down there in the mine. It's still clear.
>
> We saw what we say. These things happened. I can't explain them. I'm almost afraid to think what might be the explanation.
>
> For example, on the fourth or fifth day, *we saw this door,* although we had no light from above or from our hel-

mets. *The door was covered in bright blue light. It was very clear, better than sunlight.*

Two men, ordinary-looking men, not miners, *opened the door.* We could see beautiful marble steps on the other side. We saw this for some time and then we didn't see it. We saw other things I *can't explain.*

One thing I was always sure of. I was convinced we'd get out even if I had to dig us out myself.

A funny thing occurred on that very first day. We [Henry Throne and Louis Bova] hadn't been down in the mine five minutes that morning when my stomach started feeling a little out of whack.

I said, "Let's go out for an hour or so."

But the boys persuaded me to stay and get some work done first.

So we stayed, down at the tunnel's bottom, more than 300 feet down. Louis was on one side and me and Hank on the other.

Louis reached up to press the buzzer for the buggy [a small wagon which carries coal on tracks up to the surface]. He pressed the buzzer and stepped back. Then it happened.

Suddenly everything was coming down—timber, coal, rocks. The stuff was rushing down between us and Louis. Then it was quiet for maybe half a minute. Then the rush started again. It went on like this, starting and stopping for some time.

We sat there, listening as hard as we could for more rushes in the dark. We sat there against the wall that way 14 to 16 hours in a place about 6 feet long, 5 feet wide and about 3 feet high.

Now, you asked me about the strange things Hank saw. I actually saw more of them than he did. But I find it hard to talk about that.

I'm positive we saw what we saw. We weren't imagining them. Even before we heard from the men on the top, we had some light now and then. How else can you explain all the work we did down there? We couldn't have done it entirely in darkness.

The only time I was really scared was when we saw two men dressed like power linemen. Don't ask me what men like that were doing down on the bottom. *But I* saw them.

Hank asked me two or three times to ask the men for some light. This idea scared me down to my toes. I had the feeling this was something outside of our reach, that we shouldn't talk or do anything.

But Hank did not. Hank said to the men, "Hey, buddy, how about showing us some light?"

They didn't answer, and after a while we didn't see them any more.

Well, similar descriptions have been given from time to time by people close to death; Arthur Ford was once in that position in a hospital, and described vividly the door and the men operating it, before he was able to return to this side of the Veil once more.

Did David Fellin have a glimpse of the Other Side of Life, the Unseen World, the world of the psychic? Perhaps he did. Perhaps, too, he was being helped by these forces to return to the surface. In a television interview Fellin also claimed to have been given a message by the men, but he could not discuss it.

About the same time this happened, a millworker named Guy de Maggio had a vision of Fellin and his visitors from Beyond, and actually heard the words spoken by Fellin. So vivid was the impression that he took pains to tell people about it. This was many miles away from the scene and could be confirmed only later, after Fellin was rescued. Did both men tune in on the same supernormal wavelength?

The local psychiatrists had done their best to convince Fellin that he had a hallucination. But Fellin was convinced of his experience. And so was I.

I tried to coax the two miners to come on Pittsburgh television with me. They refused. They were afraid of being laughed at. Then a reporter from the *Philadelphia Sunday Bulletin* went to interview them on the anniversary of the event.

Yes, it was true that David Fellin had seen a door with beautiful marble steps, but there were also the people, apparently human, walking up and down the stairs. Yet somehow he and Hank Throne feared to go through the door.

"Did you see what was on the other side of the door?" the reporter asked.

"A beautiful garden, just as far as you can see. The flowers were more beautiful, the grass greener, than here on earth. I knew that was some special place."

"Did the man hold the door open?"

"No, Hank shouted for him to hold it, but the door slammed."

"What happened then?"

"Hank got mad. He said: 'Give me that hammer. I'll open that door.' The hammer was lying next to me, and I just handed it to him. He took it and ran at the door, then swung the hammer at it. That's when he broke a bone in his hand. And he bruised himself on the right cheek."

"What happened to the door?"

"It disappeared, and the light went out."

"What light? What did it look like?"

"It was a bluish light, not like daylight."

"Both you and Hank saw this door and the light?"

"Yes. Also Pope John. But Hank didn't know it was Pope John, not until we got to the hospital and the priest brought me a book with a picture of Pope John on the cover." (Pope John XXIII died June 3, 1963.)

"Let's start at the beginning."

"I was sitting here, and Hank was sitting like where you are [facing him]. He kept looking up over my shoulder. I looked up one time and saw Pope John there. He had his arms crossed and was just looking down at us. He didn't say anything."

"Did you and Hank speak to him?"

"I would say, 'Is our friend still there?' or 'How's our friend today?' Hank would grin and say he was still there."

"Didn't you tell him this was Pope John?"

"I figured Hank was a Protestant, and wouldn't know who he was anyway."

"How did he find out then?"

"When they took us to the hospital, my priest brought me a book with a picture of the Pope on it. And Hank points to the book and said, 'Hey, there's that guy we saw, Dave.' "

"Did you and Hank discuss these things while you saw them?"

"No, not too much. When we saw those people on the steps I told him we stumbled onto something. I had nicknamed the mine where we were trapped 'The Graveyard of Souls.' And I told him that we stumbled onto the graveyard of souls."

The reporter later talked to Throne, who said that he saw the door, stairway and Pope John. Pope John XXIII was, of course, on the spiritual side of the Veil at the time the two buried miners saw his apparition.

The London *Psychic News* also picked up the story and featured it. They headlined it:

ENTOMBED MINER
IS NOT AFRAID
TO DIE ANY MORE

Not after they saw where they'd be going.

SOUTHERN
MANSION GHOSTS

T HERE IS NOTHING as gracious as a Southern host or hostess, and nothing quite as colorful as a Southern ghost. Sometimes it is difficult to differentiate the true from the merely well told, but I have cut through the magnolia-scented curtain to ascertain what facts there are in a number of Southern houses, by no means more than a fraction of what there is, for the tragedies of the South, gentle though they may be in comparison with the violence of New England or the rugged West, have yielded their fair share of spectral characters.

My wife and I spent time in the Charlottesville, Virginia, area in May of 1963, and in North Carolina in April of the following year.

On both occasions we were fortunate enough to know the "right" people, so that we were received everywhere with open arms and—more important for a Ghost Hunter—open doors and secrets.

Take Castle Hill, Virginia, for instance. Its ghost wasn't much of a ghost as specters go, but it was authenticated and the names of witnesses were known. The house itself was magnificent and the only one of its kind.

At that time, it was the residence of Colonel Clark Lawrence, and it has a colorful history. I quote from information supplied to me by the Colonel:

The estate of Castle Hill passed into possession of Dr. Thomas Walker in 1741 when he married the widow of Nicholas Meriwether. It then comprised 15,000 acres and was a grant from George II, King of England.

Miss Judith Page Walker, daughter of Dr. Walker's son Francis from whom she inherited Castle Hill, married William Cabell Rives, bringing Castle Hill into the possession of the Rives family, where it remained until purchased in September, 1947, by Colonel and Mrs. Clark J. Lawrence. The estate now comprises 1,183 acres.

The house is actually two houses: the first, built in 1765 by Dr. Thomas Walker, is a frame clapboard structure, one room deep and a story and a half high, exhibiting the charm and sturdiness of the eighteenth century. Its six dormer windows and small porch with floor of solid stone blocks, belonging to an earlier structure built by Dr. Walker, look out across the old Bowling Green to Walnut Mountain, part of the estate, a continuation of the Southwest Range.

Its entrance hall runs the length of the house and is flanked on either side by spacious pine-paneled rooms.

The front of the house then faced north. In 1820 Judith Page Walker and her husband, Senator William Cabell Rives, twice Minister to France, built the formal brick addition with twelve-foot ceilings and beautiful interior trim. In 1840 he added the one-story wings with the loggias.

The 1820 structure made the front of the mansion facing the south, and the hourglass-shaped lawn and entrance box hedges were laid out and planted by Mrs. Rives and show a decided French influence.

It was at Castle Hill that Major Jack Jouett broke his famous ride, "hell for leather" from Louisa Court House to Charlottesville. He was on his way to warn Thomas Jefferson, then Governor of Virginia, and the members of the legislature there assembled that General Tarleton and his British troopers were coming to capture them.

Near Castle Hill Jouette's mount gave out. Dr. Walker remounted him on one of Castle Hill's fastest horses and bade him God Speed.

At daybreak the next morning, June 4, 1781, Tarleton and his troopers appeared at Castle Hill and demanded breakfast. Dr. Walker's potent mint juleps and an intentionally delayed breakfast made Jefferson's escape possible. Under the mellow effect of such liquid hospitality Tarleton seems to have unbent a good deal and he and Dr. Walker measured his orderly on the living-room doorjamb.

This trooper was the tallest man in the British army and proved six feet nine and one quarter inches in height. The notch cut by Dr. Walker is still visible on the old door jamb now connecting the old part of the house with the 1820 stair hall.

The old house is full of interesting memories. The youthful Jefferson played the fiddle for the still younger Madison to dance in the old living room. General Washington, General Lafayette, Dolley Madison, and in later years Andrew Jackson, Martin Van Buren and John Tyler visited at Castle Hill.

It was long the house of Amelie Rives, the authoress, who lived there with her artist husband, Prince Pierre Troubetzkoy.

The ghost had appeared from time to time to guests using a certain bedroom, known as the Pink Bedroom. In the 1930's, author Julian Green, who did not profess any belief in the supernatural, slept in the haunted room. The next morning, he packed his bags and left, cutting short an expected long stay.

Princess Troubetzkoy, who lies buried in the private cemetery on the grounds, reported smelling a certain peculiar perfume associated with the ghostly lady. As the story goes, she appears to people she doesn't like and tells them to go away. Those she likes were permitted to stay in her bedroom, however.

I questioned Colonel Lawrence as to whether he himself might have had any unusual experiences at Castle Hill. He shook his head. Either he was not psychic, or preferred not to talk about it.

Southerners can be very politely negative if they want to be and, although the Colonel was only a fairly recent addition to the Southland, he had become very much like any other owner of a Southern mansion. But he did admit that the people sleeping in the Pink Room were generally restless and disturbed for no apparent reason, for the room with its subdued, dainty elegance was surely one of the prettiest and most restful rooms I have ever been in. It has a decidedly feminine appeal, of course, and the Colonel had decided to keep it exactly as it was.

Not far from Castle Hill is one of America's most venerated historical shrines, the country house once owned by President Monroe, where he and Thomas Jefferson frequently exchanged small talk and also made big decisions. The modest-appearing house was now in private hands, but was open to visitors at certain hours.

For unexplained reasons, photography was frowned upon, and I was told in no uncertain terms by those in the know, that I should not try to take any pictures. Also, I could not have a private visit, for the very word "ghost" was unwelcome to the present owners of Ash Lawn, as the house was called.

The ghostly goings-on centered around a certain wooden rocking chair which was said to rock without benefit of human hands. With historian Virginia Cloud momentarily distracting the attention of the guide, I photographed the chair several times. It did not rock for me, but any self-respecting ghost would run for the woods, so to speak, if he had to listen to the talk of a professional museum guide every hour on the hour.

This was Monroe's favorite house even after he moved to a bigger place later in his career. Here he could "get away from it all" and, with friend Jefferson only a couple of miles away at Monticello, could really relax.

Has anyone ever seen the ghostly chair rock? Mrs. Joseph Massey, a resident of the area, whose mother once owned the house and gardens, was most emphatic about it:

"I will tell anyone, and have no objection to its being known, I have seen, not once but time and time again, the rocking chair in my bedroom rocking exactly as though someone were in it. My brother John has seen it, too. If we touched it, it stopped."

Horace Burr was a collector as well as an expert on art. His house in Charlottesville, Virginia, was filled to the rafters with art and fine furniture. Carrsgrove, as the rambling country place was called, was a wooden structure, the oldest part of which dates back at least one hundred fifty years. Soon after acquiring the property, about 1956, the Burrs realized that there was something the matter with their house.

It was haunted.

In the oldest part of the house, dead center, they kept hearing a "sighing" ghost.

Mrs. Helen Burr had just given birth to a child when she first reported hearing the uncanny noise. At 3:45 A.M. every morning she heard the mournful sighing of a woman no one could see. At first only she heard it, but one day she woke her husband and insisted that he accompany her to the spot near the inner wall. Then he heard it, too.

Burr's curiosity was aroused and he made some inquiries about the house. The previous owner, whose name was McCue, had died, but his faithful nurse was still living. She reported what had happened one terrible morning, about 1910.

McCue's daughter was staying at the house at the time with her young child. She started to imagine that the baby was not going to be normal, and in a fit of postnatal depression, she took poison. At exactly 3:45 A.M., the nurse told Burr, the father awoke and heard his daughter's dying gasp. By the time he raced to her bedroom on the other side of the house, she was dead.

It was that identical dying gasp that the Burrs had been hearing. However, once the explanation was given and the reasons for the noise in the house had been discussed, something happened to the ghost. The Burrs did not hear the noise again, but with *ghosts* one never knows.

The area was full of ghostly tales. Many of them cannot be traced to a point where a scientific inquiry would yield tangible results in terms of believability. But now and then a tale sounds so real, and the people involved are so honest and free of ulterior motives that I cannot help but feel they ought to be at least mentioned here. For the following tale, as for other invaluable help, I am indebted to Virginia Cloud, librarian and author, who lived in Charlottesville.

Not far from Castle Hill, in a less pretentious house, lived a family with a ten-year-old daughter. One night, when the child was supposed to be asleep in her upstairs room, the mother found her wide awake when she herself was going to bed.

"Why aren't you asleep?" the mother sternly asked. The little girl pointed to a corner of the room and replied, "I've been watching the little old man in the bed in the corner."

The mother insisted there was no bed in the corner, and the daughter, with equal determination, insisted that the old man was there and that he was very short of stature and had a very white beard.

All this upset the parents so much that they looked into the background of their house. To their amazement they discovered that the previous occupants had had a grandfather staying with them until his death. The room now occupied by their daughter had been his room, and the bed was exactly as the child had described it. The old man had had a very white beard and had not been very tall. He had, however, passed on long before the little girl was even born!

Some people consider Washington, D.C., neither Northern nor Southern, but the truth is that, in a historical and cultural sense, it really is a Southern city.

Our expedition to the nation's capital was aimed primarily at The Octagon, but I had read of still another haunted house and decided to pursue the matter.

On April 21, 1963, the *Boston Sunday Globe* ran a story signed by one Nick Roper and entitled, "I Lived in a Haunted House." The story was illustrated by four photographs showing Mr. Roper, his sister Anne, the police in one of the corridors, and an outside view of the famous old Georgian mansion known as Halcyon House in Georgetown.

Mr. Roper, whose family had moved into the sprawling mansion six months before, had been a nonbeliever in ghosts. Mr. Roper, Sr., was a real-estate broker who had first rented the house and then sold it to Georgetown University, which then owned it, although the Ropers still lived in it.

Young Roper made it plain that his new-found enthusiasm for things spectral was not shared by the rest of the Ropers:

Dad remained staunchly skeptical. But try as he will, even he can't explain the footsteps that tread the attics and run up and down the stairs, the lights that switch on and off without human hands, doors that open and shut themselves, ash trays that mysteriously filled with water, the Riddle of the Basement, and the Strange Affair of the Fallen Mirror—not to mention the voice in the Garden.

My twenty-one-year-old sister Anne and the three women who share Apartment 1214 will admit they've heard strange things, too. The girls report that every Thursday between 1 and 2 in the morning they hear measured pacing in the attic overhead. The "ghost" is always on schedule.

Corinne Mitchell Poole reported in the *Sunday Star* of August 9, 1959, when writing about Halcyon House:

> Perhaps the ghost of Benjamin Stoddert, the builder of Halcyon House, is responsible for the occasional mysterious opening and shutting of doors, and one likes to think it is the ghost of a twentieth century owner, Albert Clemens, which sometimes makes a clatter in the upper stories.
>
> The house has forty-five rooms, plus numerous nooks and passageways.

Of course the Ropers, Nick included, did not believe this story one bit. But they soon found out that ghosts weren't something you can sweep under the carpet. Nick wrote, in the *Globe* account:

> On two or three occasions my mother Mary, while brewing coffee in the kitchen, heard someone running down the stairs.

Convinced it was me, she poured a cup and waited. When I didn't show up, she came upstairs calling me. I was still in my room and hadn't left it.

Night after night, I have heard footsteps in the attic over my room, sometimes on the fire escape outside my French window. They pace steadily, then stop abruptly. The first time this happened, thinking it might be a prowler, I sneaked up into the attic to check. The light was on, but no one was there. The only way out of the attic was through my bedroom. I shrugged off the burning light as an electrical quirk (though the switch worked perfectly) and the footsteps as the normal creakings of an old house.

Nick Roper still would not accept the fact the house was haunted. On one occasion he found the lights burning in the basement and the atmosphere surcharged with the presence of an Unseen Person. When he shouted "Who's there?" the light went out by itself.

On another occasion he was awakened by mysterious footsteps and found himself floating above his bed, the window in his room wide open, when he distinctly remembered having it shut before he went to bed. He was gently lowered into bed again by unseen hands, but the terror of it all was enough to change his attitude towards the Uncanny.

All sorts of nocturnal noises, heard by the entire family, added to the nervous tension in the house. When a heavy mirror fell off its iron spike all by itself during their absence from the house, and a black X mark showed in the center of the glass, the Ropers were no longer amused. But what could they do?

What they could do, they did not do. That is, get the help of someone like myself to come to terms with the haunting personalities and find out what they wanted. I offered my services, free of course, and in confidence, as early as August, 1963. Mr. Roper, Sr., refused to see me, or even to discuss the matter.

A long-time Washington resident, Eleanor Baumgardner, better known to her friends as "Lady," tried to arrange things, to no avail. But she did manage to get me some background information about Halcyon House. She asked an expert friend to get me all the data I needed. Here they are:

On August 24, 1961, Bowman Jeffries wrote:

One of Georgetown's great houses, Halcyon House, has been purchased by Georgetown University. The sale was arranged by George S. Roper, real-estate broker for the University, who bought the house from Mrs. Kondrup Gray and her daughter, Mrs. H. E. Kondrup, for a purchase price reported to be in the neighborhood of $250,000.

Halcyon House, situated in the lower part of town at 3400 Prospect Street, was built in 1783 by Benjamin Stoddert, the nation's first Secretary of the Navy and one of the 18 "proprietors" of the Federal City.

The mansion is as fabulous as the myth of the bird from which its name is derived. The classic belief about the halcyon bird was that, floating on the sea in its nest, it bred at the time of the winter solstice, magically causing the water to be especially calm at that time. Hence halcyon quietude, "Halcyon Days," and Halcyon House, a name aptly selected by Secretary Stoddert.

The original Georgian structure of the house was brick laid up Flemish bond, with handsome symmetry in its two-story wings, and a widow's walk at the top.

The beautiful front door—a seven-section fanlight flanked by fluted pilasters with a rounded arch and keystone above—faced the River with Prospect Street at the back. The original façade is not visible from the street now (one can just glimpse it in winter, crossing Key Bridge), but it remains as constructed. Spreading from the front door toward the Potomac is a magnificent garden, said to be Major L'Enfant's plan.

Wisteria and boxwood are the triumphs here, with black-green magnolias, old rhododendron, mossy brick walls and walks, and ivy everywhere. The garden seems timeless, remotely walled and stranded high above Thirty-fourth Street. Various owners have added and subtracted a swimming pool, terraces, fountains, and Grecian colonnades; the dark gleaming greens of ivy, box and magnolias remain superb.

At the turn of the century Albert Clemens, eccentric *extraordinaire,* bought Halcyon House for the proverbial song. Clemens, a firm foe of electricity, refused to permit it to be installed. In addition to other changes, he had a large cigar-store Indian placed on the balcony overlooking the front door. He is said to have been buried under a chapel in the house. His ghost walks the long corridors at night.

Georgetown is the second university to have owned Halcyon House. Clemens willed it to Harvard and in 1943 the university sold it to Frederick Sterling, former Ambassador to Sweden. Not being subject to Mr. Clemens' antagonisms, he immediately installed electricity.

Georgetown University plans to turn the historic house, ghosts and all, into a dormitory for women students in the School of Foreign Service of the Graduate School and Institute of Foreign Language and Linguistics. Apartments for 60 women will be constructed.

September 13, 1963—Upon calling at Georgetown University, I found that because of zoning regulations, they were unable to turn Halcyon House into a dormitory for

women students; however, it has been turned into apartments for men and women.

If you want to discuss or visit this house, I suggest you
get in touch with George S. Roper at Georgetown
University, Thirty-seventh and O streets NW., Washington
7, D.C., inasmuch as he handles the investment properties
for the University.

This latter admonition was superfluous as Mr. Roper, Sr., had
already refused my help, advice, and even a brief visit. When I
requested the address of his son Nick, the one who had written the
newspaper piece—or at any rate, signed it—in the *Boston Globe,* I
was told, "My son Nicholas is no longer a resident in Washington."

But the Ghost Hunter is not that easily dismayed. Since we
were already in the city, I tried to telephone the house and ask permission to see it for a few minutes, just as any scientist might ask
under the circumstances. I could not reach the Ropers.

Catherine and I decided to take a chance, having heard about
and experienced lots of Southern hospitality. We felt sure that the
Ropers would at least spare us ten or fifteen minutes. It was a chilly
night and we realized that we were far from the center of the city—a
fact that caused us considerable unhappiness on our return, for taxis
were nowhere to be had.

When I rang the bell at Halcyon House, a young man in his
middle teens opened the gate. He was a cousin of the Ropers, and
most friendly. I explained my reason for not announcing our visit
and he asked my wife and me to step inside the house. We discussed
Dr. Joseph Rhine and parapsychology for a few moments, then the
young man led us farther into the house and began to show us
around. We passed the kitchen where he decided to introduce us to
his aunt, Mrs. Mary Roper.

I apologized for our unexpected visit, and asked whether we

might have the privilege of seeing the historical portion of the house before flying back to New York.

All over the world such a request would have been honored, even though our visit was unexpected. And in other days people used to visit each other without telephone announcements when Mr. Bell had not yet become lucky.

Mrs. Roper practically threw us out of the house, and only the arrival of her husband prevented an embarrassing scene.

It was evident to me at once that Mrs. Roper was suffering from extreme nervousness, due no doubt to the ghostly goings-on in the house, which had deprived her momentarily of her inbred good manners.

Mr. Roper, Sr., quietly explained that his home was his castle and that he would rather not discuss the matter of hauntings. He finally gave me the address of his son in Wheaton, Maryland, but young Roper did not see fit to either confirm or deny the material facts of the haunting, although I wrote to him a number of times. No doubt he preferred to keep quiet about it.

A Washington psychiatrist I met through famed psychic Jeanne Dixon also told us of young Roper's unusual interest in the extrasensory field, but in his view Roper's imagination was running away with him. I am inclined to accept Roper's testimony at face value. At any rate, anyone interested in finding out if ghostly Ben and Bert still haunt the corridors and rooms of Halcyon House need only go up and see. The ghosts won't object, I'm sure, but the Ropers probably will.

My sympathy, of course, is with the ghosts.

A GHOST'S LAST
REFUGE

N EAR CHARLOTTESVILLE, VIRGINIA, stands a farmhouse built during Revolutionary days, later owned by Mary W., who, some years ago, had a fleeting interest in the work of Professor Rhine at Duke University.

Her own psychic talents were acknowledged, but she insisted she had not done any automatic writing for some time, and isn't really very much interested any more. Later I realized that her waning interest must have some connection with the events at the house which we shall call Wickham, since the real name must at present remain veiled in deference to the owner's request.

Virginia Cloud had come along to serve as a combination guide and clairvoyant, and writer Booton Herndon also came along to observe what he had always found a fascinating subject. Thus a caravan of two cars made its way to Wickham one bright May morning when nature's brilliance belied the sober subject of our goal.

On arrival, my wife, Catherine, and I sat down with Mary W. to hear her tell of her own experiences in the haunted house. Only after she had done so did Virginia Cloud enter the house.

The oldest part of the house, rather skillfully connected to the rest, consisted of a hall or main room and a small bedroom reached by a narrow winding staircase.

This portion, dating back to 1781, had been the location of some uncanny happenings beginning at the time when Mrs. W. acquired the house and acreage in 1951. Whether previous owners had had any experiences couldn't be ascertained.

Mrs. W. recalled an incident for us. Emotionally keyed up at the time, she had been in a small adjoining room downstairs, which had been turned into a small home bar, when she clearly heard footsteps in the main room, and a noise like that made by riding clothes, swishing sounds; she called out, but she knew it was not her husband. The steps continued; someone was walking up and down in the room. Mrs. W. took a look through the window and saw her entire family outside near the barn, some twenty yards away.

This alarmed her even more and she stepped into the main room. There was no one there. But the eerie thing was that even in her presence the steps continued, reached the doorway and then went back across the room to the stairway where they stopped abruptly at the landing leading to the old room above.

The previous owner, by the name of Deauwell, had told Mary W. that when his predecessor at the house, Mrs. Early, had died, there had been a strange noise *as if someone were falling downstairs*.

Two years later, in 1953, Mrs. W.'s two girls, aged twelve and nine at the time, were playing in the upstairs room while the parents were entertaining some guests in the nearby cottage apart from the main house. It was 10 P.M., when the girls distinctly heard someone walk around downstairs in the empty house. They called out, but got no answer. They thought it was a friend of their parents, but later checking revealed nobody had left the party to return to the main house even for a moment.

Around 1960–61, Mrs. W. again heard the by-now-familiar

footsteps in the same spot. They started, then stopped, then started up again. Although Mrs. W. admitted some psychic talent, her automatic writing had yielded no one claiming to be connected with the house except perhaps a slave woman named Rebecca, who claimed to have been captured by Indians who cut out her tongue. She was found by the Early sons, and became their servant; Mrs. W. also claimed a guide or control named Robert.

The place had been in litigation for many years, and there are no less than three family cemeteries on the grounds. The house itself was built by one Richard Durrette in 1781. When the fireplace was rebuilt prior to 1938, before Mrs. W. owned the place, an inscription turned up explaining that Hessian-soldier prisoners from a nearby barracks had helped build the chimney in 1781. Three thousand prisoners were kept in barracks nearby. Some stayed afterwards and married local women.

This was *not* discussed in the presence of Virginia Cloud, who soon went into semi-trance in the presence of Mary W. and myself. She "saw" an Albert or Alfred, in white shirt, boots, trousers, but not a uniform, dragging himself into the house; perhaps he was an injured Hessian entering an empty house, chased here by Redcoats. "The British are farther away . . . Something was burned near here." At this point, both Mary W. and I smelled smoke.

Independent of Virginia Cloud's testimony, both of us also heard a faint knock at the entrance door, two short raps.

Virginia, in her chair near the stairway, started to shiver. "The ghost remembers his mother and calls her, but she is not here any more . . . only a memory; he may have died here, since I don't see him leave again. His arm is hurt by metal, perhaps a shell."

Mary W. had lived through tragedy in her own life. Her husband, Kenneth, had committed suicide in the very house we were visiting. I had the feeling that Mary's interest in the occult coincided with this event, and that perhaps she thought the ghostly footsteps were actually her late husband's restless movements in the room he had called his own.

But the noises and disturbances go back farther than Mary's tenancy of the house. Premeditated suicide seldom yields ghosts. I am convinced that the ghost at Wickham was not Mary's husband, but the Hessian deserter who wanted to find refuge from the pursuing British.

THE OCTAGON
GHOSTS

C OLONEL JOHN TAYLOE, in 1800, built his mansion, the magnificent building, designed by Dr. William Thornton, now known as the Octagon because of its shape. It stood, and still stands, in a fashionable part of Washington, but then housed the offices and exhibit of the American Institute of Architects. These days, it is a museum of the American Architectural Foundation.

In the early 1800's the Colonel's daughter ran away with a stranger and later returned home, asking forgiveness. This she did not get from her stern father and in despair she threw herself from the third-floor landing of the winding staircase that still graces the mansion. She landed on a spot near the base of the stairs, and this started a series of eerie events recorded in the mansion over the years.

Life magazine reported in an article in 1962 on haunted mansions that some visitors claim to have seen a shadow on the spot where the girl fell, while others refuse to cross the spot for reasons unknown; still others have heard the shriek of the falling girl.

The July, 1959, issue of the *American Institute of Architects Journal* contains a brief account of the long service record of employee James Cypress. Although he himself never saw any ghosts, he reports that at one time when his wife was ill, the doctor saw a man dressed in the clothes of 150 years ago coming down the spiral staircase. As the doctor looked at the strange man in puzzlement, the man just disappeared *into thin air.*

After some correspondence with J. W. Rankin, Director of the Institute, my wife and I finally started out for Washington on May 17, 1963. It was a warm day and the beautiful Georgian mansion set back from one of the capital's busier streets promised an adventure into a more relaxed past.

Mr. Rankin received us with interest and showed us around the house which was at that time fortunately empty of tourists and other visitors. It was he who supplied some of the background information on the Octagon, from which I quote:

> The White House and the Octagon are relations, in a way. Both date from the beginning of government in the national capital; the White House was started first but the Octagon was first completed. Both have served as the official residence of the President.
>
> It was early in 1797 that Colonel John Tayloe of Mount Airy, Virginia, felt the need for a town house. Mount Airy was a magnificent plantation of some three thousand acres, on which the Colonel, among many activities, bred and raced horses, but the call of the city was beginning to be felt, even in that early day; Philadelphia was the Colonel's choice, but his friend General Washington painted a glowing picture of what the new national capital might become and persuaded him to build the Octagon in surroundings that were then far removed from urbanity.
>
> Dr. William Thornton, winner of the competition for the Capitol, was Colonel Tayloe's natural selection of architect.

On April 19, 1797, Colonel Tayloe purchased for $1,000 from Gustavus W. Scott—one of the original purchasers from the Government on November 21, 1796—Lot 8 in Square 170 in the new plot of Washington. Although, as the sketch of 1813 shows, the site was apparently out in a lonely countryside, the city streets had been definitely plotted, and the corner of New York Avenue and Eighteenth Street was then where it is today.

Obviously, from a glance at the plot plan, Colonel Tayloe's house derived its unique shape from the angle formed at the junction of these two streets. In spite of the name by which the mansion has always been known, Dr. Thornton could have had no intention of making the plan octagonal; the house planned itself from the street frontages.

Work on the building started in 1798 and progressed under the occasional inspection of General Washington, who did not live to see its completion in 1800. The mansion immediately took its place as a center of official and nonofficial social activities. Through its hospitable front door passed Madison, Jefferson, Monroe, Adams, Jackson, Decatur, Porter, Webster, Clay, Lafayette, Von Steuben, Calhoun, Randolph, Van Rensselaer and their ladies.

Social activities were forgotten, however, when the War of 1812 threatened and finally engulfed the new nation's capital. On August 24, 1814, the British left the White House a fire-gutted ruin. Mrs. Tayloe's foresight in establishing the French Minister—with his country's flag—as a house guest may have saved the Octagon from a like fate.

Colonel Tayloe is said to have dispatched a courier from Mount Airy, offering President Madison the use of the mansion, and the Madisons moved in on September 8, 1814.

For more than a year Dolley Madison reigned as hostess of the Octagon. In the tower room just over the entrance President Madison established his study, and here signed the Treaty of Ghent on February 17, 1815, establishing a peace with Great Britain which endures to this day.

After the death of Mrs. John Tayloe in 1855, the Octagon no longer served as the family's town house. That part of Washington lost for a time its residential character and the grand old mansion began to deteriorate.

In 1865 it was used as a school for girls. From 1866 to 1879 the Government rented it for the use of the Hydrographic Office. As an office and later as a studio dwelling, the Octagon served until about 1885, when it was entrusted by the Tayloe heirs to a caretaker.

Glenn Brown, longtime secretary of the American Institute of Architects, suggested in 1889 that the house would make an appropriate headquarters for the Institute.

When the architects started to rehabilitate the building, it was occupied by ten African-American families. The fine old drawing room was found to be piled four feet deep with rubbish. The whole interior was covered with grime, the fireplaces closed up, windows broken, but the structure, built a century before, had been denied no effort or expense to make it worthy of the Tayloes, and it still stood staunch and sound against time and neglect.

Miraculously the slender balusters of the famous stairway continued to serve, undoubtedly helped by the fact that every fifth baluster is of iron, firmly jointed to the handrail and carriage. Even the Coade Stone mantels in drawing room and dining room, with their deeply undercut sculpture, show not a chip nor scar. They had been brought from London in 1799 and bear that date with the maker's name.

On January 1, 1899, the Institute took formal possession of the rehabilitated mansion, its stable, smokehouse
and garden.

So much for the house itself. I was given free rein to interview
the staff, and proceeded to do so. Some of them are white, some
black; all displayed a high degree of intelligence and dignity of the
kind one often finds in the old South.

I carefully tabulated the testimony given me by the employees
individually, and checked the records of each of them for reliability
and possible dark spots. There were none.

In view of the fact that nobody was exactly eager to be put down
as having heard or seen ghosts, far from seeking publicity or public
attention, I can only regard these accounts as respectable experiences of well-balanced individuals.

The building itself was then in the care of Alric H. Clay, a man
in his thirties, who was an executive with the title of superintendent.
The museum part of the Octagon, as different from the large com-
plex of offices of the American Institute of Architects, was under the
supervision of Mrs. Belma May, who was its curator. She was assisted
by a staff of porters and maids, since on occasion formal dinners or
parties take place in the oldest part of the Octagon.

Mrs. May was not given to hallucinations or ghost stories, and
in a matter-of-fact voice reported to me what she had experienced in
the building. Most of her accounts were of very recent date.

Mrs. May saw the big chandelier swing of its own volition while
all windows in the foyer were tightly shut; she mentioned the
strange occurrence to a fellow worker. She also heard strange noises,
not accounted for, and mostly on Saturdays. On one occasion, Mrs.
May, accompanied by porters Allen and Bradley, found tracks of
human feet in the otherwise undisturbed dust on the top floor,
which had long been closed to the public. The tracks looked to her

as "if someone were standing on toes, tiptoeing across the floor." It was from there that the daughter of Colonel Tayloe had jumped.

Mrs. May would often smell cooking in the building when there was no party. She also felt "chills" on the first-floor landing.

Caretaker Mathew reported that when he walked up the stairs, he often felt as if someone was walking behind him, especially on the second floor.

Ethel Wilson, who helped with parties, reported "chills" in the cloakroom.

Porter Allen was setting up for a meeting on the ground floor in the spring of 1962, when he heard noises "like someone dragging heavy furniture across the floor upstairs." In March, 1963, he and his colleague saw the steps "move as if someone was walking on them, but there was no one there." This happened at 9:30 A.M.

Porter Bradley reported hearing groaning, but the sound was hard to pin down as to direction. Several times he also heard footsteps.

Alric H. Clay, in charge of buildings, was driving by with his wife and two children one evening in the spring of 1962, when he noticed that the lights in the building were on. Leaving his family in the car, he entered the closed building by the back door and found everything locked as it should be. However, in addition to the lights being on, he also noticed that the *carpet edge was flipped* up at the spot where the girl had fallen to her death in the 1800's.

Clay, not believing in ghosts, went upstairs; there was nobody around, so he turned the lights off, put the carpet back as it should be, and went downstairs into the basement where the light controls are.

At that moment, *on the main floor above* (which he had just left) *he clearly heard someone* walk from the drawing room to the door and back. Since he had just checked all doors and knew them to be bolted firmly, he was so upset he almost electrocuted himself at the switches. The steps were heavy and definitely those of a man.

In February of 1963 there was a late party in the building. After everybody had left, Clay went home secure in the knowledge that he alone possessed the key to the back door. The layout of the Octagon is such that nobody can hide from an inspection, so a guest playing a prank by staying on was out of the question.

At 3:00 A.M. the police called Clay to advise him that all lights at the Octagon were blazing and that the building was wide open. Mr. Woverton, the controller, checked and, together with the police, went through the building, turning off all lights once more. Everything was locked up again, in the presence of police officers.

At 7:00 A.M., however, they returned to the Octagon once more, only to find the door unlocked, the lights again burning. Yet, Clay was the only one with the key!

"Mr. Clay," I said, "after all these weird experiences, do you believe in ghosts?"

"No, I don't," Clay said, and laughed somewhat uneasily. He was a man of excellent educational background and the idea of accepting the Uncanny was not at all welcome to him. But there it was.

"Then how do you explain the events of the past couple of years?"

"I don't," he said and shrugged. "I just don't have a rational explanation for them. But they certainly happened."

From the testimony heard, I was convinced that there were two ghosts in the Octagon, restlessly pacing the creaking old floors, vying with each other for the attention of the flesh-and-blood world outside.

There were the dainty footsteps of Colonel Tayloe's suicidal daughter, retracing the walks she enjoyed but too briefly; and the heavy, guilt-laden steps of the father, who cannot cut himself loose from the ties that bind him to his house and the tragedy that darkened both the house and his life.

THE CASE OF THE LOST HEAD

O NE OF THE MOST FAMOUS famous ghosts of the South was railroad conductor Joe Baldwin. The story of Joe and his lantern was known to me; *Life* magazine even dignified it with a photograph of the railroad track near Wilmington, North Carolina, very atmospherically adorned by a greenish lantern, presumably swinging in ghostly hands.

Then one fine day in early 1964, the legend became reality when a letter arrived from Bill Mitcham, Executive Secretary of the South Eastern North Carolina Beach Association, a public-relations office set up by the leading resort hotels in the area centering around Wilmington. Mr. Mitcham proposed that I have a look at the ghost of Joe Baldwin, and try to explain once and for all—scientifically— what the famous "Maco Light" was or is.

In addition, Mr. Mitcham arranged for a lecture on the subject to be held at the end of my investigation and sponsored jointly by the Beach Association and Wilmington College. He promised to roll out the red carpet for Catherine and me, and roll it out he did.

Seldom in the history of ghost hunting has a parapsychologist been received so royally and so fully covered by press, television and radio, and if the ghost of Joe Baldwin was basking in the reflected glory of all this attention directed towards his personal Ghost Hunter, he was most welcome to it.

If it were not for Joe Baldwin, the bend in the railroad track which was known as Maco Station (a few miles outside of Wilmington) would be a most unattractive and ordinary trestle. By the time I had investigated it and left, in May of 1964, the spot had almost risen to the prominence of a national shrine and sight-seeing groups arrived at all times, especially at night, to look for Joe Baldwin's ghostly light.

Bill Mitcham had seen to it that the world knew about Joe Baldwin's headless ghost and Hans Holzer seeking same, and not less than seventy-eight separate news stories of one kind or another appeared in print during the week we spent in Wilmington.

Before I even started to make plans for the Wilmington expedition, I received a friendly letter from a local student of psychic phenomena, William Edward Cox, Jr., and a manuscript entitled "The Maco Ghost Light." Mr. Cox had spent considerable time observing the strange light, and I quote:

A favorite "ghost story" in the vicinity of Wilmington, N.C., is that of "Joe Baldwin's Ghost Light," which is alleged to appear at night near Maco, N.C., twelve miles west of Wilmington on the Atlantic Coast Line Railroad.

On June 30–July 1, 1949, this writer spent considerable time investigating the phenomenon. The purpose was to make an accurate check on the behavior of the light under test conditions, with a view toward ascertaining its exact nature.

This light has been observed since shortly after the legend of the Joe Baldwin ghost light "was born in 1867." It is officially reported in a pamphlet entitled "The Story of the Coast Line, 1830–1948." In its general description it resembles a 25-watt electric light slowly moving along the tracks toward the observer, whose best point of observation is on the track itself at the point where the tracks, double at that point, are crossed by a branch of a connecting roadway between U.S. Highway 74-76 and U.S. Highway 19.

The popular explanation is that Conductor Baldwin, decapitated in an accident, is taking the nocturnal walks in search of his head. . . .

After testing the various "natural" theories put forward for the origin of the nocturnal light, Mr. Cox admitted:

Although the general consensus of opinion is that the lights stem from some relatively rare cause, such as the paranormal, "*ignis fatuus,*" etc., the opinions of residents of the Maco vicinity were found by this observer to be more divided. The proprietor of the Mobil Service Station was noncommittal, and a local customer said he had "never seen the light." A farmer in the area was quite certain that it is caused by automobile headlights, but would not express an opinion upon such lights as were customarily seen there before the advent of the automobile.

The proprietress of the Willet Service Station, Mrs. C. L. Benton, was firmly convinced that it was of "supernatural origin," and that the peculiar visibility of automobile headlights to observers at Maco must be more or less a subsequent coincidence.

She said that her father "often saw it as he loaded the wood burners near there over 60 years ago."

The basic question of the origin and nature of the "Maco Light," or the original light, remains incompletely answered.

The findings here reported, due as they are to entirely normal causes, cannot accurately be construed as disproving the existence of a light of paranormal origin at any time in the distant past (or, for that matter, at the present time).

The unquestionable singularity of the phenomenon's being in a locale where it is so easily possible for automobiles to produce an identical phenomenon seems but to relegate it to the enigmatic "realm of forgotten mysteries."

So much for Mr. Cox's painstaking experiment conducted at the site in 1949.

The coming of the Ghost Hunter (and Mrs. Ghost Hunter) was amply heralded in the newspapers of the area. Typical of the veritable avalanche of features was the story in *The Charlotte Observer:*

CAN SPOOK HUNTER DE-GHOST OLD JOE?

The South Eastern N.C. Beach Association invited a leading parapsychologist Saturday to study the ghost of Old Joe Baldwin.

Bill Mitcham, executive director of the association, said he has arranged for Hans Holzer of New York to either prove or disprove the ghostly tales relating to Old Joe.

Holzer will begin his study May 1.

Tales of Joe Baldwin flagging down trains with false signals, waving his lantern on dark summer nights, have been repeated since his death in 1867.

Baldwin, a conductor on the Wilmington, Manchester and Augusta Railroad, was riding the rear coach of a train the night of his death. The coach became uncoupled and Baldwin seized a lantern in an effort to signal a passenger train following.

But the engineer failed to see the signal. In the resulting crash, Baldwin was decapitated.

A witness to the wreck later recalled that the signal lantern was flung some distance from the tracks, but that it burned brightly thereafter for some time.

Soon after the accident, there were reports of a mysterious light along the railroad tracks at Maco Station in Brunswick County.

Two lanterns, one green and one red, have been used by train-men at Maco Station so that engineers would not be confused or deceived by Joe Baldwin's light.

Most helpful in a more serious vein was the Women's Editor of the *Wilmington Star-News*, Theresa Thomas, who had for years taken an interest in the psychic and probably was somewhat sensitive herself. On April 8, 1964, she asked her readers:

HAVE YOU EVER SEEN THE MACO LIGHT?

Have you ever seen Old Joe Baldwin? Or his light, that is? As far as we know, nobody has actually seen Joe himself.

But if you have seen his lantern swinging along the railroad track at Maco, you can be of great help to Hans Holzer, Ghost Hunter, who will be in Wilmington April 29th.

Either write out your experience and send it to us, or call and tell us about it.

Then the feminine point of view crashed the scientific barrier a little as Miss Thomas added:

His [Mr. Holzer's] wife is just as fascinating as he. She is a painter and great-great-great-granddaughter of Catherine The Great of Russia. Mrs. Holzer was born Countess Catherine Buxhoeveden in a haunted castle in

Meran, the Tyrol, in the Italian Alps. And she paints— haven't you guessed?—haunted houses.

My visit was still three weeks away, but the wheels of publicity where already spinning fast and furiously in Wilmington.

Theresa Thomas' appeal for actual witnesses to the ghostly phenomena brought immediate results. For the first time people of standing took the matter seriously, and those who had seen the light opened up. Miss Thomas did not disguise her enthusiasm. On April 12, she wrote:

It seems a great many people have seen Old Joe Baldwin's light at Maco and most of them are willing—even eager—to talk about it.

Among the first to call was Mrs. Larry Moore, 211 Orange Street, who said she had seen the light three or four times at different seasons of the year.

The first time it was a cloudy, misty winter night and again in summer, misty again. Her description of the light was "like a bluish yellow flame." She and her companions walked down the track and the light came closer as they approached the trestle. When they reached the center of the trestle with the light apparently about 10 feet away, it disappeared.

Mrs. Thelma Daughtry, 6 Shearwater Drive, Wrightsville Beach, says she saw it on a misty spring night. It was about 7 or 8 o'clock in the evening and the reddish light appeared to swing along at about knee height.

Mrs. Margaret Jackson, of 172 Colonial Circle, a native of Vienna, Austria, saw it about seven years ago on a hazy night. She was with several other people and they all saw the light, a "glary shine" steady and far away but always the same distance ahead of them.

Dixie Rambeau, 220 Pfeiffer Avenue, saw it about 1 A.M. Friday morning. She says it was "real dark" and the light appeared as a red pinpoint at a distance up the track, as it neared it became yellowish white, then closer still it was a mixed red and white.

She recalls that she and her companions watched it come closer to the left side of the track and that as it came close the reflection on the rail almost reached them. At about 10 feet away it reversed its process and as they walked toward it, it disappeared. Once it appeared to cross over. They watched it five or six times, she said.

Mrs. Marvin Clark, 406 Grace Street, a practical nurse, states that she and her husband saw the light 15 years ago. It was about midnight on a cloudy, rainy night. They were standing in the middle of the track and "it looked like a light on a train coming at full speed."

Mrs. Clark described the light as "the color of a train light."

"We picked up our little girl and ran. All of us have always seen reflections of automobiles but beyond a doubt it was the Maco Light."

Mrs. Lase V. Dail of Carolina Beach also has a story to tell. It seems she and her husband came home late one night from Fayetteville.

She wrote: "As we left the cut off and headed into 74-76 highway, I shall never forget the experience we had . . ." She goes on, "All at once a bright light came down the road toward us, first I figured it was a car. But decided if so it had only one light. On it came steadily toward us.

"Then I figured it was a train, yet I heard nothing, and as suddenly as it appeared it vanished. I can say it was quite a weird feeling. I have often thought of it. I have heard many versions, but never one like this."

Three days later, Miss Thomas devoted still another full column to people who had witnessed the ghost light.

Mrs. Marjorie H. Rizer of Sneads Ferry wrote: "I have seen the light three times. The last and most significant time was about a year and a half ago. My husband, three young sons and a corpsman from the United States Naval Hospital at Camp Lejeune were with me and we saw the same thing. It was about 10:30 P.M. and we were returning from a ball game. We decided to go to Maco since we were so near and the young man with us didn't believe there was anything to our story.

"The sky was cloudy and a light mist was falling. We parked the car beside the track and sure enough, there was the light down the track. I stayed in the car with my sons, and my husband and the corpsman walked down the track toward the light.

"The light would alternately dim and then become very bright. The two men walked perhaps a quarter of a mile down the track before they returned. They said the light stayed ahead of them, but my sons and I saw the light between them and us.

"It looked as if the light would come almost to where we were parked and then it would wobble off down the track and disappear. In a moment it would reappear and do the same time after time.

"When we had been there for about an hour and started to leave, a train approached going toward Wilmington. The light was a short distance away from us. As the train passed the light, it rose and hovered over the train. We could clearly see the top of the train as the light became very bright.

"It stayed over the train until it had passed then disappeared back down near the track and finally it looked as if someone had thrown it off into the woods.

"As we pulled away from the track the light came back on the track and weaved backward and forward down the track as it had been doing."

And still the letters poured in. On April 22, after half a column devoted to my imminent arrival in the area, Miss Thomas printed a letter from a young man who had taken some interesting pictures:

He is J. Everett Huggins, home address 412 Market Street, Wilmington. The letter is addressed to Bill Mitcham and reads in part: "I read with interest the articles on your 'ghost survey,' especially since I saw the Maco light less than two weeks ago and was actually able to catch Old Joe on film.

"On the nights of April 1 and 2 a schoolmate of mine and I went to Maco Station in the hopes of seeing the light. We saw nothing on Friday, April 1, but we had more success on Saturday, when it was a littler darker. Around 10:30 we saw a yellow light about 100 yards down the track from us (this distance is only a guess). It seemed to be about 10 feet above the tracks and looked as if it were moving slowly toward us for a while, then it went back and died out.

"The light appeared maybe three times in succession for periods up to what I would estimate to be about thirty seconds.

"I attempted to take two time exposures with my camera. Unfortunately I did not have a tripod, and so I had to hold the camera in my hands, which made clear results impossible. The pictures are not spectacular—just a small spot on each of the color transparencies—but they are pictures. If you are interested I will have some copies made.

"My friends had kidded me about the light, so I noted some details to try to end their skepticism. The headlights of cars traveling west on Highway 74 could be seen in the distance, and no doubt many who think they see Old Joe only see these lights. Old Joe could be distinguished in several ways, however. First, the light had a yellower tone than did the auto headlights.

"Secondly, unlike the headlights which grow brighter and brighter and then suddenly disappear, the Maco light would gradually grow brighter and then gradually fade out. Thirdly, the Maco light produced a reflection on the rails that was not characteristic of the headlights.

"More interesting was the fact that the reflection on the rails was seen only on a relatively short stretch of track. By observing the reflection, we could tell that the light moved backward and forward on the rails. It always remained directly above the tracks.

"I had seen the light once before, in 1956. It was on a cold winter night, and the light was brighter."

As the day of our arrival grew nearer, the tempo of the press became more hectic. On April 26, Arnold Kirk wrote in the *Wilmington Star-News:*

This tiny Brunswick County village, nestled in a small clearing a few miles west of Wilmington off U.S. Highway 74, is rapidly gaining acclaim as the "Ghost Capital" of North Carolina.

Its few dozen inhabitants, mostly farmers of moderate means, have suddenly found their once-peaceful nights disturbed by scores of vehicles sparring for vantage points from which to view the famous "Maco Light."

While the legend of the light and old Joe Baldwin, the "ghost" of Maco, has long been known, its popularity has become intense only in recent months.

Elaborate plans have already been made to welcome Holzer to the Port City. The mayors of all the towns in New Hanover and Brunswick counties, in addition to county commissioners from both counties, have agreed to be at the New Hanover County Airport Wednesday at 7:43 P.M. when the "ghost hunter's" plane arrives.

Lanterns at Airport—Also on hand to greet the noted parapsychologist will be 1,000 high-school students, carrying, appropriately enough, lighted lanterns! The lanterns were purchased by the city years ago to offer warmth to trees and plants during blustery winter months.

Adding to the fanfare of the event will be the first public offering of "The Ballad of Old Joe Baldwin," written by the senior English class of New Hanover High School.

The reception was a bash that would have made Old Joe Baldwin feel honored. A little later, we tried to sneak out to Maco and have a first glance at the haunted spot. The results were disappointing.

It was not so much that the ghost did not show, but what did show up was most disturbing. *The Wilmington Star* summed it up like this:

> An unwilling Old Joe Baldwin exercised his ghostly prerogative Wednesday night by refusing to perform before what may have been his largest audience.
>
> Huddled in small clusters along the railroad tracks near the center of this tiny Brunswick County village, an estimated 250 persons stared into the gloomy darkness in hopes of catching a glimpse of the famous "Maco Light."

But the light would not offer the slightest flicker.

Holzer's announced visit to the scene of Baldwin's ghastly demise gave no comfort to the few dozen residents of Maco. By 10 o'clock, dozens of cars lined both sides of the narrow Maco road and scores of thrill-seeking teenagers had spilled onto the railroad track.

If Joe Baldwin had decided to make an appearance, his performance no doubt would have been engulfed in the dozens of flashlights and battery-powered lanterns searching through the darkness for at least a mile down the track.

Several times, the flashlights and lanterns were mistaken for the "Maco Light," giving hope that the mysterious glow would soon appear.

A large portion of the track was illuminated by the headlights of a jeep and small foreign car scurrying back and forth along both sides of the track. A young girl created an anxious moment when she mistook a firefly as the "Maco Light" and released a penetrating scream that sliced through the pitch-darkness.

Holzer's visit to Maco on Wednesday night was mostly for the benefit of photographers and reporters who met the noted parapsychologist at the New Hanover County airport earlier that night.

His second visit to the crossing will be kept a closely guarded secret in hopes the "ghost hunter" will be able to conduct his investigation of the light without being interrupted by pranksters and playful teenagers.

Soon I realized that it would be impossible for us to go out to the tracks alone. Crowds followed us around and crowds were ever present at the spot, giving rise to a suspicion in my mind that these people were not in a working mood while we were visiting their area. Evidently we were the most exciting thing that had happened to some of them for some time.

Finally, the day of a scheduled press conference arrived, and at ten o'clock in the morning, before a battery of klieg lights and microphones set up at the Blockade Runner Hotel on the beach, I started to talk in person to those who had come to tell me about their encounters with Joe Baldwin's ghost.

In addition to those who had written to Miss Thomas and reaffirmed their original stories, others came forward who had not done so previously. There was William McGirt, an insurance executive, who called the light "buoyant," flicking itself on and off, as it were, and fully reflected on the iron rails. But you cannot see it looking east, he told me, only when you look towards Maco Station.

Margaret Bremer added to her previously told story by saying the light looked to her "like a kerosene lantern swaying back and forth."

Her husband, Mr. Bremer, had not planned on saying anything, but I coaxed him. He admitted finally that twelve years ago, when his car was standing straddled across the track, he saw a light coming towards him. It flickered like a lamp and when it came closer, it flared up. As an afterthought, he added, "Something strange— suddenly there seemed to be a rush of air, as if a train were coming from Wilmington."

"Was there?" I inquired cautiously.

"No, of course not. We wouldn't have had the car across the track if a train were expected."

Mrs. Laura Collins stepped forward and told me of the time she was at the trestle with a boy who did not believe in ghosts, not even Joe Baldwin's. When the light appeared, he sneered at it and tried to explain it as a reflection. Six feet away from the boy, the light suddenly disappeared and reappeared in back of him—as if to show him up! Mrs. Collins, along with others, observed that misty weather made the light appear clearer.

Next in the parade of witnesses came Mrs. Elizabeth Finch of Wilmington, who had offered her original testimony only the day before.

"It appeared to me many times," she said of the light, "looked like a lantern to me. Two years ago, we were parked across the tracks in our car—we were watching for a train of course, too—when I saw two dazzling lights from both sides. It was a winter evening, but I suddenly felt very hot. There was a red streak in front of the car, and then I saw what was a dim outline of a man walking with a lantern and swinging it. Mind you, it was a bare outline," Mrs. Finch added in emphasis, "and it did have a head . . . just kept going, then suddenly he disappeared inside the tracks."

"Did you ever have psychic experiences before, Mrs. Finch?" I wanted to know.

"Yes, when we lived in a house in Masonborough, I used to hear noises, steps, even voices out of nowhere—later, I was told it was haunted."

I thanked Mrs. Finch, wondering if the local legend had impressed her unconscious to the point where she did see what everyone had said was there—or whether she really saw the outline of a man.

I really had no reason to doubt her story. She struck me as a calm, intelligent person who would not easily make up a story just to be sensational. No, I decided, Mrs. Finch might very well have been one of the very few who saw more than just the light.

"I tell you why it can't be anything ordinary," Mr. Trussle, my next informant, said. "Seven years ago, when I saw the light on a damp night about a mile away from where I was standing, I noticed its very rapid approach. It disappeared fast, went back and forth as if to attract attention to something. It was three foot above the track, about the height of where a man's arm might be.

"At first, it seemed yellowish white; when I came closer, it looked kind of pinkish. Now an ordinary car headlight wouldn't go back and forth like that, would it?"

I agreed it was most unlikely for an automobile headlight to behave in such an unusual manner.

Mrs. Miriam Moore saw it three times, always on misty, humid nights. "I had a funny ringing in my ears when I reached the spot," she said. She was sure what she saw was a lamp swinging in a slow motion. Suddenly, she broke into a cold sweat for no reason at all. I established that she was a psychic person, and had on occasion foretold the death of several members of her family.

E. S. Skipper was a dapper little man in the golden years of life, but peppery and very much alert. He used to be a freight shipper on the Atlantic Coast Line and grew up with the Maco Light the way Niagara kids grow up with the sight of the Falls.

"I've seen it hundreds of times," he volunteered. "I've seen it flag trains down—it moved just like a railroad lantern would. On one occasion I took my shot gun and walked towards it. As I got nearer, the light became so bright I could hardly look. Suddenly, it disappeared into the old Catholic cemetery on the right side of the tracks."

"Cemetery?" I asked, for I had not heard of a cemetery in this area.

Mr. Skipper was quite certain that there was one. I promised to look into this immediately. "Since you came so close to the light, Mr. Skipper," I said, "perhaps you can tell me what it looked like close up."

"Oh, I got even closer than that—back in 1929, I remember it well. It was two o'clock in the morning. I got to within six foot from it."

"What did you see?"

"I saw a flame. I mean, in the middle of the light, there was, unmistakably, a flame burning."

"Like a lantern?"

"Like a lantern."

I thanked Mr. Skipper and was ready to turn to my last witness, none other than Editor Thomas herself, when Mrs. E. R. Rich, who had already given her account in the newspaper, asked for another minute, which I gladly gave her.

"Ten years ago," Mrs. Rich said, "we were at the track one evening. My son Robert was in the car with me, and my older son went down the track to watch for the light. Suddenly not one but two lights appeared at the car. They were round and seemed to radiate, and sparkle—for a moment, they hung around, then one left, the other stayed. My feet went ice cold at this moment and I felt very strange."

"Miss Thomas," I said, "will you add your own experiences to this plethora of information?"

"Gladly," the Women's Editor of the *Star-News* replied. "There were three of us, all newspaper women, who decided a few weeks ago to go down to the trestle and not see anything."

"I beg your pardon?"

"We'd made up our minds not to be influenced by all the publicity Joe Baldwin's ghost was getting."

"What happened?"

"When we got to the track, dogs were baying as if disturbed by something in the atmosphere. We parked on the dirt road that runs parallel to the track, and waited. After a while, the light appeared. It had a yellow glow. Then, suddenly, there were two lights, one larger than the other, swaying in the night sky.

"The lights turned reddish after a while. There was no correlation with car lights at all. I thought at first it was a train bearing down on us, that's how big the lights appeared. Just as suddenly the lights disappeared. One light described an arc to the left of the track, landing in the grass."

"Just as those old tales say Joe's lantern did, eh?"

"It seems so, although it is hard to believe."

"What else did you notice?"

"I had a feeling that I was not alone."

And there you have it. Mass hysteria? Self-hypnosis? Suggestion? Could all these people make up similar stories?

Although the Maco Light was unique in its specific aspects, there are other lights that have been observed at spots where tragedies have occurred. There are reports of apparitions in Colorado taking the form of concentrated energy, or light globes. I don't doubt that the human personality is a form of energy that cannot be destroyed, only transmuted. The man who heard the sound of a train, the psychic chill several people experienced, the flame within the light, the two lights clearly distinguished by the newspaper women—possibly Joe's lantern and the headlight of the onrushing train—all these add up to a case.

That evening, at Bogden Hall, before an audience of some five hundred people of all ages, I stated my conviction that the track at Maco Station was, indeed, haunted. I explained that the shock of sudden death might have caused Joe Baldwin's etheric self to become glued to the spot of the tragedy, re-enacting the final moments over and over again.

I don't think we are dealing here with an "etheric impression" registered on the atmosphere and not possessing a life of its own. The phantom reacts differently with various people and seems to me a true ghost, capable of attempting communication with the living, but not fully aware of his own status or of the futility of his efforts.

I was, and am, convinced of the veracity of the phenomenon and, by comparing it to other "weaving lights" in other areas, can only conclude that the basic folklore is on the right track, except that Joe isn't likely to be looking for his head—he is rather trying to keep an imaginary train from running into his uncoupled car, which of course exists now only in his thought world.

And until someone tells Joe all's well on the line now, he will continue to wave his light. I tried to say the right words for such occasions, but I was somewhat hampered by the fact that I did not have Mrs. Ethel Meyers, my favorite medium, with me; then, too, the Wilmington people did not like the idea of having their town ghost go to his reward and leave the trestle just another second-rate railroad track.

The folks living alongside it, though, wouldn't have minded one bit. They can do without Joe Baldwin and his somewhat motley admirers.

Suddenly the thought struck me that we had no proof that a Joe Baldwin had ever really existed in this area. The next morning I went to the Wilmington Public Library and started to dig into the files and historical sources dealing with the area a hundred years ago. Bill Mitcham and I started to read all the newspapers from 1866 onwards, but after a while we gave up. Instead, I had a hunch which, eventually, paid off. If Joe Baldwin was physically fit to work on the railroad in so hazardous a job as that of a train man, he must have been well enough to be in the Armed Forces at one time or another.

I started to search the Regimental Records from 1867 on backwards. Finally I found in volume V, page 602, of a work called *North Carolina Regiments,* published in 1901, the following entry:

Joseph Baldwin, Company F, 26th N.C.T., badly wounded in the thigh. Battle of Gettysburg. July 1, 1863.

It was the only Joseph Baldwin listed in the area, or, for that matter, the state.

I also inquired about the old Catholic cemetery. It was, indeed, near the railroad track, but had been out of use for many years. Only oldsters still remembered its existence. Baldwin may have been

Catholic, as were many residents of the area. Time did not permit me to look among the dilapidated tombstones for a grave bearing the name of Joe Baldwin.

But it would be interesting to find it and see if *all* of Joe Baldwin lies buried in sacred ground!

THE ARDMORE
BOULEVARD GHOSTS

ARDMORE BOULEVARD WAS in a highly respected and rather beautiful section of Los Angeles. It was a broad street, richly adorned by flowers, and substantial homes lined it on both sides for a distance of several miles north and south.

The people who lived here are not prone to ghost stories, and if something uncanny happens to them, they would prefer that their names be kept secret.

Since that was the only condition under which I could have access to the house in question, I reluctantly agreed, although the names and addresses of all concerned in this case are known to me and to the American Society for Psychic Research, represented, in the investigation I made, in the person of its California head, Mrs. George Kern.

It all started unbeknownst to me when I was a panelist on a television program emanating from the Linden Theatre in Los Angeles in December of 1963.

Shortly after, I received a letter from a lady whom we shall identify as Helen L. She wrote:

I consider myself lucky that I tuned in on the show you appeared on. You see, I live in a haunted house, and I do need help desperately.

I have heard a terrible struggle and fight in the middle of the night when I have gotten up to go to the bathroom! The other night I was reading in bed and smoking a cigarette. It was about 9:30, and I was completely engrossed in my book. Suddenly, I would say about a couple of feet to my right, a champagne cork popped loud and clear and then I heard it [champagne] being poured into a glass! I saw nothing, yet heard it all, and the horror of it is that it all took place right beside me.

I telephoned Helen L. as soon as I received a second letter from her.

There was no immediate possibility of going to Los Angeles to help her, but I wanted to establish personal contact and perhaps get a better idea of her personality in the process.

Miss L. struck me as a person of good educational background; her voice was well modulated and not at all hysterical. She sounded rather embarrassed by the whole thing and begged me to keep her name and exact address confidential. I explained that unfortunately there was no Foundation to pay for an expedition to Los Angeles posthaste, nor was there as yet a television series to finance such a trip as part of its legitimate research.

Consequently, I had to provide the funds myself, and an author's funds are never enough.

I would go as soon as there was an opportunity to do so—an engagement to speak or to appear on television which would take me to the Coast. Meanwhile, would she write me whenever anything new was happening in the house. Also, could she give me a chronological account of the strange goings-on in her house, blow by blow.

On January 23, the lady obliged. Her letter seemed a bit more composed this time; perhaps the promise of my coming out to see her had helped calm her nerves.

Just as I had asked her, she started at the beginning:

> My mother bought our home around thirty-eight years ago. It had just been completed when we moved in. My mother had been widowed a few years previously and she brought my two sisters and myself from the Middle West to California because we were always sickly due to the fierce winters that we left behind.
>
> About a couple of years after we moved in, we unfortunately lost almost everything. My mother then rented our house furnished and we lived elsewhere. She rented the house on a lease basis to five different tenants over an eight- or nine-year period.
>
> There was an oil man who had a young wife and baby. My mother can only describe him as a great brute of a man with a surly disposition.
>
> Our next-door neighbors called my mother while these people were living here and said that there had been a terrible fight at our house the night before and four other men were involved. They said that they could hear furniture being broken, and that they had almost called the police.
>
> As to furniture being broken—it was all too true—as my mother discovered when they moved out.
>
> In the back of the house are two bedrooms and a small room that we use as a den. These three rooms all have French doors and then screened doors that open onto a good-sized patio.
>
> Things didn't start to happen right away after we

moved back. It was quiet for a while, but then it started.

The first thing I remember was when I was about nineteen or twenty years old. Everyone had gone to bed, my sister had gone out, and I was writing a letter in my bedroom. Suddenly my locked French doors started to rattle and shake as if someone were desperately trying to get in. It just so happened that we had had our outside patio floor painted that very afternoon. I couldn't wait until I got out there the next morning to look for footprints in the paint. There weren't any. There wasn't even a dent.

I touched my finger to the freshly painted patio floor and a little of it adhered to my fingers.

We would also keep hearing a light switch being pushed every now and then, and no one in the room!

Sometimes my mother would ask me in the morning why I had been rapping on her bedroom door at night. I have never rapped on her door and she knows it now because that's another thing that goes on every now and then. Three raps on your bedroom door, usually late at night. I was married during World War II, and after the war my husband and I lived here for three years. I had a most unhappy married life and eventually we separated and I secured a divorce.

One night, while I was still married, my mother and sister were visiting relatives in the Middle West.

I was all alone, as my husband had gone out for a while. I had locked all the doors that lead to the back of the house as I always did when I was alone. It was only around 9:00 P.M. Suddenly I heard someone slowly turning the knob of the door that leads from the laundry to the den. Then it would stop and a few minutes later "it" would try again, turning and turning that knob!

My husband came home less than an hour later and we both went through the house together. Every window was bolted, every door was locked.

Then later, there was the man I kept steady company with for a long time. We met about eleven years ago and I remember so well after we had been out and he'd walk me up to my front door at night we would both hear these footsteps inside the house making a great deal of noise running to the front door as if to meet us!

Then, sometimes for weeks at a time, every night tapping on my furniture would start while I'd be in bed reading. "It" would go around and tap on all of my furniture, usually two or three taps at a time. I used to get so fed up with it all I'd yell out "Get out and leave me alone!" That didn't do any good because "it" would always come back.

When I used to sleep with my lights out up to five years ago, three times I was nearly smothered to death.

I always sleep on my left side—but for some strange reason I would slowly wake up lying flat on my stomach trying desperately to breathe.

Something seemed to have me in a vise wherein I absolutely could not move any part of my body, and would keep pressing my face into the pillow! I would try desperately to scream and fight it off, but I was absolutely powerless. Just when I knew I couldn't stand it any longer and was suffocating to death—I would be released, slowly!

But each time this happened—"it" would suffocate me a little longer. I felt that I would never live through it again, and hence have slept with my lights on ever since.

The same thing happened to my mother once when she had that room prior to my having it. She never told me about her own experience, however, until I told her of mine.

The champagne cork popping and the liquid being poured (it even bubbled) right beside me, without being seen, happened three times last year at approximately six-week intervals.

That too was in my bedroom; it happened once in my mother's bedroom also.

The loud shrill whistling in my right ear occurred last March or April when I came home one evening around 10:00 P.M. It was so loud it was more like a blast. It started as a whistle into my right ear just as soon as I opened the front door and stepped into the darkness of the house. I screamed and ran to the kitchen and when I turned the light on it stopped. The whistling sounded like the beginning of a military march, but there were just a few notes.

Occasionally we hear a whistling outside our house at night—but it is a *different* tune and sounds more as if it is calling to us.

My mother has heard articles on her dressing table being moved around while she was in bed at night. This happened twice last year.

Noises in our kitchen wake me up at night. They sound as if something were moving around, kettles being handled, and cupboards being opened.

One night about three years ago, I got up around midnight to go to the bathroom. While I was in the bathroom, I heard loudly and clearly a terrible fight going on in the living room. It was a wordless and desperate struggle!

How I got the courage to open the door to the living room I'll never know, but I did. It was completely dark—I saw nothing and the fighting stopped the instant I opened the door!

Some months later, my mother, sister, and I were

awakened at night by a terrible fight going on right outside of our bedroom's French doors. It sounded as if every stick of our patio furniture were being broken by people who were fighting desperately but wordlessly. It lasted all of several minutes.

We didn't go outside, but the next morning we did. None of our furniture on the patio had been touched, everything was in its place and looked as pretty as it always had. Yet we had all been awakened by the terrible noise—and what sounded like the complete destruction of everything on our patio.

This blasted ghost even walks around outside in the back yard and on our driveway and sidewalks.

Several times when we have had relatives staying with us for a few days, my mother and my sister slept in our double garage on some of our patio chaise longues. They have always been awakened at night by heavy footsteps walking up to the garage door and then they hear nothing else. There are never any footsteps heard that indicate "it" is walking away! Let me also mention it would be almost impossible for a human intruder to get into our back yard. Everything is enclosed by high fences and a steel gate across the driveway.

Several years ago when I had fallen asleep on the couch in the den while looking at television, I awakened around 11:00 P.M. and turned the television off. Then I stretched and was just walking to my bedroom when I heard a voice enunciating most distinctly, and saying loudly and clearly, but slowly—"Oh woe—woe—woe—you've got to go—go—go!"

Last month I heard footsteps every night in the den, even after I had left that room only five minutes before.

I decided to seek verification of the experience with the footsteps from inside an empty house. The young man Helen had mentioned, William H., was a chemist and rather on the practical side.

"On quite a few instances upon returning to Helen's home and entering the house I heard what sounded to me noises of footsteps approaching to greet us as we entered the living room. I investigated to assure myself as well as Helen that there was no one there. I cannot explain it, but I definitely heard the noises."

I had encouraged Helen L. to report to me any further happenings of an uncanny nature, and I did not have to wait long. On February 3, 1964, she wrote me an urgent note:

On February 28th I woke up about 11:30 P.M. to go to the bathroom for a glass of water. As I turned on the light I pushed the bathroom door open, and I heard a loud, screeching, rusty sound. It sounded like some heavy oaken door that one might hear in a horror movie! I examined the bolts at the top and the bottom of the door and there was nothing wrong; the door was as light to the touch and easy to open as it always had been.

Incidentally, while the door was making those terrible noises, it woke my mother up. She had heard it, too.

On Friday night, January 31, I was in the small room that we call the den, in the back of the house.

I suddenly heard footsteps outside, walking very distinctly on the sidewalks right by the den windows and then suddenly they just ceased as they always do—outside!

They are definitely a man's footsteps, and I would say the footsteps of a man that knows exactly where he's going! It's always the same measured pace, and then they suddenly stop!

I asked Miss L. whether anyone had ever died in the house, whether by violence, or through ordinary ways. "As far as we know, nobody ever died," she replied.

I promised to make arrangements soon to visit the house with a medium. Miss L. meanwhile wanted me to know all about her mother and sister:

> My sister here at home is mentally handicapped due to an injury at birth. Also, my mother is 80 years of age, an arthritic with crippled hands and feet and suffers from the added complication of heart disease.
>
> Last night, February 2, I was reading in bed. It was around 10:30 P.M. Suddenly it sounded as if a body were thrown against my bedroom door.

Since this was the first I had heard of the sister's mentally handicapped condition, I naturally questioned her role in creating the strange phenomena. Knowing full well that a mentally handicapped person is often exactly like a youngster prior to puberty as far as the poltergeist phenomena are concerned, it occurred to me that the girl might be supplying the force required to perform some of the uncanny actions in the haunted house.

I tactfully suggested this possibility to Helen L., but she rejected any such possibility:

> Her power of concentration is impaired and her nervous system more or less disorganized. You must also bear in mind that every door in this house that leads to another room is locked. There is only one door that we don't lock and that is the door that leads from the kitchen to the laundry.
>
> She couldn't possibly produce the phenomena that even other friends of mine have witnessed when my sister

has been over 3,000 miles away visiting relatives in Minnesota.

One thing I haven't told you is that I seem to have inherited a tendency of my mother's. We both dream dreams that come true—and have all of our lives. Many of them don't concern me at all or even people that are close to me, but they always come true.

One night I dreamt I saw this ghost who has been haunting our house. I was in bed and he was sitting on my cedar chest just looking at me. He seemed to be dressed in some early Grecian style—had rather curly hair—a frightfully mischievous expression and the most peculiar eyes. They were slanted up at the corners but he was not Asian. His eyes were rather dark and very bright but his face looked bloated—an unhealthy-looking pasty white skin—and it was too fat. He was a pretty big young man. He looked anything but intelligent, in fact the expression on his face was quite idiotic! Now—can you make anything out of this?

The picture began to get clearer. For one thing, Helen L. had not understood my references to her mentally handicapped sister. I never suggested conscious fraud, of course. The possibility that her energies were used by the ghost began to fade, however, when Helen told me that the manifestations continued unabated in her absence from Los Angeles. Poltergeists don't work long distance.

Then, too, the incidents of earlier clairvoyance and premonitory dreams in Helen's life made it clear to me at this point that she herself must be the medium, or at least one of the mediums, supplying the force needed for the manifestations.

Her strange dream, in which she saw the alleged ghost, had me puzzled. Could he be an actor? The Grecian dress was not so impossible for Los Angeles, where young men of peculiar habits abound.

As I began to make preparations for my impending visit to California, I was wondering about other witnesses who might have heard the uncanny footsteps and other noises. Helen L. had told me that a number of her friends had experienced these things, but were reluctant to talk:

> There was only *one* time in my life that I was glad that this wretched ghost around here made himself known. I had a close lady friend for a number of years with whom I used to work. After I had known her a few years I took her into my confidence and told her that our house was haunted. She laughed and said of course there was no such thing as a ghost, and that I must be the victim of my own imagination. I didn't argue the point because I knew it was useless.
>
> About one month later she called me on the phone on a Sunday afternoon and asked me if she could stop by and visit. She came by around 4:00 P.M., and I fixed a cup of coffee which I brought to my bedroom. She was sitting in my bedroom chair jabbering away—and I was sitting on my bed drinking my coffee. It was still daylight. Suddenly, this ghost started walking and thumping from the living room right up to my bedroom door and stopped. Margaret looked up at me brightly and said, "Why, Helen, I thought you said you were all alone—who on earth could that be?" I said, "Margaret, I am all alone here—no living person is in this house except you and me, and what you hear is what you call my imagination!"
>
> She couldn't get out of this house fast enough, wouldn't even go out through the living room, but rushed out of my French doors that lead to the patio and that's the last I saw of her.

On February 23, Helen L. wrote again. There had been additional disturbances in the house, and she was able to observe them a little more calmly, perhaps because I had assured her that soon I would try to get rid of the nuisance once and for all.

Since I last wrote to you two or three weeks ago—for almost one solid week I would hear someone moving around in the den which adjoins my bedroom; sometimes within only 5 or 10 minutes after I would leave the den, lock the door, climb into bed and read—I would keep hearing these *furtive movements*. This time the walking would be soft—and "it" would keep bumping into the furniture; of late I am awakened quite frequently by someone that has thrown himself forcibly against the den door leading to my bedroom. This has happened several times at exactly 11:30 P.M., but has also happened as early as 8:30 P.M. The only way I can describe it is that someone is pretty damned mad at me for closing and locking that door and is registering a violent reaction in protest.

It actually sounds as if the door is about to be broken down. Then "it" has begun to rap loudly on the bedroom walls, two loud raps.

A week before I was due to arrive in Los Angeles, I had another note from Helen. On April 9, she wrote:

Last Saturday night I got home around midnight and went to bed with my book as usual. I was just about ready to doze off when a "bull-whip" cracked right over my head! The next night someone hit the bedboard of my bed real hard while I was sitting there in bed trying to read.

I've told you about the heavy man's footsteps outside,

what I neglected to tell you is that my mother and sister are both awakened every once in a while between 3:00 and 4:00 A.M. by a woman's fast clicking shoes hurrying up our driveway and stopping at the gate that crosses the driveway towards the rear of the house! The last time was less than two weeks ago.

I wonder what the neighbors think when they hear her!

I arrived in Los Angeles on April 16 and immediately called Helen L. on the phone. We arranged for a quick initial visit the following day. Meanwhile I would make inquiries for a good medium. Once I had found the right person, I would return with her and the exorcism could begin.

The quick visit after my lecture, delivered to the Los Angeles branch of the American Society for Psychic Research, was of value inasmuch as I got to know Helen L. a little better and could check on some of her reports once again. The house on Ardmore Boulevard was as comfortable and pleasant-looking as its owner had described it, and I would never have guessed that it had a sinister history.

That's the way it is sometimes with haunted houses; they just don't look the part!

Dick Simonton, an executive deeply interested in extrasensory perception studies, accompanied me to the house. He, too, was impressed by Miss L.'s apparent level-headedness under trying conditions.

Fortunately, I did not have to look far for a suitable medium or, at least, clairvoyant. Several months before my California trip, I had received a letter from a Mrs. Maxine Bell, who had seen me on a local television show:

I am a sincere medium willing to offer my talents for your research and experiments. For the past 20 years I have been doing much work for individuals with definite problems. Not once have I run into a poltergeist type, for my work is more spiritually oriented. Deep trance is not even necessary for me to work as I am extremely sensitive.

I am a woman in her late 40's who has had the gift of perception since 1938 and I have worked on the most serious cases of possession and some haunted-house cases as well. I would be most happy to serve you in any way.

I called Mrs. Bell and asked her to meet us the following day in front of the house. The time was 3:00 P.M. and it was one of those lovely California afternoons that are hard to reconcile with a ghost.

Obviously, Mrs. Bell had no chance to dig into the past of the house or even get to know the present owner. I told her to meet us at the corner but volunteered neither name nor details.

Soon she had seated herself in the living room across from Helen L., myself, Mrs. George Kern of the American Society for Psychic Research, and an associate of hers, Mr. G., who was psychic to a certain extent.

The house impressed him strongly. "I felt chilly on entering this house," he said. "There are two people here—I mean ghosts—one is a man in his middle years, and a young female who died by suffocation."

I immediately thought of Helen L.'s report of how she was almost suffocated a number of times by unseen hands!

"These two seek each other," Mr. G., an engineer by profession, continued. "The young person is about ten or twelve years old, feminine or a male with feminine characteristics. This child is lost and asking for help. There is wildness, she wants to do 'things,' she says, 'I want. . . .' "

Mr. G. was now breathing heavily, as if he were assuming the personality of the young ghost.

"This child may be a little older," he finally said, "maybe as much as fifteen years. She is very nervous . . . crying because of unexpressed emotions . . . this child lived in this house but had sad times here, too much discipline. I think both people died about the same time. I'd say at least fifteen to twenty years ago."

I thanked the engineer and turned to Mrs. Bell, who had quietly watched the "reading" of the house.

"I never interfere with another medium's impressions," she finally said, "but if he's finished, I'd like to add mine."

I nodded for her to go ahead.

"A Philip Stengel died here in nineteen thirty-four," she began. I looked at Helen L. The name did not register. But then her mother did not recall all of their tenants. There were quite a few.

"Ten years ago a person was murdered here," Mrs. Bell continued. "No—in nineteen forty-eight. There were violent arguments. Two men, one of them named Howard. Arguments in the driveway outside. The neighbors heard it, too. Two parties came here, there was that violent argument, and one was killed. Wounded in the abdomen. The body was lifted into a vehicle. One of them is staying here in this house, but there is also another person in the house. I feel sudden violence and money involved. A lady fled. Lots of money was at stake. Two people were here, the woman, however, had the house. The quarrel was due to a misunderstanding about money."

I was amazed. Unless Mrs. Bell had read Helen L.'s letters to me or spoken to her before coming here, she could not have known many of these details. The description of the quarrel and the attitude of the neighbors were exactly as described to me by Helen L.

I looked at the owner of the house who sat somewhat stunned by what she had heard.

"Well," she finally said to me, "there are two different kinds of footsteps—the ones in the back of the house sound like those of a man, while the ones in front are certainly more like a child's steps, very fast. The steps we hear around three or four in the morning are also a woman's, I think. I'm sure the whistler we've heard is a man."

What were the facts around that quarrel?

Helen L. had looked into the matter further since my arrival.

"There was a fight," she said quietly. "An oilman lived here, he was married to a much younger woman, and they had a baby. He went away and a friend came to the house. There was a wild fight here."

"What about those rather quaint words you heard?" I questioned Miss L.

"You mean, 'Woe, woe, woe, you've got to go, go, go!'—why, they were spoken with a definite British accent."

"Or a theatrical phony British accent?"

"Perhaps."

We moved on to the bedroom where so much commotion had been observed. Mrs. Bell stood opposite the bed and the rest of us formed a circle around her. I asked the entity to leave, in a ritual known as Rescue Circle, a verbal exorcism, which usually works. There are exceptions, of course.

I then took some photographs with my Super Ikonta B camera, a camera which was double-exposure proof because of a special arrangement of the transport and shutter systems. I used Agfa Record film and no artificial light. There was enough light coming in from the French windows. To my amazement, two of the pictures showed figures that were not visible to the naked eye, at least not to mine. One of the two clearly shows a female figure, rather young and slender, standing near the window in what looks like a diaphanous gown. Evidently the ghost wanted us to know she was watching us. I have since enlarged this picture and shown it on television.

There was no doubt about the figure, and I didn't put it there, either.

We returned to the living room and took our leave. I felt sure the evil entity had been dislodged or at least shaken up. Sometimes an additional visit is necessary to conclude the deed, but I could not stay any longer.

I had hardly touched New York soil, when a letter from Helen L. arrived:

> I haven't written you sooner because I wanted to be sure that "it" has left, and I feel that "it" hasn't left entirely. I am suffering from a dreadful fatigue of mind and body and soul—and I'd like to cry and cry and never stop! On the Saturday night you were here, I woke up about 11:30 P.M. and walked into the kitchen, when I heard heavy foot-steps walking in the dining room to the swinging kitchen door. Needless to say, I got out of there fast.

On May 17, Helen L. finally wrote to me some of the corroboration I asked her for. I wanted to know if any more of the material obtained by Maxine Bell could be checked out, and if so, with what results:

> When Miss Bell was here, she said there was a kindly gray-haired man standing before her who had died suddenly in my bedroom, years ago, of a heart attack. He hadn't expected to die, and had so much unfinished business. In talking to my mother later she feels that it was a man she had as a tenant here who was married for the second time, to a much younger woman. She said he had been ill with a heart condition and he was an extremely busy man with more than one business, including a railroad he owned. He

had a baby daughter by his second wife and was quite cheerful and happy—and confident that he was over the heart attack he had previously suffered.

Nevertheless he did die suddenly and my mother always felt that he did die in this house, although his wife denied it. Even so, my mother released her from the lease. He was a gray-haired, very distinguished-looking man.

Now about the murder that Miss Bell mentioned and the terrible fight that took place that our neighbors reported to my mother.

Miss Bell was right when she said that the fight started toward the back of the house on the driveway. In fact, our neighbor came out and asked what was going on and the man he asked, whom he didn't know (probably a guest of our tenant's at that time) said, "Oh, nothing," and gave him his card which had an address on this street. Nevertheless the fight started again, and it was terrible—furniture being broken, etc. The neighbors didn't call the police because they didn't wish to become involved. My mother said that this particular tenant was a big brutish-looking man, married also to a young woman, and they too had a baby daughter.

The wife and baby were not here, according to our neighbors. They were away visiting relatives over the weekend.

My mother also told me that after they moved she did find blood spots on our floors.

For a while, I heard nothing further from the haunted address on Ardmore. Then a letter arrived, dated July 4. It was no fireworks message, but it contained the melancholy news that Helen L. was being plagued again by footsteps, thuds, movements, and other poltergeist manifestations.

I explained that I thought her own mediumistic powers made the manifestations possible and her fear of them might very well bring back what had been driven out. Such is the nature of anxiety that it can open the door to the Uncanny where the strong in heart can keep it closed forever.

I also hinted that her own emotional state was extremely conducive to paranormal occurrences. Frustrations, even if unconscious, can create the conditions under which such manifestations flourish.

But Helen L. could not accept this.

"They'll always come back, no matter who lives here," she said, and looked forward to the day when she would sell the house.

What was needed was such a little thing—the firm conviction that "they" *could* be driven out, never to return. Instead, through apprehension as to whether the Uncanny had *really* left, Helen L. had turned the closed door into a revolving door for herself.

GHOSTS, GHOSTS, EVERYBODY'S GOT GHOSTS

B Y THIS TIME my wife and I had become so imbued with the spirit of the spirit hunt, we looked at everything from *our* point of view.

"Look at that old house," I would say. "Isn't it lovely?"

I was just admiring the scenery. But Catherine's mien would become pensive.

"I wonder if it's got a ghost," she would say, but of course we never would find out, since we don't go around asking people in old houses if perhaps, like termites, they have ghosts.

Living with the Uncanny, as we do, one becomes conditioned to the reflexes that come with the trade. The other day, the nineteenth-century New England clock in my study stopped.

"The clock has stopped, darling," I said, matter-of-fact like, ready to wind it up.

"I wonder who died," Catherine shot back. Nobody we knew had died. But we realized with a smile how much psychic research had become part of our everyday existence.

People have stopped me in the street to tell me *their* ghost story. If I thought they had something worth looking into, I invited them to put it in writing, with their real names attached. Few did, but those who wrote to me got fast action, one way or another. My telephone was listed. For a few years it was an unlisted phone and I felt terribly superior about it all. Imagine being among the elite who are so popular they cannot allow their telephone number to be known to the masses.

Then I wanted to get off the hook and be listed again. Why? Because nobody could find me. People began to wonder if I had not become a ghost myself. The telephone company said it could be done just like that—I mean the re-listing of our number.

Since then I have always been tempted to sign my telephone-bill checks in invisible ink.

There are so many bona fide cases worthy of investigation that I simply cannot follow up on all of them. There was also a category of reports where it might be impossible to interview the original witnesses because they are no longer living, are far from New York, or are unavailable for a number of reasons. Nevertheless, some of the testimony by my sources was so compelling that I felt I should include a few of these cases here, even though I was not myself present when they happened. Instead, I will vouch for the sanity, reliability and general truthfulness of those who had the experiences.

I have in these cases investigated the witnesses rather than the ghost and, in the face of the testimonies, have no reason to doubt these occurrences.

The Ancram Poltergeist was reported to me by the owner of a house in New York State which he very much wanted to sell. Consequently, he asked me not to visit the house until he had sold it. How could I resist such a firm disinvitation?

Here, however, is the report for what it is worth—and I would like to point out that a similar occurrence was investigated by me in a farmhouse in Switzerland the summer of 1964. About that, later.

Herbert Rockefeller was a young man of urbane tastes and not a believer in the occult. Nevertheless, he started wondering, after becoming the owner of a haunted house quite by accident. That is, *apparently* by accident.

Four years ago he was passing through Columbia County, New York, when he stopped at a little town called Ancram. He was in the market for a country house and someone directed him towards an old sheep farmhouse in the outskirts of the little town. The house had for generations been called "Never Sweat" because the position of the house was such that there was always a breeze cooling it even during the hottest summer days.

The house was old all right, for a 1790 map shows it. Mr. Rockefeller took one look at the house and fell in love with it. At the same time, he felt there might be something sinister about it.

Soon he became its owner, but from the very start he realized there was something strange about the place.

One night he was washing dishes in the kitchen, while the only other person in the house, his friend Charles S., was in another part of the building where neither could hear the other. The kitchen had a window next to a pantry, and through the window one can see a retaining wall outside, near the house, on the hillside, about a yard high and extending all the way around the old house.

Suddenly Rockefeller heard a sound "like a heavy club hitting a board hard" against the outside of the pantry wall. This went on for some time. Charles S. came into the kitchen at this moment, and he, too, heard the beating sound. Rockefeller decided to investigate the source of the strange noise, for there was no one to be seen outside the kitchen window. He walked into the living room adjacent to the kitchen, when he was stopped in his tracks by a loud, whimpering sound seemingly emanating from the basement.

Following the strange noise, he found himself next to the old stairway leading into the basement. Between the fireplace and the wall he located a recess, about 3 feet wide. He dug a little into it, but found nothing. Promising himself to dig deeper when he had a chance, he was momentarily distracted by a rapping sound from the bathroom window. Still convinced that there must be a natural explanation for the uncanny sounds, Rockefeller decided to trap the intruder by fast action. Quickly he flung open the bathroom door. There was enough light coming in through the window and from the living room to see fairly well.

To his amazement he saw a heavy wooden stick, outside the bathroom window, come down with extreme violence, hitting the screen. There was no arm holding the stick. A few moments later, the phenomenon had ceased. It was late fall and there was snow on the ground on the shaded side of the house where the bathroom was located. Rockefeller dashed outside and looked in the snow. There were no footprints of any kind.

Meanwhile, the whimpering from the chimney continued. Three people, including his mother, clearly heard it and remarked on it. Nobody had a natural explanation.

Several months went by. Charles S. and Mr. Rockefeller were talking in front of the fireplace one evening. There was a friendly argument such as happens among close friends. Suddenly the discussion was interrupted by the swishing noise of a broom, which had up to now stood motionless and unnoticed in the corner, but which now somehow flew right into Rockefeller's hands. Rockefeller caught it and put it down. The two men looked at each other in silence for a moment, then Charles swallowed hard and said, "We must not tell anyone about this."

Mr. Rockefeller started to think of selling the house. Somehow he could not account for the poltergeist phenomena he had witnessed by ordinary logic. Was someone still living a shadowy dream in the old pre-Revolutionary house, someone who had been clubbed to death and the body stuffed into the chimney?

Some ghost stories are the by-product of nonghostly activities, such as my work on television. That's how I heard about *"the TV Studio Ghost."*

I have appeared at least seven or eight times on Station KDKA-TV in Pittsburgh, but I never knew until recently that a ghost had been noticed in the station building itself. If it weren't for Joanne O., secretary to the program manager of the station, Bob Novak, who had a weather eye (and ear) open for likely tales a ghost hunter might want to know, I would not have known about the sad and strange case of artist Julian Drob, who died suddenly of a heart attack in May of 1963, aged fifty, leaving behind a lot of unfinished business, both personal and television, and an office with all but two panels completed.

His official title was that of Facilities Director of the station, but his duties were artistic and he was actually a supervisor of art work, sets and such. Early in 1963, when he had started to embellish his smallish office off the main floor of the modern studio building, one of his fellow executives commented on the perfectionist slowness with which he was completing the decorations.

"If you don't finish this office, Julian," he said laughingly, "it'll finish you." Today he wishes he had not spoken those prophetic words, for Julian Drob was, indeed, finished first.

Shortly after Drob had been buried, two porters working for the station noticed the lights burning in his office. What was strange about it was that they were *sure* they had turned them off. Another time, they came in only to see the papers still on his desk turn and move by their own volition, as if touched by unseen hands.

The two porters never moved as fast as when they ran out of the office. Next thing, an exorcising service was held and strange candles were found in the room the next morning.

A painstaking and responsible man, Julian Drob may have been chagrined over the problems arising for the station because of his sudden death—and tried to help out from his side of the Veil. But we'll never know for sure.

I am not sure if the next report belongs under American ghosts or Irish ghosts, since it happened to an Irishman in Ireland, although I first became aware of him when he resided in New York City. My Celtic friend had another brush with the Uncanny a little later in life when he passed through our own South, I feel safe in putting down his ghostly experiences in this chapter. He's *"the man who meets High-Society ghosts."*

Charles McGarvey was a man in his late middle years, soft-spoken with a touch of the Irish brogue, which was no surprise, since he was born on the Old Sod. He lived comfortably at the Hotel Tudor in Manhattan, and pursued a career as a management consultant.

When McGarvey was a lad of about nine or ten, he lived in his native village of Rothmullen, County Donegal, Northern Ireland. There was a particularly interesting ruined castle nearby, known locally as "Mac Swyne's Castle," the latter name related to "Sweeney" rather than pigs.

This old castle boasted a tower with a circular staircase, but time had destroyed the steps above the first floor. Although the tower rose farther and traces of the winding stairs were still there, the actual steps had long disappeared above the first floor. One day, McGarvey and a friend of about his own age decided, as boys will, to explore in the old castle. He had frequently managed to get to the top despite those missing stairs, using ingenuity and sheer courage instead. But this time, his friend refused to accompany him beyond the first floor, and, frightened, remained behind at the level where the steps ended. Cheerfully, McGarvey continued toward the top, unaware that he was quite alone now.

A bit farther on, he suddenly had to make room for a lady in expensive eighteenth-century-type dress coming down the nonexisting stairs. Without thinking there was anything unusual about this visitor, he tried to step aside towards the wall. Thinking that his friend was coming up, somewhere below him, he yelled out, "Make way for the lady." Downstairs, looking up, the other boy saw nothing. No lady coming down. McGarvey thinks it might have been Elizabeth I of England, who used to rendezvous with Lord O'Neil, whose castle this was.

He recalls vividly how he thought the fine lady would bawl him out for getting in the way.

The second uncanny experience in McGarvey's life took place much later, when he was sent to Birmingham, Alabama, on an investigation of a business nature. The hotel he went to seemed too expensive to him, so he started to look for private lodgings. About five miles outside the city proper, he found, through a real estate agent, a house that seemed to suit his purpose and was extremely inexpensive to boot. Strangely enough, this two-story house had a ground floor all sealed off, the furniture and windows covered as if long in disuse. The renting agent assured him the ground floor was not available, but the second story was. So McGarvey took it and moved in. The staircase leading to the upper story started from the living room of the ground floor.

The first day nothing special happened, but on the second night, he was aroused around 1 A.M. by the sound of voices and music coming from downstairs.

"That's strange," he said to himself. "I had no idea there were people below me. The renting agent must have leased the downstairs after all." He couldn't sleep with all that noise going on, so he got up and started to walk down the stairs. What met his eyes was a wondrous sight indeed.

The entire living room was ablaze with the light of chandeliers, the furniture was all uncovered, the curtains plainly visible, and a party was in full swing. A room full of happy people were dancing to the strains of a waltz, and voices filled the room.

Everybody was formally dressed, but, as McGarvey later recalled, their clothes seemed a bit odd, somewhat old-fashioned, but not an awful lot, perhaps belonging to a period ten years prior to when this took place.

As McGarvey took a few more steps down the stairs, the better to see, one of the men at the party looked up at him, and instantly the whole scene vanished into thin air!

Again, the living room was dark and empty, except for the covered furniture and secured curtains. McGarvey rubbed his eyes, but the apparition had vanished.

The next evening a very puzzled McGarvey said to himself, "It must have been a dream." But again, come the middle of the night, the music woke him, and he went down the stairs, only to find the same party in full swing.

When the ghostly dancers appeared to him for the third time, shortly thereafter, McGarvey went to see the renting agent and told him what he had seen.

Real-estate people have no use for ghosts. The agent accused McGarvey of being crazy, and when that wouldn't stick, of being drunk. But, of course, McGarvey was neither. Without further explanation, the agent canceled his lease, and McGarvey looked for other lodgings.

He asked around the neighborhood about the house, but no one who knew anything could be found.

One thing though—McGarvey's ghosts are always dressed in the height of fashion of whatever century that may be.

Mina Lauterer was a person of the highest integrity and had a keen intellectual gift of observance.

She was a model and a writer of novels, and had an interest in the occult mainly because so much had happened to her that could not be explained within the confines of narrow logic. Of her many experiences with clairvoyance, perhaps this one involving a *"Dream Man"* was most remarkable because of the unusual details she was able to observe.

"One night not long ago, in New York, as I was in bed, halfway between sleep and being fully awake," she said, "I saw a face as clearly as one sees a picture projected on a screen. I saw it with the mind's eye, for my eyes were closed. This was the first experience that I can recall, where I saw, in my mind, a face I had never seen before.

"About six weeks later, I received an invitation to go to Colombia, South America; I stayed on a banana plantation in Turbo, which is a primitive little town on an island or peninsula in the Gulf of Uruba. Most of the people who live there are the descendants of runaway slaves and Indian tribes. Transportation is by launch or canoe from the mainland to the tiny cluster of nearby islands. The plantation was located near the airport on the mainland, as was the customs office.

"One Sunday afternoon I went into town with my host, an American, and my Colombian friend. As we walked through the dirty streets bordered with sewerage drains and looked around at the tin-roofed hovels and the populace of the place, I thought: This is the edge of the world.

"Sunday seemed to be market day; the streets were crowded with people mostly of two hues, black and red-skinned. As we passed a drugstore, walking single file, a tall, handsome, well-dressed young man caught my attention. He seemed as out of place as I and my companions did. He did not look at me, even as I passed directly in front of him. It struck me as strange. South American men always look at women in the most frank manner.

"Also, he looked familiar, and I realized that his was the face that I had seen in my mind, weeks before in New York!

"The following day we were invited to cocktails by our neighbor, the Captain of Customs. He told us that a young flyer arrived every month around the same time, stopped in Turbo overnight and then continued on his regular route to other villages. He always bunked in with his soldiers, instead of staying at the filthy hotel in the village. He mentioned that the young man was the son of the governor of one of the Colombian states, and that he had just arrived from Cartagena, the main office of his small airline.

"He brought the young man out and introduced him to us. It was the young man that I had seen in the village! I asked him if he had really arrived Monday morning and he later proved beyond all doubt that he had not been in Turbo on Sunday afternoon, when I saw him. He was dressed in the same clothes on Monday, as those that I had seen him wearing on Sunday, in my vision.

"I do not know why I saw him when he wasn't there. Later he asked me to marry him, but I did not.

"When I and my companions went to Cartagena later on we checked and again confirmed the facts—he was miles away when I had seen him!"

The Quick and the Dead aren't always as different as you might think. Take, for instance, the case of the Restless Advertising Executive who insisted on his usual martini even after he had committed suicide.

It all started when my friend and fellow ghost devotee, the late *New York Daily News* columnist Danton Walker, ran the following tantalizing item:

West 56th Street agitated by what purports to be the ghost of a former Madison Avenue ad executive who was ruined by drink. Makes his pre-dawn presence known by scribbling advertising slogans on the building walls and leaving an empty Martini glass on the bar of his former restaurant hangout.

It didn't take me long to track down the restaurant, which turned out to be a posh eatery known as DaVinci's. I arranged with the owner to hold a séance in the place, and to find out what it was that disturbed our drinking ghost.

The DaVinci owners were very co-operative. After all, why not? If the place was so good that even the dead want to return there for a visit, the living ought to be lining up, too. And apparently this was not the clanking variety of ghost, but a jolly fellow with a keen sense of humor.

I telephoned Ethel Meyers. She agreed to come along, although I told her nothing of our destination. We met late at night, after the usual dinner guests and even the late-hour tipplers had gone, and the DaVinci was practically empty. The last persistent barflies I chased myself by telling them the place was haunted. Rather than wait to find out if it really was, they departed in great haste.

Present in the longish room there remained the eminent Broadway director Harold Clurman, with his silver cane and imperturbable mien, who really didn't care at all for ghosts; and his fiancée and later wife, actress Juleen Compton, who very much cared, especially since she had seen the ghost of the advertising man in what had once been his apartment and had become hers. There he was, she related, here one moment, gone the next.

That's how ghosts are, I assured her.

Alas, she knew him well—when among the Quick—and felt that any help she could give him now, she would gladly give. The man deserved a rest, after all. Apparently he had committed suicide while not entirely sober, and that is frequently the cause of a haunting—

when the ghost wakes up dead, so to speak, and doesn't like it!

The lights were doused, and we seated ourselves behind the long table on one side of the room. I was next to Mrs. Meyers. Within minutes, she was in deep trance, completely oblivious to what went on around her. In this state of total dissociation, the psychic is lending her vocal apparatus and body to a discarnate entity, and it is his or her personality that speaks through the facilities of the medium. This is easy to check: If the information obtained in this manner is unknown to all present, especially to the psychic, and is of a personal nature rather than general and obtainable without too much trouble, then we have a genuine communication.

No sooner was Mrs. Meyers in deep trance, than our friend took over. In a creaking voice very unlike Mrs. Meyers' own soft-spoken tones, he demanded a drink—*any drink*—refusing to talk about anything until his drink had been brought. We went through the motions of putting a glass into the medium's hands, but evidently the ghost was also using her smelling faculties, for he immediately bellowed that the glass was empty!

With that, he began to rock the table rather violently, all the time insisting on his drink. Remember, Mrs. Meyers was not told that the ghost had been an alcoholic or that this was his favorite place. We finally put a martini before Mrs. Meyers (who doesn't drink herself and would have been horrified at the sight). Our ghost calmed down somewhat, enough for me to ask some questions. When I brought up the fact that he had killed himself, he started to cry for "Allan, Allan," and I quickly looked at Miss Compton's face to see if it meant anything. It did. Later, she told me that the ghost had spent his last day on earth drinking with Allan, his closest friend.

As is usual in these investigations, once contact is made, I tell the Restless One that he should leave and go to what Dr. Joseph Rhine of Duke University called the "World of the Mind," that wider horizon where human memory continues to live beyond the confines of space and time, and, certainly, of the physical body.

Then I proceeded to awaken Mrs. Meyers from her "alcoholic" trance, while the DaVinci waiters and staff stood transfixed behind the rear door, watching in awe.

"Where am I? Hic!" my psychic lady said, and looked properly amazed.

It was the first time in my long career as a Ghost Hunter that anyone had become inebriated by a ghost. But the fact was, Mrs. Meyers had a king-size hangover.

THE GHOST GOES
EAST, OR AN
AMERICAN GHOST
HUNTS IN ENGLAND

E VER SINCE I SAW René Clair's incomparable motion picture
satire, *The Ghost Goes West*, I have wondered about those
British ghosts.

Do they really travel? You bet they don't. Ghosts, as my readers
must realize by now, are tied to their earthly abodes and cannot
accompany the old masonry to a new country. What was fantasy in
that motion picture, however, was grim reality to me now.

There are lots of English ghosts all right, but I don't know that
there are any more specters per capita in the British Isles than in the
United States. It is just that tradition treats the subject with more
respect and as a matter of course rather than something so offbeat
one must not admit it. Still, England is the traditional place where
the ghosts are, and I decided to see for myself if what they said about
haunted castles and houses in Britain was true.

With the help of William Houlton of the British Travel

Association and, of course, my own extensive file of material on British haunts, I set about attacking my objective by letter. I wrote to about seventy-five bona fide haunted places and asked for permission to visit. I also asked for specifics, witnesses, all the earmarks of my own brand of investigation. Some answered me, welcoming me to their hearth; others could not see me for various social reasons; and still others did not reply at all.

I soon realized that the willingness to talk about one's *own* ghosts is not as great as relating ghost stories in general. The English are a bit shy at times when it comes to the specter of Uncle Reginald walking the moat, inasmuch as a ghost usually was involved in a spot of trouble at one time or other, and families being what they are, they would rather not discuss it.

Eventually, I hope to return to many of the places my wife and I visited and do a series of documentary films on each one of them in such a manner that even the most reluctant witnesses to ghostly happenings wouldn't hesitate to relate them. Also, to pay them a decent sum for their troubles, because many of the stately homes of Britain need just that to remain stately.

In particular, the Crown was adamant in not permitting this parapsychologist on any of the Royal properties. I began to pine for the days of Macbeth, when a ghost at least had some standing in the community. The *New York Daily News* of December 29, 1963, carried a "special" report from Sandringham, England, concerning the ghost that haunted that Royal residence in the northeastern part of the country:

> The Sandringham ghost had introduced an atmosphere of uneasiness into the great country house. So far, the ghost has not been encountered in the royal rooms and corridors, but there is no doubt about its haunting the staff quarters.

Hollow footsteps along corridors when no one is walking there, door handles stealthily turned and doors opened to reveal nothing or no one entering or leaving, lights going on and off without human hands ever touching the switches—these are some of the alarming things that happen.

So far, the worst area of haunting has been in the Sergeant Footman's corridor on the second floor, and no housemaid will go there alone to clean and dust. One footman refused to sleep in the room allocated him, insisting that a large paper sack put there for rubbish "breathed in and out" before his eyes. The horrified man swore he could hear the sack breathing, quite apart from seeing it.

Other uncanny manifestations have included the transfer of Christmas cards from one wall to another and the stripping of beds which had been left made. In each case the occupant of the room left it locked and took the key.

The Sandringham hauntings, which only began a year ago, appear to begin on Christmas Eve and continue for from six to eight weeks.

Whenever there is a domestic accident, such as the breaking of a dish or a plate, or something not readily explainable goes wrong below stairs, it is customary for the staff to exclaim: "Oh that's that ghost again!" Any loud bang or thump whose origin cannot be explained is likewise attributed to the ghost.

There has been some talk among the household staff of asking for a local clergyman to be called in to exorcise the ghost, but the majority of the clerics are still trying to pass it off as a joke. If it should prove to be a specter that is no respecter of persons, however, and should extend its hauntings to the royal corridors, then something drastic will have to be done.

I approached the proper authorities for permission to visit the house for a few minutes. The Assistant Keeper of the Privy Purse answered me on July 15, 1964.

> Your letter came as something of a surprise to me, since I personally had no idea that there were ghosts in the house. However, I have looked into the matter, and have been informed that the house was only built in 1870, and there are no substantiated accounts of ghosts having been seen there.
>
> In view of this, it is felt that the proposed visit would be a waste of your time, and I am instructed to write to you accordingly.

Well, of course, I don't want to waste my time, even on ghosts, so I merely wrote back quoting the reports I had researched. This time, the Privy Purse was a little less talkative:

> Further consideration has been given to your request to visit Sandringham House: the area you mention, the Sergeant Footman's Corridor, is, of course, within the main house.
>
> Permission to visit Sandringham, which is a private residence of Her Majesty The Queen, is rarely given, and I regret that it has not been found possible to make an exception in your case.

To add to my frustrations, the Brown Lady of Raynham Hall, a mere stone's throw from Sandringham, at Fakenham, Norfolk, also wasn't having any ghost hunting.

The Marquess Townsend of Raynham, whose house Raynham Hall is, evidently had had his fill of her, seeing that she had not only been encountered hundreds of times by people staying at the Hall, but even photographed in 1936 and her picture published in some of the leading magazines.

The Brown Lady, in case you haven't heard, is the shade of Lady Dolly Walpole, sister of the politician Robert Walpole. She died "of an unsound mind" in 1726, upstairs at Raynham Hall, where the family had shut her up for the last few years of her life.

My request for a simple visit was turned down flatly even after I promised to send the Brown Lady packing. "Raynham Hall is not open to the public," the Marquess wrote and that was that. But it sure was open to ghosts.

Then there was the tavern ghost at the Ferry Boat Inn, Holywell, Huntingdonshire. Her name was Juliet Tousley. She was quite a cutup some nine hundred years ago, and allegedly lies buried approximately underneath the spot where a piano now stands. She is supposed to have killed herself there after a lover's quarrel and her ghost has been seen by many at regular intervals.

True or not, I wanted to look into the matter, and contacted the owner of the Inn. I received a reply from a Mr. D. Forrest, present owner of the old Inn:

> Whilst admiring your enthusiasm for the occult, I myself am not a bit interested and am not personally interested whether or not a ghost exists here. In the circumstances, therefore, I have to inform you that I would not allow you to carry out your researches here with or without assistance from the Press or TV.
>
> I regret that you are an interesting person and that I will not be meeting you.

Evidently, Mr. Forrest's sense of hospitality stopped short of parapsychologists, or perhaps he figured that ghosts don't really drink very much, do they, so why bother? At any rate, if Juliet has any ghostly sense at all, she haunted Mr. Forrest, but badly, from then on.

Imagine taking away her telephone.

Then there was that aborted attempt to conclude a most interesting investigation right in the heart of London. Thanks to the alert eye of my good friend, the Baron Adam Konopka, I was introduced to a Mr. Donald W., an American editor residing in England, who lived with his family in a wonderful old house in Regent's Park, a section abounding in wonderful old houses.

When I interviewed the family in April, 1964, they were fascinated by the idea of living in a haunted house.

"I've heard footsteps in this room," Mr. W. related, as we were seated in the comfortable sitting room on the second floor of the rather narrow house.

The building was the work of architect John Nash and dated back to the 1820's, when the area was a most fashionable part of London as, indeed, it is today. A ghost had been reported here for over sixty years, it seems.

"Yes, I've heard those footsteps," Mr. W. repeated, "and my boy downstairs, in the other room, also heard them. On one occasion, the door to this room we're in flung itself wide open."

"By itself?" I asked.

"By itself. I saw it with my own eyes."

I examined the door. It did not move easily and could not have slid open by itself unless someone pushed it.

Did anyone else hear the ghost?

"The cleaning woman did. I think the ghost always greets the new tenants here. It seems to me it's a pretty old ghost."

Mr. W. was a man of great calm and level-headedness, not easily convinced that the supernatural could have a basis of fact. But there it was happening in his own home.

"You know," he added, "there is still another peculiar thing about this house. During the recent war years, the War Ministry was right next door, so naturally we were a prime target for bombs. In all those years of aerial bombardment, practically the entire neighborhood was hit at one time or other. Our house is the only one that didn't get a scratch. Looks as if the ghost is protecting her own."

I smiled, and addressed myself to Mrs. W., who had just joined us.

"I had one particularly impressive encounter with the ghost," she related. "It was during the black-out, and I had to take a friend to the hospital at four o'clock in the morning. I dressed in the dark, of course, and as I did so, I definitely felt a presence in the room with me, although I was quite alone at the time. When I returned to the house an hour later, there was nothing or no one here."

I thanked the W.'s for their hospitality and left for New York. We agreed that we would return with a good medium in the summer to see what the ghost wanted.

When I telephoned Donald W., in September of 1964, he recalled our plans, of course. I obtained a suitable trance medium, told her nothing of our plans, as always, and waited for the Thursday of the séance. Wednesday night I received a special-delivery letter from Donald W.

I'm very sorry to inform you that I've had a change of heart about the séance. I've decided not to have it. One chief reason is that it will be profoundly upsetting to my little boy, who already got wind of it and I am now determined to cancel anything to do with ghosts or the spirit world. Frankly, we are a skeptical family, anyway.

Fortunately, there were many haunted houses eagerly awaiting our arrival. With a map in hand, I set about planning our visits in such a way that we could cover the maximum number of locations. Assisted in this plan by Harper-Ellis cars, we managed to lay out a pretty imposing schedule for our "safari for ghosts" in the coming weeks.

Mr. Ellis not only supervised our routing, he gave us a gem of a chauffeur by the name of Brown, who was that rare person among drivers, a true professional. Mr. Brown never intruded himself on anything, yet he was always present when needed, and brought us safely over some of the most harrowing roads in Britain.

On the second day of our English stay, we went to bed in our comfortable apartment at the White House Club, secure in the knowledge that all was well with English ghosts after all.

Tomorrow we would have our first encounter with the denizens of the nether world, United Kingdom division.

THE GRAY LADY OF
SAWSTON HALL

S AWSTON HALL LIES a few miles south of the great English
university town of Cambridge, and can be reached from
London in about two and a half hours. When I heard that reliable witnesses had seen a ghost in this old manor house, I contacted
the owner, Captain Huddleston, about a visit. The Captain's
nephew, Major A. C. Eyre, wrote back saying how delighted they
would be to receive us. Like so many British manor houses, Sawston
Hall was open to the public at certain times and, of course, I wanted
to avoid a day when the tourists were sure to interfere with our
quest. Although I usually avoid getting secondhand information on
hauntings, and prefer to talk to the witnesses directly when I see
them, I like to know the general background of a haunted house
before I approach it. This gives me a better idea as to what I might
encounter in the way of atmosphere, mementos, and such. As a
trained historian, I have no trouble finding my way around English
history. I picked up one of the little booklets the Major had prepared
for the visitors, to familiarize myself with the history of Sawston Hall
while the car, driven by the unperturbable Mr. Brown, rolled quietly
through the picturesque countryside. The booklet read:

Sawston Hall has been the home of the Huddleston family for over 400 years and is noteworthy for being one of the few old manor houses in Cambridgeshire built out of stone. In 1553 Edward VI was ailing and entirely dominated by the ambitious Duke of Northumberland. The King was already dead, when his half sister, Princess Mary, afterwards Queen Mary Tudor, who was living in Norfolk, received a message purporting to be from him, begging her to come to him. Mary immediately set out for London and at Hoddesdon she received word that the message was a trap. On her way back, she accepted the hospitality of John Huddleston, the then Squire of Sawston, and spent the night at the Hall. During the night, however, the Duke's supporters from Cambridge who learnt she was there, set out to capture her. John Huddleston just got her to safety in time by disguising her as a dairy maid.

When we arrived at Sawston Hall, it was already four o'clock, a little late for tea, but our gracious hosts, the Huddlestons, had waited tea specially for us, and a delicious English brew it was. By now the light was not quite so strong as I would have liked it for the sake of my motion-picture camera. But I never use artificial lighting, only the available natural light.

We started up the stairs, and Mrs. Huddleston explained the treasures of the house to us. We admired, but quickly passed through the imposing Great Hall with its magnificent portrait of Queen Mary Tudor, the drawing room with its harpsichord in perfect playing condition, as if Queen Mary were about to use it, and proceeded past the Little Gallery and a paneled bedroom into the Tapestry Bedroom, so called because its walls are hung with a set of Flemish tapestries showing the life of King Solomon. Dominating this room was a four-poster bed in which Queen Mary was said to have slept, back during the dark days of 1553 when she was running for her life. To the right of the bed, there was a small marble fireplace and farther down the wall an oaken door opening onto a passage which ultimately leads to the priest's hiding hole. I think these connections are of some importance if the ghost was that of Queen Mary, who was Catholic.

We stood in front of the four-poster, when I started my examination.

"Tell me, Mrs. Huddleston, what are the facts about the hauntings here?"

Mrs. Huddleston, a soft-spoken, well-organized lady in her middle years, smiled a friendly smile. "Something always seems to take place in this room we're standing in. The original story is that in the middle of the night you suddenly hear three slow knocks at the door, and the door slowly swings open and a lady in gray slowly floats across the room and disappears into that tapestry. A great many people have slept in this room and there are a great many different stories of various things that have happened to them."

"What sort of things?"

"One girl woke up in the night very frightened, because she heard someone next to her in the bed breathe very heavily."

"What did she do, scream?"

"No, she just crawled to the bottom of the bed and tried to forget all about it."

"I can't say that I blame her under the circumstances. Did anyone else have trouble in this bed?"

"Well, there was a young man who was sleeping in this room, and he wasn't very well when he went to bed. When he came down to breakfast the next morning, he said, 'You know I was quite all right last night, you needn't have bothered to come to see me.' So I said, 'But I didn't.' He insisted, 'Oh, yes, you did; you knocked on the door three times, and rattled on the latch, and I got awfully frightened, and kept saying, "Come in, come in," and nothing happened, and I suddenly felt really, really frightened, so I crept down to the bottom of the bed and tried to forget all about it.'"

"Seems habit-forming," I said, "that bottom of the bed business. Of course, it *is* a huge bed."

"Well, he insisted, 'it must have been you; you must have come to see me,' but I told him, 'No, I'm sorry. I never came near you; you weren't nearly sick enough.' That was that."

"How long ago did this take place?"

"Four years ago."

"Did you yourself ever hear or see anything unusual?"

"When I was first married and came here as a bride, I heard distinctly some very tinkly music rather like a spinet or virginal, and I asked my husband who it was, and he said, oh, he had heard nothing and that it was all nonsense. However, I heard it again the next night and again a little later. He kept telling me this was all rubbish, so I felt very triumphant when about a month later a visitor came down to breakfast, and said, 'Do tell me, what is this music I keep hearing.'"

"Who do you think is playing the instrument?"

"The general opinion is that it is Queen Mary Tudor herself."

"You mean her ghost?"

"Yes. Of course, you know she slept in this bed and was very fond of this house. But the reason I think that it is really she is that she was a very good performer on the virginal, in fact she was so good that her father, Henry VIII, had her brought down from the nursery as a child to play for the Flemish ambassadors when they came over."

"And you are sure you heard the music?"

"Absolutely. It was quite clear."

"Has anyone else had psychic experiences in this room?"

"Oh, yes; quite a few, really," Mrs. Huddleston said with typical

English understatement. To her, a ghost was no worse than a famous actor or politician in the family. In England, one need not be looked at askance just because one believes in ghosts. It is rather respectable and all that.

"One day I was taking a rather large group around the house, and when we were in this room an old lady suddenly stepped forward, and said, 'You know, I knew this house long before you did! You see I was employed here as a young girl, as a house maid. Once I was kneeling down, attending to the fire, and suddenly I felt very cold, looked up, and I saw the door slowly opening and a gray figure swept across the room and disappeared into the tapestry there. I was so frightened I flung myself out of the room and fell headlong from the top to the bottom of the stairs and hurt myself so badly that I've never dared come back to this house until this very day.'"

"That's quite a story," I said. "Did you check on it?"

"Yes. You see, you can't see the bottom of the stairs, when you're upstairs, and so she must have been absolutely right in the way she remembered things, because when we'd finished the round, and were at the bottom of the stairs, she suddenly called out, 'Oh, that's the place, I remember it, that's where I fell!'"

"And there was such a place?"

"Yes, there was."

"Have there been any manifestations here lately?"

"Not long ago, Tom Corbett, the well-known psychic, slept in this bed. He reported a presence bending over him every hour of the night. His alarm clock, which he had set for seven o'clock, went off at one, two, three, four, five, six. When it did so this presence kept bending over him. Mr. Corbett had the impression the ghost was that of a night watchman with one eye, and a name that sounded to him like Cutlass or Cutress."

"Did this make sense to you?"

"Well, I thought it simply meant he was carrying a cutlass with him, but Tom Corbett insisted it was a name. I made inquiries after Mr. Corbett had left, and I found to my amazement there was a man named Cutress living in the village. I had never heard of him. But the people who did the research for me said, 'That can't possibly have any connection with the night watchman, since he's only just arrived from London.'

"About a month later, the butler here was standing next to a stranger in the local pub, and he said, 'What is your name?' The stranger replied, 'Oh, my name is Cutress, and I've just come here a short time ago.' The butler wondered why he had come to this rather out-of-the-way place. 'Oh,' the man replied, 'my family's lived in Sawston for generations. I wanted to come back to the old family place.'"

"Tom Corbett certainly hit the nail on the head on that one," I acknowledged. "Any other interesting witnesses to uncanny phenomena?"

"I was taking an old lady round, and it was broad daylight, and I was showing her the tapestries, and was so busy with that, I didn't notice the change that had come over her face. When I looked around at her, she looked simply terrible, as if she were going to pass out. I asked her if I should get a doctor, but she assured me she would be all right.

" 'It's really this room,' she explained. 'It's the ghosts in this room.' "

We left the haunted bedroom and went along the Long Gallery to the priest's hiding hole, which was ingeniously hidden in the thickness of the wall, barely large enough for a man to sit in, and accessible to the outer world only through a small trapdoor which could easily be covered during a raid.

I wondered if any hauntings had been observed in connection with the hiding hole, since so much tragedy and emotional turmoil adhered to the atmosphere around it.

"Not by the hole itself, but there is a nearby bedroom where there have been some ghostly experiences during the last few years. That room just above the staircase. A friend of ours, a well-known Jesuit priest, was sleeping in it, and he had so much disturbance during the night, knocking at the door, and noises outside, that he got up several times to see what was happening."

"Did he find anything or anyone?"

"No, of course not. They never do."

"Was there anyone else who experienced anything out of the ordinary around that staircase?"

"A lady from South Africa came here for a first visit. She arrived rather unexpectedly, so we put her into the haunted room, but the next morning she reported that she had had a good night and not been disturbed at all. Maybe the ghost had moved away? 'Anyway,' she bragged, 'I always know when there is a ghost around, because I get very cold and get goose pimples all up my arms.' So we forgot all about the ghost and started to show her around the house. But when she got to this same big staircase, which leads to this room I have just talked about, she suddenly gave a little scream and said, 'Oh, there's no doubt about it, *this* is where the ghost is!' I hurriedly looked at her arms, and she was, in fact, covered with goose pimples.

"Tom Corbett also went up these stairs and he distinctly felt someone walking after him, so much so, he turned around to speak to him, but there was nobody there."

There we had it.

The Gray Lady floating across the haunted bedroom, and the haunted staircase.

During the years of religious persecution, Sawston Hall was the principal refuge for those of the Catholic faith, including a number of priests and lay brothers. Many atrocities were perpetrated in those days in the name of the Reformed Religion, and the atmosphere at Sawston Hall is soaked with the tragedy and suffering of those martyrs.

Then, too, one must realize that Mary Tudor, later known as Bloody Mary, had found the old manor house her salvation when the Huddlestons saved her life by hiding her. Her ghost might, indeed, be drawn back there even though she did not die there. I don't think the Gray Lady was merely an etheric impression without personality; the behavior was that of a bona fide ghost.

Perhaps at some future time I may be privileged to sleep in the big four-poster, and if I hear someone breathe heavily next to me, it had better be my wife!

THE HAUNTED
MOTORCYCLE
WORKSHOP

L EIGHTON BUZZARD SOUNDED like a species of objection-
able bird to us, when we first heard it pronounced. But it
turned out to be a rather pleasant-looking English country
town of no particular significance or size, except that it was the site
of a poltergeist that had been reported in the local press only a short
time before our arrival in England.

The *Leighton Buzzard Observer* carried a report on the strange
goings-on at Sid Mularney's workshop.

When Leighton motorcycle dealer, Mr. Sid Mularney,
decided to extend his workshop by removing a partition,
he was taking on more than he anticipated. For he is now
certain that he has offended a poltergeist.

Neighbors were blaming "Mularney's Ghost" for weird
noises that keep them awake at night, and Mr. Mularney, who
claims actually to have witnessed the poltergeist's pranks, is
certain that the building in Lake-street, Leighton, is haunted.

It was about a fortnight ago when he decided to take down the partition in the workshop which houses racing motorcycles used by the world-champion rider, Mike Hailwood.

The following morning, said Mr. Mularney, he went to the door, opened it, and found three bikes on the floor. The machines, which were used by local rider Dave Williams, had their fairings smashed.

A few days later Mr. Mularney was working on a racing gear box, and when he realized he couldn't finish it unless he worked late, he decided to stay on. And it wasn't until three o'clock that he finished.

As he was wiping his hands, weird things started to happen.

"I felt something rush by me. I looked round and spanners flew off hooks on the wall and a tarpaulin, covering a bike, soared into the air," he declared.

"You would have to see it to believe it. I was scared stiff. I grabbed a hammer, got out of the room as fast as I could and made straight for home. My wife was asleep and I woke her up to tell her about it."

Since then other peculiar things have been taking place, and neighbors have been complaining of weird noises in the night.

Mrs. Cynthia Ellis, proprietress of the Coach and Horses Restaurant, next door in Lake-street, said she had been woken during the night several times "by strange bangings and clatterings."

"I looked out of the window, but there was never anything there."

She said her young son, Stephen, was the first to wake up and hear noises.

"We thought it was just a child's imagination, but we soon changed our minds," she said.

"The atmosphere around here has become very tense during the past fortnight. It's all very odd," said Mrs. Ellis.

Since his strange experience Mr. Mularney has discovered odd happenings in the workshop. One morning he found a huge box of nuts and bolts "too heavy for me to lift," scattered all over the floor. Since then he has discovered petrol tanks which have been moved about and even large bolts missing, which, he claims, he could never mislay.

I contacted the editor of the *Observer*, Mr. McReath, who confirmed all this information and gave me his private estimation of Mr. Mularney's character and truthfulness, which were A-1. I then arranged with Mr. Mularney to be at his place at noon the next day to look into the matter personally.

Located on a busy main street, the motorcycle workshop occupied the front half of a large yard. Much of it was rebuilt, using some very old timbers and bricks. Mr. Mularney, a large, jovial man with a bit of an Irish brogue, greeted us warmly and showed us around the rather crowded workshop. There were three rooms, leading from one into the other like a railroad flat, and all of this space was chock-full of motorcycles and tools.

"What exactly happened, Mr. Mularney?" I opened the conversation.

"When we finish off in the evening, my partner and I clean our hands and put all the tools back onto the bench. Just then, for some unknown reasons, the spanners [wrenches] jumped off the hooks on the bench and landed on the bench in front of me."

"You mean, the wrenches flew off the hooks by themselves?"

"Yes."

"You saw this with your own eyes?"

"Oh, yes, definitely."

"There was enough light in the shop?"

"Yes, the shop was lit."

"What did you think it was?"

"Well, at the moment I didn't take much notice of it but, later, there was a noise in the rear of the workshop, something came across the floor, and caught my foot, and my toe, and my eyes, and so I began to look around; on the other side of the shop we had some metal sprockets which were standing there. They started to spin around on a pivot bolt. Later, a huge piece of rubber foam came off the wall and flew into the middle of the room."

"By its own volition?"

"Yes."

"Did you think it was something unusual?"

"I did then, yes. Then we had a racing motorcycle covered by a waterproof sheet, and this rose completely up—"

"You mean, in the air?"

"Yes, it stayed up. By that time I was ready to leave the shop."

"Did you think something supernatural was taking place then?"

"I did. I sat in the van for a moment to think about it, then went home and woke my wife up. I explained to her what I had seen, and she thought I'd been drinking."

"Did anything else happen after that?"

"Yes, we had the Swedish motorcycle champion leave his motorcycle here for repairs. He left some pieces on the bench and went to have tea. When he went back, they had completely disappeared and could never be found again. There was no one in the shop at the time who could have taken them, and we had locked up tight.

"I had the same experience myself," Sid Mularney added. "We were taking a cycle apart, two of us working here. One compartment, big enough to see, just disappeared."

"You have, of course, looked into the possibility of pranksters?"

"Oh, yes, we have. But there's only two of us who use the shop. About five weeks ago, the two of us took another motorcycle to pieces. We put some of the nuts and bolts into a waterproof pan to wash them. We locked up for the night, but when we returned in the morning, the whole lot was scattered all over the room."

A number of amateur "ghost chasers" had offered Mr. Mularney their services, but he turned them all down since the shop housed some pretty valuable motorcycles and they did not want to have things disappear by natural means on top of their supernatural troubles.

I realized by now that a mischievous spirit, a poltergeist, was at work, to disrupt the goings on and call attention to his presence, which is the classical pattern for such disturbances.

"Tell me, what was on this spot before the repair shop was built?"

"Years ago it used to be an old-fashioned basket works, and there used to be about fourteen men working here. After that, the shed stood empty completely for five or six years. When we came here to open the shop, it was full of old baskets and things. We rebuilt it and made it into this workshop."

"I understand the phenomena started only after you knocked down a wall?"

"Yes, we knocked down that wall on a Saturday evening. We came back Sunday morning and three motorcycles were in the corner, as if somebody had thrown them there. As if in anger."

"Did something dramatic ever take place here before you took it over, Mr. Mularney?" I asked.

"Somebody hanged himself here years ago when it was the basket works. That's all we know."

I went back into the third of the three rooms and examined the spot where the wall had been removed. The wooden beams still left showed signs of great age, far beyond the current century.

Quite possibly, in removing the partition wall, Sid Mularney had interfered with the memory picture of a ghost who did not wish to leave the spot. The three of us stood quiet for a moment, then I addressed myself to the poltergeist, asking that he discontinue annoying the present owners of the place. I left my card with Mr. Mularney and instructed him to telephone me the moment there was any further disturbance.

All has been quiet in the years that have followed, so I can only assume that the poltergeist accepted the redesigning of the place. Then, too, he might have become offended by the kind of clientele that rides motorcycles nowadays. Basket weaving is a gentle art, and "mods" and "rockers" are best avoided by gentle folk. Even ghosts.

ENCOUNTERING THE GHOSTLY MONKS

W HEN KING HENRY VIII broke with Rome as the aftermath of not getting a divorce, but also for a number of more weighty reasons, English monastic life came to an abrupt halt. Abbeys and monasteries were "secularized," that is, turned into worldly houses, and the monks thrown out. Now and again an abbot with a bad reputation for greed was publicly executed. The first half of the sixteenth century was full of tragedies and many an innocent monk, caught up in the turmoil of a new wind in matters religious, was swept to his doom.

The conflict of the abolished monk or nun and the new owners of their former abode runs through all of England, and there are a number of ghosts that have their origin in this situation.

The "act of dissolution" which created a whole new set of homeless Catholic clerics also created an entirely new type of haunting. Our intent was to follow up on a few of the more notorious ghosts resulting from the religious schism.

I should be happy to report that it was a typically glorious English fall day when we set out for Southampton very early in the morning. But, it was not. It rained cats and dogs, also typically

English. I was to make an appearance on Southern TV at noon, and we wanted a chance to visit the famed old Cathedral at Winchester, halfway down to Southampton. My reason for this visit was the many persistent reports of people having witnessed ghostly processions of monks in the church, where no monks have trod since the sixteenth century. If one stood at a certain spot in the nave of the huge cathedral, one might see the transparent monks pass by. They would never take notice of you; they weren't that kind of ghost. Rather, they seemed like etheric impressions of a bygone age, and those who saw them re-enact their ceremonial processions, especially burial services for their own, were psychic people able to pierce the Veil. In addition, a rather remarkable report had come to me of some photographs taken at Winchester. The *Newark Evening News* related the incident:

> Amateur photographer T. L. Taylor thought he was photographing empty choir stalls inside Winchester Cathedral, but the pictures came out with people sitting in the stalls.
>
> Taylor took two pictures inside the cathedral nearly a year ago. The first shows the choir stalls empty. The second, taken an instant later, shows thirteen figures in the stalls, most of them dressed in medieval costume. Taylor swears he saw no one there.
>
> Taylor's wife, their 16-year-old daughter Valerie, and a girl friend of Valerie's said they were with him when he took the pictures. They saw nothing in the stalls. "It gives me the creeps," Valerie said.
>
> Taylor, a 42-year-old electrical engineer whose hobby is photography, is convinced that the films were not double exposed. He said his camera has a device to prevent double exposures and the company which made the film confirmed the ghosts were not caused through faulty film.

As I already reported in *Ghost Hunter,* I take psychic photography very seriously. Not only John Myers, but others have demonstrated its authenticity under strictest test conditions, excluding all kinds of possible forgery or deception. The camera, after all, has no human foibles and emotions. What it sees, it sees. If ghostly impressions on the ether are emotionally triggered electric impulses in nature, it seems conceivable that a sensitive film inside the camera may record it.

The camera I used in those days was a Zeiss-Ikon Super Ikonta B model, which had a device making double exposures impossible. I used Agfa Record film, size 120, and no artificial light whatever except what I find in the places I photograph. I didn't use flash or floodlights, and I always had my films developed by commercial houses. I wouldn't have known how to develop them myself, if I had to.

When we arrived at Winchester, it was really pouring. My wife and I quickly jumped from the car and raced into the church. It was eleven o'clock in the morning and the church was practically empty, except for two or three visitors in the far end of the nave. Light came in through the high windows around the altar, but there was no artificial light whatever, no electricity, only the dim light from the windows and the faraway entrance gate. The high wooden chairs of the choir face each other on both sides of the nave, and there were three rows on each side. Prayer books rest on the desks in front of each seat. The entire area was surrounded by finely carved Gothic woodwork, with open arches, through which one can see the remainder of the nave. There wasn't a living soul in those chairs.

The solitude of the place, the rain outside, and the atmosphere of a distant past combined to make us feel really remote and far from worldly matters. Neither of us was the least bit scared, for Ghost Hunters don't scare.

I set up my camera on one of the chair railings, pointed it in the direction of the opposite row of choir chairs, and exposed for about two seconds, all the while keeping the camera steady on its wooden support. I repeated this process half a dozen times from various angles. We then left the cathedral and returned to the waiting car. The entire experiment took not more than fifteen minutes.

When the films came back from the laboratory the following day, I checked them over carefully. Four of the six taken showed nothing unusual, but two did. One of them quite clearly showed a transparent group or rather procession of hooded monks, seen from the rear, evidently walking somewhat below the present level of the church floor. I checked and found out that the floor used to be below its present level, so the ghostly monks would be walking on the floor level *they* knew, not ours.

I don't claim to be a medium, nor was my camera supernatural. Nevertheless, the ghostly monks of Winchester allowed themselves to be photographed by me!

We left Southampton after my television show, and motored towards Salisbury. South of that old city, at Downton, Benson Herbert maintained his "paraphysical laboratory" where he tested psychic abilities of various subjects with the help of ingenious apparatus. One of his "operators," a comely young lady by the name of Anne Slowgrove, also dabbled in witchcraft and was a sort of younger-set witch in the area. Her abilities include precognition and apparently she was able to influence the flickering of a light or the sound of a clock by willpower, slowing them down or speeding them up at will. A devoted man, Benson Herbert was introduced to me by Sybil Leek, medium and "White Witch" of the New Forest. We witnessed one of his experiments, after which we followed his car out of the almost inaccessible countryside towards our next objective, Moyles Court, Ringwood.

The ghostly goings-on at Moyles Court had come to my attention both through Sybil Leek, and through an article in *Fate* magazine.

The original house goes back to the eleventh century and there is a wing certainly dating back to the Tudor period; the main house is mostly sixteenth century, and is a fine example of a large country manor of the kind not infrequently seen in the New Forest in the south of England.

Lilian Chapman, the author of the *Fate* article, visited the place years ago, before it was sold to the school which now occupies it. The Chapmans found the house in a sad state of disrepair and were wondering if it could be restored, and at what cost.

Mrs. Chapman, wandering about the place, eventually found herself seated on the window sill near the landing leading to the second floor, while the rest of the party continued upstairs. As she sat there alone, relaxing, she felt herself overcome with a sense of fear and sadness:

As I looked toward the doors which led to the Minstrels Gallery, I was amazed to see, coming through them, a shadowy figure in a drab yellow cloak. There seemed more cloak than figure. The small cape piece nearly covered a pair of hands which were clasped in anguish or prayer. The hands clasped and unclasped as the apparition came towards me. I felt no fear, only an intense sorrow. And I swear I heard a gentle sigh as the figure passed me and drifted to the end of the landing. From there it returned to go down the stairs, seeming to disappear through a window facing the chapel.

I, too, have sat on that spot, quietly, relaxed. And I have felt a chill and known a heaviness of heart for which there was no logical reason.

The Chapmans did not buy the house, but the Manor House School did at the subsequent auction sale. Unknown to Mrs.

Chapman at the time, Dame Lisle, onetime owner of the manor house, was tried and executed at nearby Winchester by the notorious "hanging judge" Jeffreys in 1685. The sole crime committed by the aged lady was that she had given shelter overnight to two fugitives from the battle of Sedgemoor. The real reason, of course, was her Puritan faith. As described by Mrs. Chapman in detail, it was indeed the apparition of the unfortunate lady she had witnessed.

I contacted the headmistress of the school, Miss V. D. Hunter, for permission to visit, which she granted with the understanding that no "publicity" should come to the school in England. I agreed not to tell any English newsmen of our visit.

When we arrived at Moyles Court, it was already five o'clock, but Miss Hunter had left on an urgent errand. Instead, a Mrs. Finch, one of the teachers, received us.

"What is the background of the haunting here?" I inquired.

"Dame Lisle hid her two friends in the cellar here," she said, "where there was an escape tunnel to the road. There were spies out watching for these people, they discovered where they were, and she was caught and tried before Judge Jeffreys. She was beheaded, and ever since then her ghost was said to be wandering about in this house."

"Has anyone ever seen the ghost?"

"We have met several people who had lived here years ago, and had reared their families here, and we know of one person who definitely has seen the ghost at the gates of the house—and I have no reason to disbelieve her. This was about twenty-five years ago, but more recently there has been somebody who came into the house just before we took it over when it was covered in cobwebs and in a very bad state. She sat in the passage here and said that she had seen the ghost walking along it."

"How was the ghost described?"

"She has always been described as wearing a saffron robe."

"Does the ghost ever disturb anyone at the house?"

"No, none. On the contrary, we have always heard that she was a sweet person and that there is nothing whatever to be afraid of. We've had television people here, but we don't want the children to feel apprehensive and as a matter of fact, the older children rather look forward to meeting the ghostly lady."

I thanked Mrs. Finch, and we were on our way once more, as the sun started to settle. We were hoping to make it to Beaulieu before it was entirely dark. As we drove through the nearly empty New Forest—empty of people, but full of wild horses and other animals—we could readily understand why the present-day witches of England choose this natural preserve as their focal point. It was an eerie, beautifully quiet area far removed from the gasoline-soiled world of the big cities.

We rolled into Beaulieu around six o'clock, and our hosts, the Gore-Brownes, were already a bit worried about us.

My contact with Beaulieu began a long time before we actually arrived there. Elizabeth Byrd, author of *Immortal Queen and Flowers of the Forest,* introduced us to the Gore-Brownes, who had been her hosts when she spent some time in England. Miss Byrd was keenly aware of the psychic elements around us, and when she heard we were going to visit Beaulieu—it consists of the manor house itself owned by Lord Montague and known as the Palace House; "The Vineyards," a smaller house owned by the Gore-Brownes and, of course, the ruins of the once magnificent Abbey and gardens—she implored me to have a look from a certain room at "The Vineyards."

"When you go to Beaulieu please ask Margaret to take you up to 'The Red Room'—my room—and leave you alone there a while. It is not the room but the view from the window that is strange. If even *I* feel it, so should you have a very strong impression of static time. I have looked from that window at various seasons of the year at various times of day and always have sensed a total hush . . . as though life had somehow stopped. The trees are as fixed as a stage-set, the bushes painted. Nothing seems quite real. As you know, I am a late riser, but I was always up at dawn at Beaulieu when that view was nearly incredible to me—not just fog, something more, which I can only call permanent and timeless and marvelously peaceful. I would not have been surprised (or afraid) to see monks tending the vineyards. It would have seemed perfectly natural. If one could ever enter a slit in time it would be at Beaulieu."

The vivid description of the view given us by Elizabeth Byrd was only too accurate. Although it was already dusk when we arrived, I could still make out the scenery and the ruins of the Abbey silhouetted against the landscape. My wife was rather tired from the long journey, so I left her to warm herself at the comfortable fireplace, while Colonel Gore-Browne took me down to the Abbey, to meet a friend, Captain B., who had been a longtime resident of Beaulieu. The Palace House, comparatively new, was not the major center of hauntings.

A modern Motor Museum had been built next to it by Lord Montague, and had become a major tourist attraction. I have no objections to that, but I do find it a bit peculiar to have a washroom built into an ancient chapel, with a large sign on the roof indicating its usage!

The Abbey itself had not been commercialized, but lay tranquil on the spot of land between "The Vineyards" and an inlet of water leading down to the channel called "the Splent," which separates the Hampshire coast from the Isle of Wight. Here we stood, while the Captain looked for his keys so we could enter the Abbey grounds.

"What exactly happened here in the way of a haunting, Captain?" I asked, as we entered the churchyard surrounding the ruined Abbey walls.

"A young lady who lived in Beaulieu was walking across this little path toward what we call 'the parson's wicked gate,' when she saw a brown-robed figure which she thought was a visitor. She had been walking along with her eyes on the ground and she raised them when she got near to where she thought the man would be so as not to run into him—but he just wasn't there!"

We were now standing in the ruined "garth" or garden of the Abbey. Around us were the arched walls with their niches; back of us was the main wall of what was the Beaulieu church, but which had once been the monks' dining hall or refectory.

"Has anyone seen anything here?" I inquired.

"Well, there were two ladies who lived in the little flat in the *domus conversorum.* One of them, a retired trained nurse of very high standing, told me that one Sunday morning she came out onto the little platform outside her flat and she looked, and in the fifth recess there she saw a monk sitting reading a scroll."

"What did she do?"

"She watched him for a minute or two, then unfortunately she heard her kettle boiling over and she had to go in. When she came out again, of course, he was gone."

"Did it ever occur to her that he was anything but flesh and blood?"

"Oh, yes, she knew that he couldn't have been flesh and blood."

"Because there are no monks at Beaulieu."

"Yes."

"Was she frightened?"

"Not in the least."

"Are there any other instances of ghosts in this area?"

The Captain cleared his throat. "Well, old Mr. Poles, who was Vicar here from eighteen eighty-six to nineteen thirty-nine, used to talk of meeting and seeing the monks in the church, which was the lay brothers' refectory and which is now behind us. He also used to hear them as a daily occurrence."

We walked back to the church and entered its dark recesses. The interior was of modern design hardly consistent with its ancient precursor, but it was in good taste and the mystic feeling of presences persists.

This was the place where the Vicar had met the ghostly monks.

"He not only heard them singing," the Captain said, "but he also saw them. They were present."

"Has anyone else seen the ghostly apparitions in this church?"

"A few years ago," the Captain replied in his calm, deliberate voice, as if he were explaining the workings of a new gun to a recruit, "I was waiting for the funeral procession of a man who used to work here, and two ladies came into the church. We got to talking a little, and one of them said, 'When I came to this church about thirty years ago, with my friend, she saw it as it was.'

"I didn't quite understand what she meant and I said, 'Oh, I know, the church was completely altered in eighteen forty.'

"'Oh, no,' she said, 'I mean—we both saw it—as it was, *when the monks had it.*'

"I questioned her about this.

" 'We came in,' she said, 'and we saw the church laid out apparently as a dining room. We were rather surprised, but we really did not think anything very much of it, and then we went out. But when we got home, we talked it over, and we came to the conclusion that there was something rather extraordinary, because we hadn't seen it as a parish church at all. Then we made inquiries and, of course, we realized that we had seen into the past.' "

The ladies had evidently been catapulted back in time to watch the monks of Beaulieu at supper, four hundred years ago!

I walked out into the middle of the nave and in a hushed voice invited the monks to show themselves. There was only utter silence in the darkened church, for it was now past the hour when even a speck of light remains in the sky.

As I slowly walked back up the aisle and into the present, I thought I heard an organ play softly somewhere overhead. But it may have been my imagination. Who is to tell? In that kind of atmosphere and having just talked about it, one must not discount suggestion.

Others have heard the ghostly monks in the garden, burying their own. Burial services were very important to a monk, and King Henry had deprived them of the privilege of being laid to rest in the proper manner. Where could the dead monks go? The Abbey was the only place they knew on earth, and so they clung to it, in sheer fear of what lay Beyond the Veil.

Quite possibly, too, the ghostly brothers cannot accept the strange fact that their sacred burial ground, their cemetery, has never been found! There was a churchyard around the Abbey, but it belonged and still belongs to the people of Beaulieu. The monks had their own plot and no one knows where it is. I have a feeling that there will be ghostly monks walking at Beaulieu until someone stumbles onto that ancient burial ground, and reconsecrates it properly.

The massive manor house, or Palace House, also incorporates much of the abbot's palace within its structure. Monks have been seen there time and again. When I appeared on the Art Linkletter program in January of 1964, I was contacted by a Mrs. Nancy Sullivan, of the Bronx, New York, who was once employed as a cook at Palace House.

"Palace House used to have a moat all around," she explained, "and a spiral staircase running down from the top to the bottom. It was claimed Mary Queen of Scots escaped down that staircase, and a man was waiting in the moat in a boat, making good her escape. Some say her ghost still runs down those stairs!

"The help had their rooms on the top floor; there were five girls then, and every night we heard someone walking down those stairs, although we knew that the doors were safely locked, top and bottom. We were scared stiff, so much so, we all moved into one room."

Whether it was Mary Stuart getting away from Beaulieu, or perhaps an older ghost, is hard to tell. What is interesting is that the steps were heard where no one was seen to walk.

Television cameras have overrun Beaulieu in quest of the supernatural. When all has quieted down, I intend to go back and bring a good trance medium with me. Perhaps then we can find out directly what it is the monks want.

NELL GWYNNE AND THE GHOST OF THE CAVALIER

F OUR MILES SOUTH of St. Albans, and about an hour's drive
from London, lies Salisbury Hall, small as manor houses go,
but perhaps more ancient than most of them. Probably the site
of a Roman outpost when nearby St. Albans was an important
Roman city, Verulamium, it was developed uninterruptedly from
Saxon times onward, passing through many stages and families'
hands. The Earl of Warwick, known as "the kingmaker," Charles II
and Nell Gwynne, Sir Winston Churchill, and many lesser names
are associated with the Hall.

Its owner, artist Walter Goldsmith, who lived there with his wife
and children, restored the manor house to its original Tudor
grandeur after it had served as an aircraft shop during World War II.

The house was surrounded by a very old battlement and moat,
to this day filled with water. From the moat Mr. Goldsmith had
recovered numerous medieval swords, unquestionably left there by
dead soldiers in the battle of Barnet, which was fought around the
property in 1471. Soldiers were then billeted at the manor house,

which passed into the hands of one John Cutte after the Civil War ended. Cutte rebuilt it completely around 1550, but only the center portion of the house was now extant, the wings having disappeared over the years. Far from hurting the appearance of the house, this diminished size makes Salisbury Hall warmer and more like a home.

I went to Salisbury in the company of a reporter from the *Daily Sketch*, Rodney Burbeck, who wanted to watch me ghost hunting. We were met at the Hall by a photographer, and Mr. Goldsmith, who showed us around the house.

The large room downstairs was called The Crown Chamber; it had a fireplace on one side, next to which there was a heavy oaken door, and a staircase leading to the upper floors.

The Goldsmith family have lived here for about ten years, and they take their unseen guests in their stride.

"Where in this house has the ghost been seen, Mr. Goldsmith?" I asked when we had seated ourselves in the large room.

"The main recorded incident has happened in this great hall you're in," he said, "and it happened at the turn of the century, when an apparition very much like the accepted appearance of Nell Gwynne came down the staircase here and appeared to Sir Winston Churchill's stepfather, Mr. Cornwallis-West, sitting in the hall here. She disappeared into that wall over there."

He pointed at the oaken door near the fireplace, which seemed to me as solid as could be.

"Did he realize she was not something of flesh and blood?" I asked.

"At first he thought that it was his old nanny, who was very like the pictures and prints of Nell Gwynne, and he got very worried because he thought that something had happened to her, so he immediately rang up his sister, but learned that she was in perfectly good health. Then he suddenly remembered that people always said how very much like Nell Gwynne his nanny, whose name is Old Girlie, was considered to be."

"How did he know this was an apparition, a ghost, and not a person who had walked in from outside?" I wanted to know.

Mr. Goldsmith was not the least bit perturbed at my insistence on proof.

"On recollection," Mr. Goldsmith continued, "Mr. Cornwallis-West was aware of a very unusual perfume which he could not account for, also that the apparition was dressed in a pale cream dress with blue tissue, found very often in the authentic portraits of Nell Gwynne. He was aware, too, of a rustling sound of silk which also was quite unaccountable."

"Had he had psychic experiences before?" I asked.

Mr. Goldsmith shook his head. "None whatsoever. He wasn't that sort of man; he was a Guards Officer, practical and matter-of-fact."

"Has anyone else had psychic experiences in this house?"

"Yes, many people, particularly elderly people who've either spent their childhood here, or been in service in the house towards the end of the last century, the eighteen eighties and nineties. They have written and told us of their experiences, and Mrs. Goldsmith is the person who really knows about this side of it."

I promised to take the matter up with Mrs. Goldsmith, who was watching us patiently from a corner of the room. First, however, I wanted to know if he himself had ever been involved in any actual experience since he came to live here.

"The only thing I notice is that the atmosphere of the house, which is usually very happy, changes considerably when I happen to be alone in the house or in the gardens."

"What do you think is the reason for that?"

"I don't think the house is haunted by anything evil, but when the house gets back to itself, so to speak, when the family is not about, possibly some other influences come out. Certain parts of the garden have a frightening atmosphere, probably of great antiquity."

I thought of the murderous battle fought on this spot, and the intrigues of the War of the Roses, and could readily see that some of that could hang on in the etheric atmosphere of the place.

"Nell Gwynne actually lived in this house, didn't she?" I said, changing the subject.

"Yes, she did," Goldsmith replied. "The house was a romantic ruin by the time Charles II saw it. Evidently it charmed him, for he saw the possibilities of making it into a little country retreat. He pulled down what remained of the old wings, kept the central portion, and made it into what you see today. He borrowed the money, and built this as a little hideout for himself and Nell Gwynne."

"Then Nell Gwynne lived here for a number of years?"

"Yes, it's all rather shrouded in mystery, for naturally the King did not want to have this known throughout the country, the monarchy having just been restored with great rejoicing by the English people, and he was anxious not to have any undue scandal associated with him."

"Nell Gwynne didn't die here, did she?"

"No, she died in poverty in London. She is buried in Lincoln's Inn Fields, in what is today the City or legal district of London."

"Was this her favorite retreat?"

"I think it was."

I walked around the great hall, then up the stairs which led to the upper floor. To my right, a perfectly preserved set of armor stood erect as if guarding the approaches.

"Nell Gwynne certainly isn't the only ghost here," Mr. Goldsmith remarked casually. "There is a very well-authenticated one of a cavalier who committed suicide in a room which you will see presently."

The term "cavalier" is applied in England to the soldiers fighting for the monarchist cause and King Charles I, against the Roundheads or Parliament troops of Oliver Cromwell during that bloody and protracted Civil War which culminated in the beheading of Charles I in 1649.

"What about this cavalier? Who was he, and why did he take his own life?"

"They say he took refuge here during one of the many battles of the Civil War, and the Roundheads chased him into this house; he was carrying certain vital secrets which he was afraid of giving away under torture, so he shot himself."

Mrs. Audrey Goldsmith, an ash blonde looking far younger than the mother of a seventeen-year-old son, which she is, came over and I asked her about the ghost of the cavalier.

"I've been here eight years now. One night I heard footsteps quite definitely going along the passage which is said to be haunted by the ghost of the cavalier, and I've heard these footsteps since then on several occasions."

"When did you hear them the last time?" I asked.

"About two years ago. They were very definitely a man's heavy footsteps. There was nobody in the house at the time who could have made those footsteps."

"It wasn't a prowler? Did you check?"

"Yes. Besides, the dogs would have barked if there had been anybody."

"Did you feel anything peculiar that time?"

"I had a prickly feeling in the back of my neck, and a cold sensation all over. The first time it happened I didn't."

"What were the circumstances of the first experience with those uncanny footsteps?"

"The first time, about three years ago, I was sleeping in a room upstairs along the passage. I had a very bad cold at the time, and I heard those footsteps passing my door about two o'clock in the morning. I was wide awake at the time, and reading, because I couldn't get to sleep. I thought possibly it was my husband going along to the bathroom, which is the only room at the end of the passage, but when I asked him the following morning, he said that he never stirred throughout the night."

I examined the passage, which is what we would call a corridor in America. It was narrow and straight and anyone walking in it could neither hide nor dash out quickly without being seen. Evidently the bathroom at the end of the passage of the corridor was built rather recently into masonry that was very old. The passage used to continue into what was once another wing of the house, but which was demolished around 1819. At the time of the Civil War, in the 1640's, it still stood.

Mrs. Goldsmith had never had any psychic experiences either before or beyond the happenings at Salisbury Hall. She had no interest in the supernatural and was a well-adjusted English homemaker.

"It seems to me," I said, "that you would have tried to see who it was when you heard those footsteps."

"Well, the first time, three years ago, when I assumed it to be my husband, I had my bedside light on already, and I assumed that when he saw the light on from under the door, he would come in and see how I was, since I had a cold. *But the footsteps did not return.* They vanished into the distance. If it had been someone going to the bathroom, I would have heard them return."

"Quite so," I nodded, "and did you hear the footsteps at a certain time?"

"Yes, always about two o'clock, and always in that passage. Various families who have lived here before us had the same experience."

"Did you make any alterations in this part of the house?"

"The only alteration that was made since the seventeenth century was when we came here and put the bathroom in because there was no existing bathroom at the time. This blocked off the passage which originally led through into the older wing of the house."

"Did the footsteps occur before you made the alterations, or only after?"

"As far as I'm concerned, after. Other families, however, have heard them here before we made the changes."

"To your direct knowledge, has anyone else had a ghostly experience here other than the footsteps you've just described?"

"Yes," Mrs. Goldsmith said. "There was a governess who worked here in nineteen fourteen for a family called Price. I had a letter from the lady who was Miss Price. She was quite a young girl at the time, but she remembers her governess being very frightened one night because she actually saw somebody come out of the wall and he stood by her bed. She was so terrified, she left the house the next day."

"Which room was that?"

"That was the room in which I was sleeping when I heard the footsteps."

"Did she describe this apparition in any detail?"

"No, she didn't, as far as I know."

"You were sure the footsteps you heard were those of a man?"

"Yes, they were too heavy to be a woman's. But I saw nothing."

I walked around the bedroom, back into the passage and to the bathroom at the far end of it. It felt unseasonably cold. Outside, it was sunny and mild. Even with the early fall dampness that sometimes besets England at this time of year, I could not account for the chilly feeling.

"What about the ghost of Nell Gwynne? You haven't seen her, have you?"

"No, I haven't," Mrs. Goldsmith replied, "but I have here a letter from an old lady who used to live here in the eighteen nineties with her mother, and older sisters, and brothers. It was a very big family, and she told me that on several occasions her mother met a young girl in her late teens, rather beautiful, dressed in an old costume with a blue shawl around her shoulders like the one mentioned in Cornwallis-West's story. The first time this happened she took it for granted that it was one of her older daughters playing a trick on her, so she followed the girl up to the top landing, where she vanished. She then investigated all the bedrooms and found all her family fast asleep. This happened on several occasions."

"And the lady in question is still living?"

"Oh, yes, she came to see us a short time ago."

"Is she a woman of sound mind, and balanced?"

"Oh, definitely! Far more sound and balanced than most of us, I think," Mrs. Goldsmith replied with a smile.

Frequently, animals will behave strangely when confronted with psychic occurrences. The Goldsmiths have two large dogs. I wondered if anything unusual had ever been observed in the behavior of the two animals. Mrs. Goldsmith nodded.

"Once, when I heard these footsteps in the bedroom, I had one of the dogs in bed with me, and she was right down under the bedclothes at my feet and could not have heard anything, yet at the very moment when I heard the footsteps, she let out a blood-curdling growl which frightened me almost more than the footsteps."

The Goldsmiths have two boys, one of whom was away when I called. But the elder boy, Christopher, aged seventeen, readily talked to me about his own experiences in the house. He sleeps in a room in the attic, two flights up the haunted stairs.

"Nothing ever happened in my room, but my brother Robin has the room next to mine, and I have experienced something very unusual while in his room."

"What exactly did you see or hear?"

"A couple of years ago, one night, the only night I've ever slept in that room—Robin happened to have been staying away and I thought I'd sleep there for a change—I had a very frightening dream. It was something about a terrible fight between two men."

"Speaking of dreams," I said, and returned to Mrs. Goldsmith, "didn't you mention something about a dream also? A very unusual kind of dream?"

"Yes," Christopher's mother said. "The lady who wrote to us about the governess and her frightening experience came to visit us about six months ago and brought along a friend who'd stayed with the family a lot in her childhood. This friend told us that she'd always used this little room—it was the spare bedroom at the time— and she never had a good night's sleep here but always had terrible dreams, always of two men bursting out into the room from the wall, and fighting."

Had Christopher and those who used that room before him "tuned in" on a tragedy far back in time? Did the cavalier not die by his own hands but in battle?

I wonder how Nell Gwynne must feel about all this fighting going on in what was after all her quiet country retreat.

But then ghosts are terribly self-centered and don't care much about other people. Not even other ghosts.

SOMERSET, DORSET, WILTSHIRE—GHOSTS THAT NEVER CEASED WALKING

WHEN I LAID out the route for our two-day safari to western England, the driver just shook his head and smiled a grim smile, the kind English drivers use when they want to tell you even Sir Winston couldn't do it. I insisted that we could. If the ghosts could stand our pace, so could we.

I telephoned the Marquess of Bath and made a date with him for noon, the following day. Before the tourists swarmed over his magnificent family seat and made ghost hunting all but impossible.

Longleat, as the palace was called, can't live on ghosts, of course, and the thousands of visitors who wander through its treasure-filled rooms and corridors contribute handsomely towards its upkeep.

Promptly at noon, we rolled into the surrounding park at Longleat. It had taken us a full three hours' driving to make it from London, but make it we did. We didn't even stop for tea, and in England, that's driving.

We were now in the very heart of Salisbury Plain, famed battle ground for centuries, near a town called, appropriately, Warminster.

After our car had entered "the grounds," it took us a full ten minutes to reach the main house. Anyone getting lost at night in this park might never be found until daylight.

We stopped on the last hill looking down into the plain on which stood the fantastic palace called Longleat like a breathtaking vista from the Arabian Nights.

Named after the small River Longleat that runs through the grounds, the palace had been the home of the Thynne family for four hundred years. It was built originally, in the years before 1580, by Sir John Thynne, ancestor of the present Marquess of Bath. His portrait—showing a determined man with a strong forehead and clothed in the rather peculiar dark costume of the period, sporting a very high collar—hangs among the many other family portraits in the many galleries and corridors. Comparable in size and grandeur to Versailles, Longleat was filled with art treasures assembled over the years by the family. Later additions to the great house, up to the time of Charles II mainly, have created the never-never land aspects of this building which appears as a stunning example of exquisite civilization amid the greens of the countryside.

But the vastness of Longleat was such that we had to restrict ourselves to the areas which were haunted.

When we arrived, the genial public-relations man for Lord Bath, and Lord Bath's thirty-year-old son, Lord Christopher Thynne, were already waiting in the large drawing room–library to the right of the magnificent staircase downstairs. The most incongruous sight that caught my eye was the stacks upon stacks of empty soda bottles piled neatly against one of the walls, but tourists do get thirsty, and there were so many of them!

While we were awaiting the arrival of the Marquess of Bath, Lord Thynne introduced the old family nanny, the nurse who had taken care of the Bath children for years and years and who had seen the ghosts—or one of them, anyway—many times. Miss Marks, the nurse, now in her seventies, used to look at the many portraits in the palace with the little girl named Caroline, and talk about them.

Often, as she stood in one of the rooms, she would look up and see a man standing in front of her.

"A tall scholarly-looking man," the nurse said, "walking along and looking as if he might be reading something. I only saw his back and he had a high collar; the wings of it I distinctly saw standing out. I would say, 'I think perhaps that's Grandpa. Shall we hurry up and speak to him?' We would follow him up the room, but when we got to the door at the end, which was shut, *he just wasn't there!*

"I don't think anything of that; I saw it lots and lots of times, and then at last, I thought it isn't a person at all. I didn't discuss it with anyone, but I knew it was friendly to me. I loved seeing this person, even after I discovered it was only a ghost."

"Did he ever actually disappear before your eyes into nothingness?" I questioned.

The nurse nodded emphatically. "Well, he was there, and he just dissolved as I got to the door. Just melted."

"Was there anything unusual about his costume?"

"The thing that was unusual was this collar that stuck out. People don't wear collars like that."

"Who do you think this ghost is?"

"I have no idea."

Perhaps Miss Marks felt it to be disrespectful to accuse a member of her employer's family of being a ghost, but her description of him, and that given by clairvoyant Tom Corbett who also visited the house recently, tallies pretty strongly with the appearance of the builder of Longleat, Sir John Thynne. Considering that Thynne had had a rather checkered career in his day and was known as an immensely headstrong man, it would appear not entirely impossible that his ghost was still being seen at his house simply because he wanted to "take it with him," and, failing in that as so many before him, elected to "stay with it," rather than let go.

"How often did you see this apparition, Miss Marks?" I asked.

"Every time I walked through the Red Library, in the evening. Between seven and eight, roughly. There was still some light."

I thanked the aged nurse, and greeted the Marquess of Bath, who had joined us. He took us upstairs into the haunted corridor, which was now bare even of carpets. This long, narrow passage parallels the sleeping quarters of some of the Thynne family, and it was here that Tom Corbett, the clairvoyant, felt a ghost also.

I questioned Lord Bath about the corridor.

"In this corridor," Lord Bath began, "a duel was fought by one of my ancestors, the second Viscount Weymouth, because he found that his wife, who was Louisa Carteret before he married her, had been unfaithful to him. He found her in a state, unfortunately, in which he thought a duel ought to be fought with the man she was with. He fought this duel in the corridor and killed the man, after which he buried him in the cellar. His skeleton was accidentally found when the boiler was put in downstairs, six years ago."

"Has there been any haunting reported in connection with this skeleton of the slain lover?"

"No, nothing in regard to the skeleton at all," Lord Bath said, "but people have seen what is assumed to be the ghost of Louisa Carteret, who was very unhappy when her lover was killed here in this corridor."

"Have you yourself ever seen a ghost?"

"No, I'm afraid not. I don't have that power. But my mother did see the ghost in the Red Library, downstairs. But not this one."

"Have any of the many visitors who come here ever reported seeing a ghost or experienced anything unusual?"

"Well, they haven't, but then I must say that visitors are never taken to that part of the house where the ghosts exist."

I took a good look at the portrait of Louisa. She was, indeed, something to fight a duel over—lovely young face, beautiful eyes, slim in her green dress.

I arranged with the Marquess to come back with a trance medium sometime and see if we can't get Louisa to join either her husband or her lover—whichever she prefers. For even a ghost lady has the privilege of changing her mind.

We left Longleat with hungry stomachs but a high degree of satisfaction at having seen so magnificent a haunted house.

It was after two, and if you have ever tried to get lunch in the English provinces one minute after the appointed hour, you know what it's like. It would be far easier to get a young eaglet away from a baldheaded eagle, or to open up a stock exchange in Moscow, than to persuade an English innkeeper that serving a meal at a quarter after two is not inconsistent with good hospitality. We finally managed to get fed, and were on our way again, this time setting course for a town called Sherbourne, due south, hard by the Blackmoor of Dorset.

The reason for this detour was a bit of intelligence I had received the night before from Clementina Bentine, wife of my old friend, the television star and writer Michael Bentine. Michael and Clementina used to live at Holwell Manor, Dorset, for many years, before the distance from London made it impractical for Michael to continue there. The Manor had been the property of Clementina's family and was left to her by her grandmother, Minnie Gadesen. Situated on the Bournemouth road, it had a priest's hiding hole, and was originally built as a hunting lodge for King John. It was, of course, haunted. The then-owners, who were in the process of remodeling the house to their needs, were Mr. and Mrs. Harry Digby, a kindhearted country squire and his practical wife.

We proceeded to Holwell with some difficulty, but managed to get there around four in the afternoon. The house sits behind an old moat on a rather large piece of land, and was one of those very ancient country houses of the gentry found rather frequently in the southern part of England. From the bedroom upstairs one could overlook a garden started in the days of King John, thirteenth century, but most of the house dated back to the Tudor period, sixteenth century.

My wife, Catherine, and I took innumerable photographs and films, none of which showed any ghosts. But then, the house was now so torn up that any self-respecting specter would keep from walking the familiar paths out of fear of stumbling over workmen's tools.

The following evening, when we joined the Bentines at their home in Esher, Surrey, after a truly Lucullian meal Clementina had whipped up, we started to discuss their experiences while residing at Holwell Manor.

"Clementina," I finally said, "what exactly did you hear?"

"Well, I used to hear what I was sure were my grandmother's footsteps walking down the passage. About a year before she died, she broke her hip, and she had to learn to walk again with a stick. It was a sort of distinctive step. I would hear this at odd times of the day or night."

"You mean, after her death?"

"Yes, of course. I always felt that if I were only brave enough to rush to the door and open it, I would see her."

"Did you?"

"No, I'm a terrible coward and I never did."

"But you heard these footsteps more than once?"

"Yes, I often used to hear her. There seemed to be no rhyme or reason for it. Sometimes when I was with people and sometimes without. Of course, it is difficult to be sure, an old house creaks and groans a lot."

"But a house doesn't walk with a cane," I interjected.

Clementina laughed. "No, that's true."

"Have there been any other manifestations at Holwell Manor?"

"Well, the maids used to say they would constantly meet a monk wandering along their passage. I don't know if they were slightly hysterical or whether they did see one. At any rate, they used to scream loudly."

"I understand, Michael, that you also had an experience with a monk. Am I correct?"

"Why, yes, on the top floor of the house. Of course I didn't know anything about a monk at the time. I became suddenly aware of an intense cold. Then, out of the corner of my eye, I saw this sort of brown habit, and I felt the presence of another human. I got out of there dead fast!"

"Have there been monks at Holwell at any time during its earlier history?"

"During the persecution of the Jesuits in England, Holwell had a priest's hiding hole built into the walls. It was used again later during the Civil War under Cromwell. Cavaliers used it as a hideout. The present owners, I understand, are trying to find this secret room, and turn it into a bathroom."

"Is there anything else at Holwell of unusual character?"

"The passages at night are continually cold. It's rather more than just the cold of stone. In fact, the stones used in Dorset pick up an enormous amount of heat during the day, so it should be warmer at night, but it just isn't. I've noticed when getting up at night— rather reluctantly, I might add—to go to the bathroom, at the end of a very long passage, it has required a considerable amount of courage, because the feeling really is that you're walking past and through a large number of people."

We left Holwell Manor and drove back towards the Bristol Channel, some hours distant. In fact, our chauffeur doubted we could reach it in time for bed, but I knew we would. My schedule was only an hour or so off, and that could be managed. Our next stop was Glastonbury Abbey, called the holiest spot in all England, because here is the tomb of King Arthur and Queen Guinevere, as well as the miraculous tree planted, allegedly, by Joseph of Arimathea. What made the stopover at Glastonbury interesting was the fact that a psychic named Bond was responsible for the rediscovery of the Abbey, which had fallen into total ruin after it had been burned to the ground during the Dissolution period under Henry VIII. For years, the walls of the majestic cathedral lay buried under grass, until a communicator who identified himself as "one of the monks of Glastonbury" told Bond, through automatic writing, where to look for the Abbey, and what to expect. He gave a very detailed description of the layout, all of which turned out to be correct when the Abbey was finally excavated, upon the urging of scholar Bond.

From Glastonbury, we continued on towards the sea. By seven o'clock, two hours late by now, we finally reached our destination, a little town called Banwell, where there was a ghost waiting for me.

It all started when a Californian, Dick Simonton, visited us and told us of his experiences at Banwell Abbey. Mr. Simonton was an executive in the communications field and a man of keen observation, so I listened attentively as he told us of his visit to the Abbey, which was then the property of Stella and Jim Hawthorne, who have since sold it. It was the chapel area which to Dick seemed haunted, and he spoke of his uncanny feelings while standing in that vaulted room.

The Abbey had been subdivided into three apartments, occupied now by Albert Russell, Ian McDonald, and a Mr. Martin, respectively. It was Albert Russell who answered my request for a visit in the most cordial terms.

"Twelve years ago," he wrote, "the local paper did a piece on the ghosts at Banwell Abbey. But do come."

We had a little trouble making out the Abbey from the many old buildings in this town, but finally drove into the yard surrounded by the buildings of the Abbey itself. Mr. Russell came to greet us, and took us inside the part of the Abbey he owned.

The Russells had lived here for nine years and when they took over their part of the house, knew nothing of any hauntings.

Across the yard, there was a very old building which was originally the coachman's house in the days when the bishops lived here. Mr. Russell had made this into a workshop. One ascends on a somewhat rickety staircase to the upper floor, lighted only by a couple of naked electric bulbs. The beams overhead were very strong and blackened from the exposure to the centuries.

We stood in the former coach house, and Mr. Russell proceeded to tell me of an eerie experience that had occurred to him here only six months ago.

"I entered one end of this building and switched the light on. I then walked up the wooden stairway to the room above. I didn't switch the light on in that room but walked through it—it's a fairly long room, as you can see—and then to the room at the end of this one, in which I switched on the light. I put some wood on my bench and was preparing to work on it, when I heard quite distinctly heavy footsteps coming up the stairway I had just ascended!

"I immediately went to the door, expecting to see someone appear in the doorway at the far end of the darkened room, but no one did, so I walked immediately through the room and to the stairway. There was no one on the stairs, and no one in the room below. I ran down the stairs, out into the courtyard, and I looked both ways and all around the courtyard, but there was no one at all. I can't explain this."

"They were a man's footsteps?"

"Yes, quite heavy."

"You are sure it wasn't a human intruder?"

"Impossible. There wasn't a car or other vehicle outside."

We went across the yard into the main house, where we seated ourselves in front of a comfortable fireplace. It was September, but the fire was going; it was one of those English nights when its warmth was very necessary indeed. "I understand there is a haunted staircase here," I began.

"All I know is that there is a stone stairway and a priest's hiding hole at the top of it."

"Have you noticed anything unusual about it?"

"Well, no, that part of the building belongs to my neighbor, Mr. McDonald."

We rose and went next door to see the McDonalds, who received us with curiosity and warmth. They were somewhat younger then the Russells, perhaps in their late thirties, and Mr. McDonald was the liberal candidate for Parliament from the area.

We were now standing in the old chapel which was built over the original Abbey. This part of the building dated from the fifteenth century.

"Then this is the actual chapel in which services were performed for many hundreds of years?"

"That is correct," Mr. McDonald said, and pointed at the Gothic church windows framing the paneled room. "We have made the upper half into our bedroom and this lower half into a sitting room."

Being a liberal, sleeping in a chapel did not disturb Ian McDonald at all.

"What about the ghost?" I said.

"There is the story of the bishop who died here and another bishop who came to see him, and who also died as he came in, and these two old bishops are reputed to walk in the Abbey at various times. I've never seen either of them."

It was late, and I did not wish to keep the McDonalds and the Russells up to the witching hour, which was close at hand. I had a feeling they were sorry to see us go, after having come so far on so unusual a quest, bringing, as it were, a spark of excitement into this far-off place.

We drove on to a seaside town called Weston Super Mare, where we bedded down for the night.

The next morning we started out on the long trip home. Our first stop was a sixteenth-century house in the little town of Keynshaw, on the Bath-Bristol road. This house, called Ellsbridge, was now occupied by a social-service agency for the county, but in former years belonged to Colonel and Mrs. Gore-Browne of Beaulieu.

During the last war, Margaret Gore-Browne lived here in charge of an auxiliary unit serving people in need, or displaced from their homes because of the war. It was then that she noticed something peculiar about the house, especially the big stairway leading up to the upper floor smack in the middle of the house. At all times, she had the impression of people coming to the house, walking up and down that staircase, some in sorrow, never to leave again. She also heard a child crying when there was positively no child about. Humphrey, the head gardener, shared some of these eerie experiences. Mrs. Gore-Browne made inquiries about the old house and discovered that it had served as a hospital during the Civil War between Charles I and Parliament forces. The people she felt going up and down those stairs were wounded soldiers from a nearby battlefield!

We pressed on for our next stop, the ancient city of Bath, known since Roman times as a spa and pleasure resort to the wealthy and famous. What drew us there, however, was not the mild climate or the famous Regency buildings in which it abounds. What attracted me was a newspaper account of strange goings-on that had all the overtones of a poltergeist—or rather of a ghost given to poltergeist manners:

> Spooks are shivering both the timbers and the guests of an 18th century inn reconverted from a labyrinthine gambling den.

Guests said the nether-world nothings threw a glass across a room during a party (the glass didn't break up but the party did), sent squeaky footsteps down a secret passageway (no prints showed up on the dust-covered floor, except those of a fleeing guest) and frightened the wits out of an elderly woman.

The woman, who said she could tell a spirit from an actor because her son's an actor, reported seeing a heavy-jowled man in a Georgian costume and a long, full brown wig.

Another guest at the inn, the Garrick's Head, also saw the nocturnal visitor, who was stepping into a secret tunnel at the time. It was the landlord's son, Henry Barron Fox, a former sea captain and Royal Air Force squadron leader, who reported the invisible footsteps incident.

Another article added that no footprints could be seen in the heavy dust of the corridor where the steps had been heard! That was enough of an incentive for me, so we drove up to the Garrick's Head Inn, which was no longer an inn but a bar catering primarily to theater folks from the next-door playhouse and others residing in the area.

A new owner greeted us, fortyish, soft-spoken Bill Loud, who had bought out Mr. Fox some time before.

Alterations in the bar, which was the center of the eerie goings-on, include a wall where a stairway leading to the upstairs used to be. The connecting links between the inn and next-door theater no longer exist as they once did when Beau Nash, the gambling king, owned the place, back in the eighteenth century.

Upstairs, there was a window which somehow was difficult to keep closed. There was a tradition that a woman threw herself out of that window. She was a "lady in gray" whom various actors and actresses have seen sitting in a box high above the audience. I was wondering whether the ghost of the Theatre Royal was responsible for Mr. Loud's troubles.

The bar was half filled with people having a beer or some other drink, and Bill Loud answered my questions between serving them.

"When we came here, we had heard about this ghost and I didn't really believe it. But within the first two months, firstly the till came off the counter and smashed a chair—"

"You mean this heavy cash register took off by itself? Did you see it?"

"Yes, I did. I was serving in the bar and there was nobody near the till at all."

I was all ears.

"This till weighs about sixty, seventy pounds," Mr. Loud emphasized.

"And this happened in good light?"

"Oh, yes, quarter past twelve on a Sunday morning. About a year ago now."

"Anything else that's unusual?"

Bill Loud thought for a moment.

"Oh, we've heard noises in the night, people walking about, that sort of thing," he finally said casually, as if having unseen people walk around were the most natural thing in the world.

"There was no one there when you checked?"

"No one."

"You live in this building?"

"Oh, yes. For two years now."

"Outside of those frequent footsteps, have you noticed anything else you could not account for in the normal way?"

"Twice when I walked through the cellar, something came along and stroked the back of my head. I thought it was cobwebs, but of course it wasn't. It's ridiculous really. And we do smell perfume about at times—in the cellar, mind you."

"It appears then that you've got a female ghost?"

"This as you know used to be a gambling house run by a famous character, Beau Nash, who made Bath what it is today. That was in the eighteenth century. He had all the Lords and Ladies down from London to take the waters and come gambling.

"Once there was an argument in what is now the bar, but which was a private house in those days. And two men had a duel over a woman, I believe, and one man was killed. The other man went rushing up the stairs obviously to claim his prize. The woman heard him coming and hanged herself on the bedroom door! That is authentic; she did hang herself. Whether it is her ghost that walks in this place or the man who was killed, I don't know.

"This house used to have a communicating door to the theatre next door, and there is a ghostly 'gray lady' in the theatre."

"Then you think there is a connection between those two?"

"There must be; the buildings used to be connected."

"Outside of yourself, has anyone else had experiences in this building?"

"The previous landlord, Mr. Baron Fox, as you know, heard the footsteps quite often. Several customers have heard things, footsteps mostly. Mainly in the bar, the cellars, and also in the residence lounge which used to be the old gambling room. We had a reporter staying here and he heard a great deal."

"I'll look into that," I promised, "but tell me, does it worry you to have a ghost here?"

"Gracious no, it's a friendly ghost, really—apart from the till."

I took my leave of Bill Loud, and checked into the newsman's story. It appeared in the *Western Daily Press* of Bristol, July 5, 1963. The reporter, John Duller, stayed at the inn to listen for the ghostly noises.

I can vouch for loud and mysterious bumps in the night.

It happened when I was staying at the pub two months ago,

before I heard the story of the ghost. Several thuds woke me as I was dozing in the first-floor sitting room. I searched the room and the corridor outside for ten minutes. But I found nothing except that the sounds seemed to have come from behind the paneling in a corner of the room.

Bill Loud asked the help of a study group of parapsychologists at Cambridge University under the leadership of Tony Cornell. But the spooks continue to have their merry way. Less than a month ago, the stage lights dimmed and a grandfather clock chimed in the middle of a performance at the Theatre Royal—although no one could have been at the switches at that time.

If the "gray lady" committed suicide by leaping from the top window and the other woman by hanging herself from her door, they can't be one and the same ghost. Since the evidence for the hanging is pretty sound, we may safely assume that there were, indeed, several specters roaming the corridors of the old Garrick's Head Inn—not forgetting the cavalier who started the whole mess!

We continued on toward London after a delightful luncheon at the St. Francis Hotel. The road now took us through the rolling Berkshire hills, past Marlborough, the ancestral seat of the Churchills, along the Vale of Kennet to Great Marlow, near the Thames River.

Here was one of the finest of Tudor buildings, called Bisham Abbey. It was once a priory, but towards the end of the sixteenth century it belonged to one Sir Thomas Hoby and his wife, Elizabeth. Tradition has it that she went to London, one fine day, having forgotten that she had shut up her child as punishment—and when she returned, the child had died. Her remorseful spirit is said to haunt the Abbey, with a basin floating ahead of her in which she keeps washing from her hands the blood of her child.

Now a National Recreation Center for physical recreation, the building abounds in magnificent fireplaces and Tudor halls. The Warden, Mr. Taylor, who had given me permission to look the house over, was absent when we arrived rather unexpectedly. We were shown around by the bursar, Mrs. Cecily de Havas, who occupies a room on the upper floor.

The room had a wall which hides a secret: behind the wooden paneling there can still be seen the original Tudor wall. This was the spot where the ghost of Lady Hoby is said to have appeared. I questioned Mrs. de Havas about this.

"Have you ever noticed anything unusual in this room?"

"There are noises constantly during the day, sometimes at night, tapping noises, sometimes very loud, sometimes I ask 'them' to stop, and they do."

"Are they the kind of noises that might be explained by natural means?"

"I don't think so. They appear from underneath the floors or behind the walls."

"Is this the haunted room where the ghost has appeared from time to time?"

"Yes, it is."

Mrs. de Havas had not encountered the lady, however. All she experienced were those tapping noises. I examined the wall and bed. Nothing was loose, no floorboards, or anything else that would creak or cause noises of this type.

We drove on, past Hurley, where there is a haunted house called "Lady Place," allegedly the site of a ghostly monk, and past Windsor Castle where there may or may not be ghosts, depending on who is right—the librarian who denies it all, or the tradition which says there is something there to be looked into.

But it was much too late in the day to find out, so we hurried on to London, and the warm, comfortable beds of our apartment at the White House Club.

THE STRIP-TEASE
GHOST

I F YOU THINK MEDIEVAL castles and stately homes are where
the ghosts are, you have a rude awakening coming. Sure, there
are haunted castles and dungeons all over England, and for that
matter, all over the world. But the tragic phenomenon called "ghost"
can and does occur in strange places. Take, for instance, the
Gargoyle. For those who don't know what a gargoyle is, it isn't
someone's unfriendly mother-in-law but a heraldic or fabled animal
said to have existed underground in olden times. One meets it mostly
on the walls and steeples of Gothic churches where it forms a rather
formidable adornment, presumably to remind the faithful of the
pleasures denied them should they stray from The Path.

But the Gargoyle I am referring to was a night club in the
London section known as Soho. When this part of the capital was
still green, the huntsmen used to yell to each other "Soho!" very
much as today they say "Tally-ho!" or whatever they do say when
they chase after one miserable fox in what is laughingly called sport.

As London grew, Soho became a city within the city, specially
favored by the foreigners who were drawn to London, especially
Italians, Spaniards, and other foreign nationals. At this time, the

strip-tease dancers in the numerous cellar clubs that had all but driven the legitimate "naughty" revues out of business.

The oldest and probably the best produced of these shows took place twice an evening at the little house in Deane Street housing two attractions—the Gargoyle night club and the Nell Gwynne Theatre. The Gargoyle continued after ten where the Nell Gwynne left off, and leaving off was the word here. Both were shows populated by a procession of young ladies who display their natural attributes in varying degrees and forms of undress. There was never any doubt where it will all end—only how it gets there. This brain child of Jimmy Jacobs was, however, immensely popular, not only with American tourists, but with the English out-of-towner who had heard about wicked London town and wants something to tell the boys back in Upper Rickenham when he gets home.

I did not know about the ghost at the Gargoyle until Sabrina called my attention to it. Sabrina, herself well-endowed by Mother Nature, was a night-club singer with a keen interest in the supernatural. When she lived in New York for a few years, I found that her East Side apartment was slightly haunted. It terrified her greatly, even though she never saw anything herself.

Not only was Jimmy Jacobs, the owner of the Gargoyle, happy to co-operate; it turned out that he was himself a medium and a spiritualist—imagine!

When we arrived at the Club, the second "house" had just ended and the plush, red-upholstered reception room on the fourth floor of the building was empty, except for the receptionist. You had to be a "member" here to enjoy the fun, but membership, happily, was available quickly and painlessly by paying a nominal sum. This was definitely not the Union League Club.

I asked Mr. Jacobs to have present any witness to the ghostly goings on, and waiting for me was a tall brunette, fully dressed now, who led us into the almost darkened Nell Gwynne Theatre which occupies the upper floor. The woman's name was Cherry Phoenix, and she took her new role as scientific witness very seriously.

"I joined the Nell Gwynne Theatre club about a year and four months ago," she began with a slight tinge of provincial accent, "and I had been working here for about four months, when one day I happened to come in fifteen minutes early. There were no lights on the staircase anywhere and as I went upstairs, I felt my way. As I reached my dressing table, I heard peculiar sounds, like someone flicking over pages of a book. I looked around. The whole place was in darkness, there was nothing else about, yet there was this horribly cold atmosphere. I went goosey all over and I thought maybe somebody was in the top dressing room, so I called the two girls to see if they were there—Barbara? Isabelle?—but there was no answer. Still, this flicking of the pages sound carried on. I was so petrified I just stood there for about fifteen minutes. Finally one of the girls came in and I told her about it.

" 'Oh,' she said, 'that's nothing. That's just Nelly.' "

Tradition has it that the ghost is Nell Gwynne, who lived in this house for a number of years.

"Did you hear this just once?" I asked.

"This kind of noise, yes, but there are other things. Frequently the door to the roof will open of its own. Normally the bolt is quite stiff and you can't move it. It has slipped down by itself and just opened. There was nobody at all about."

"How long ago the last time?"

"About six months ago."

"Did you ever sense a presence you could not account for?"

"Yes, sometimes during the hot summer it has been really freezing in the dressing room, and it feels as if there is 'something' hanging over you. Like a mist. I've also heard noises that sound like chain rattling. One night, after the cabaret was finished and everybody else had gone home, I was still on my own upstairs and I heard rattling sounds as if somebody was locked in a cage, rattling the bars to get out! Many times I would look up and down the stairs to see if there was anyone there and there never was."

"Have you ever seen a ghost here?" I finally asked while straining my ears for some stray chain rattling which, however, did not materialize.

"Not I, but one friend of mine who used to work here went into the Gargoyle kitchen one day and came out screaming in horror. She saw a ghost—the outline of a figure wearing a pale lilac costume. She'd also often heard voices calling when there was nobody about."

"What sort of voices?" I wanted to know.

"On several occasions she heard her name being called. By a woman. She thought it was the girl she used to dress with, but when she went downstairs, there was nobody there. My friend's name is Tracy York."

"Did you have psychic experiences before you came to work here?"

"No, never."

I next turned to Terry Brent, choreographer and one of the leads in the revue, a young man in his late twenties, who was somewhat cautious about the ghost business.

He was outside the kitchen at the time of the incident involving Tracy York.

"She was quite articulate about it. She said it was a lady, age indeterminate, in a gray period costume, and there was a sort of mistiness about the whole apparition. She just appeared and stood and smiled."

"Has anyone else complained about a ghost?"

"Several girls who used the upstairs dressing room, which is somewhat isolated from the rest of the building, have told me either of seeing the apparition or experiencing this intense cold they could not account for."

"Did these people know this was a very ancient building and that it had a reputation of being haunted?"

Terry Brent shook his head with emphasis.

"No, they would not know about this. It is not the sort of thing we talk about, especially when a girl is quite new, we don't want her to be frightened. We always wait for them to find out, and then we explain."

"Have you yourself experienced anything unusual here?"

"Well, one evening when I came in to do the cabaret, one of the young ladies, Isabelle Appleton, was dressing in that upstairs dressing room that seems to be a center of ghostly activities. I came in through the theatre where you're sitting now, and I heard laughter upstairs and thought, oh, the girls are in early tonight. So I went up and before I actually reached the dressing room at the top of the stairs, I said, 'Hello, girls, how are you this evening?' "

He paused.

"What happened then?" I asked.

"Much to my surprise, when I turned the corner and looked into the dressing room, Miss Appleton was in there alone. The laughter was not hers."

"How did she take it?"

"Well, I had been extremely skeptical about the whole business until then, while she was somewhat psychic, I'm sure. She was glad that I had heard it, too. She thinks it was the 'lady in gray.' "

Jimmy Jacobs, a dark-haired, smallish man who moves quietly and deliberately, had just joined us.

I thought it was time to find out why this building would have a ghost. What was its background? Mr. Jacobs turned out a veritable fountainhead of information.

"The Club itself is Europe's oldest night club and was founded by Noël Coward and the artistic aristocracy of the nineteen twenties. The room downstairs was designed by Henri Matisse."

I was secretly wondering how the founders would feel about the changes in policy that had since taken place at the Gargoyle.

"I came here about eight years ago," Mr. Jacobs continued. "Although I was always interested in psychic phenomena, I had not bargained on purchasing a ghost as well. But next door to where we are now stood the Royalty Theatre, one of London's oldest, which was destroyed by bombs in the last war, and subsequently pulled down, and it had housed one of our most famous theatre ghosts, the 'gray lady' who was seen and heard in the wings on many occasions.

"The building in which we are now dates from about sixteen thirty-two and Nell Gwynne is reputed to have lived here. In this very room in which we are sitting we once held a séance, because a girl who was left behind here one night by mistake heard such an amount of noise and human voices that she attempted to jump out of the window!"

"Did she do it?" I asked. I had heard rumors that the ghost was hers.

"No, the fire brigade got here in the early hours of the morning and released her. But I was so interested in her story I arranged for the *Psychic News* to have a séance here. We found out that the Royal Stables used to be in the basement of this building, but nothing more definite about the 'gray lady.' "

"What about the 'gray lady,' then? Who do you think she is?"

"My own experience leads me to think she is not Nell Gwynne. It is somebody who pretends she is Nell Gwynne—a ghostly imposter."

"You mentioned you yourself saw the ghost. When did that happen?"

"Some two years ago," Jacobs said, "I was standing in the reception room which is separated from us by this plaster-of-Paris wall, when I heard the elevator come up and I went towards it. It would be impossible for it to be operated except electrically by someone pressing a button to bring it up, somebody inside it, that is. I was in the building all alone, it was three o'clock in the morning, and I was wondering if someone had forgotten something here and had come back for it. The elevator came to a stop. The doors did not open. Nobody got out. I opened the gates; it was empty. Then suddenly, to my right, about five yards away from me, across the room, I saw a gray, shadowy figure that seemed like a little old lady, dressed in what I can only describe as a period dress, high-waisted, a large flowered hat, her face turned away from me—and she seemed to glide across the floor like one of those little dolls that one sees on wheels. The most amazing thing about it was the very strong, pungent odor of a perfume which lingered in my nostrils for many days afterwards. It was gardenias, and this overpowering perfume filled the room as the little gray lady glided past me and then disappeared just a yard or so from me into what is now the elevator shaft."

"Did she speak to you?"

"I had the feeling she was turning her face to avoid being seen. She did not want me to know who she was."

"Did she come back after that night?"

"No, not so far anyway. But one never knows with ghosts."

Had the ghost of the Royalty Theatre simply moved next door when her old home was no more? She must be an actress for surely so well staged an appearance as the mystery ghost managed on several occasions seems to point to a thespian talent that neither time nor space was able to diminish.

So if you are at a strip-tease club one of these evenings, watching the show—if you happen to see an extra woman with her clothes *on*—she just may be a ghost!

THE HALL PLACE GHOSTS

HALL PLACE IS A thirteenth-century manor house, largely rebuilt in Tudor times, which had very little publicity either as a historic shrine or, indeed, as a haunted house. Tourists do not overrun its beautiful grounds as they do so many other stately homes open to the public. In fact, were it not for painstaking research and a tip from the British Travel Association, I might have never stumbled onto it. As it was, it seemed the perfect setting for an experiment in ghost hunting that I had been contemplating ever since I had come to England. I wanted to find an experienced psychic or medium, and take that person to a place where he (or she) had never been; a place the psychic was not likely to have heard of. Hall Place lies off the main road in a small Kentish town called Bexley, about an hour from London proper. The area is associated with the Black Prince, Edward, and his ghost allegedly had been seen there, although this had very little basis in fact. There is the tradition, also, of one Lady Atte-Hall, who threw herself to death from one of its towers when she saw her husband killed by a stag. The Librarian of Bexley, whom I consulted, was sure this happened in another manor house—not this one. Be this as it may, moans and groans had been reported from the tower area, and also a woman "in white" had been seen there; voices out of nowhere were heard, and in 1931 a certain Canon Wicksteed conducted exorcism ceremonies in the house, according to the local newspaper of April 19, 1950, when the nearby Lewisham Psychic Research Society entered the case. Three of their members spent the night at Hall Place, but their report was not conclusive. Evidently, the ghosts were not in a mood to show themselves. The matter then died down, and I could find nothing about the place in more recent years.

I asked Brigadier Firebrace, President of the British College of Psychic Science, to suggest a reliable psychic with the ability of trance. He named Douglas Johnson, and I called him to ask him to accompany us to a place of my selection, on a given date, to which he readily agreed. Until the morning of the expedition, I myself did not know which of three possible places we would visit, so that thought transference would have been extremely difficult. We did not discuss our destination at all as we drove along. I asked Manning Ross, who was driving us, to take certain roads which would eventually get us to Bexley. Only when we arrived did Mr. Johnson learn where we were, and it meant nothing to him.

The buildings were now used as a school, and we had to come after 4:00 P.M. so as not to interfere with the youngsters who throng the ancient rooms and corridors before that hour.

We quickly walked through the garden that surrounds the manor house on all sides and ascended the stairs that led to a great hall on the first floor of the house. There we paused, as Douglas Johnson got his bearings.

"Tell me," I finally asked. "When we came into this building, did you have any psychic impressions?"

"Well, I had one," Mr. Johnson answered in his usual quiet, cultured voice. "As we were walking along the passage into this beautiful banqueting hall, I saw a figure in front of me, and I thought at first that it was one of you. But then I noticed that there was a shaven head, and I believe that he was a monk and that this part of the building at one time was either a monastery or was connected in some way with a religious fraternity."

"Was this an impression, or did the monk look to you as if he were solid?" I wanted to know.

"Exactly as solid as you are, Mr. Holzer," Johnson replied.

"What did he do? Just walk by or did he disappear?"

"He had his back to me. He appeared to walk through this door; when I got into the room, I could not see anything further at all."

"Did it appear strange to you to see this man here?"

"No, not really. I go into many old houses, as part of my profession, and I do see all sorts of apparitions."

"But you weren't prepared for a monk, were you?"

"No, I wasn't."

I turned to the slender man in his thirties, who had come with us from Bexley, and introduced him to Johnson. "We're fortunate to have with us the Librarian of Bexley, Mr. Paul Morris, who can either confirm or deny what we have just discussed."

I turned to Morris. "Has there been any association that would explain the presence of a monk in this building?"

"Well, it's very difficult to say precisely," the librarian said in his cautious manner. "The building itself is from reclaimed stone from the monastic dissolution. There is a chapel in one of the rooms upstairs; as in many houses, it is highly likely that at some time or other monks were associated with it."

We proceeded up the stairs to the second floor. We were walking along the corridor and were about to bypass one of the rooms, when Johnson halted us and insisted on entering the room itself.

"Do you feel anything in here?" I asked.

"I feel very strongly indeed," he said. "A man in a later time than Tudor times—in the eighteenth century—with a wig; stout, rather red-faced; he either took his own life—I have a rather choked feeling in my throat at the moment—could be he hanged himself or it could possibly have been apoplexy—a very unhappy man, I think. His name sounded like Gwayne. Perhaps the librarian can check on it."

We continued our tour of the old mansion, going up the back stairs which, in Johnson's view, were freer from later impressions, since they were not ordinarily open to the public. The stairs led up to the attic floor. We found the attic almost in the original state in which it was four hundred years ago. Little or no restoration had taken place here, and the ceilings showed the old beams exactly as in Tudor times.

"Somebody certainly hanged himself up here," Douglas Johnson muttered as he walked about the area at random.

We entered the servants' quarters, dating back about three hundred years.

"I feel someone hanged himself from a beam here—a servant," Johnson declared, and continued the search for the elusive ghosts of Hall Place. We were now following him through the narrow passages, through ancient archways, still within the confines of the servants' quarters up under the roof of the manor house.

"I have an impression of a woman," Johnson suddenly said, and stopped. "Dressed in a gray gown, and something white around the face, rather like a nun's veil, but she isn't a nun. There is great unhappiness, and she is walking about, crying, wringing her hands, and she is worried about a child or baby."

I asked Johnson to "stay with her," so to speak, and try to establish some sort of contact. Johnson's face became tense and his eyes took on a faraway look.

"There was a child that belonged to this woman," he finally said, slowly, as if someone were dictating to him.

"Yes. Go on!" I urged.

"This child either died or was murdered—and it made her desperately unhappy. She was a rather beautiful woman. I feel I want to link her up with somebody with the initial M. Possibly her own name; I don't know for sure. I can see her walking down these stairs, crying and wringing her hands."

"Let us follow her downstairs," I suggested, and we swiftly descended the stairs again, winding up in a suite of Tudor rooms on the ground floor, now used as classrooms.

Johnson suddenly froze in his tracks. We grouped ourselves around him to better hear the faint voice now coming from his trembling lips. " 'The baby is dead! The baby is dead!' she keeps saying. 'What am I to do? What am I to do?' Pacing and walking." Johnson bent over now. Finally, he straightened up.

"We must help her," he said. "We will ask for help for her." There was a minute of silent prayer.

"Mr. Johnson," I finally said, "do you feel her near you now?"

"I felt her very near a moment ago," the medium replied. "I think she is realizing now that it is unnecessary to be attracted to this place; a contact from the other world may have already been made— for the whole atmosphere now feels lighter, and I don't believe that she is here at this moment."

"Then our visit here has done some good?" I asked.

"I really think so," Johnson replied very seriously. "I am glad you asked me to come with you."

The librarian, Paul Morris, excused himself. He could not deny nor confirm the story, but then the death of a servant woman's child is hardly the sort of historical event one might find in the records. A white figure was seen at Hall Place; moans were heard. The explanation of the suicide of Lady Atte-Hall, or the apparition of Edward, the Black Prince, is infinitely more romantic than a servant woman's tragedy. But I am inclined to accept the latter as the more valid possibility. None of the children in the school had yet encountered the unhappy one. She seems to confine her activities to the tower area. Since our visit there have been no further reports of uncanny happenings. Perhaps the girl had found peace among her own kind, and Hall Place belongs once more only to the living.

There were two other haunted spots to which I wanted to take Douglas Johnson. One of them is the Old Manor Hotel, Midhurst, Sussex, a very old and picturesque house which was once a manor house and still showed the original construction—beams and walls—with very few alterations. There was, however, a sealed-up doorway between a bay window and a square window, and it is here that a ghost had been observed. The ghost is a monk, tradition has it, who used to have clandestine rendezvous with a girl, the daughter of the lord of the manor. Evidently she died, and he couldn't take it. November is his particular haunting month—when he had most frequently been seen.

I questioned Mrs. Stackey, the Manager, about all this. She admitted that there was some truth in it, but that she herself had not seen the ghostly monk.

Did she know anyone who had? . . . That is when I got to know Mrs. Primrose Withers, a nurse, who had lived at the Manor House Hotel for the past five years.

"There is a subterranean passage," she said, when I talked to her in London where she had gone for the weekend to be with kin, "and it's not an ordinary girl—it was a nun he kept visiting."

Perish the thought, I said to myself, there we have it. The classical Borley Rectory situation again. Boy monk meets girl nun. Bang.

"Did you ever see the ghost?" I asked Mrs. Withers.

"Yes, I did," she said in a pleasant, matter-of-fact voice. "Last November I saw this nun at the bottom of the stairs that lead to my room."

"Was that the only time?"

"No, the November before last, that is, in nineteen sixty-two, the door to my room—which must have been theirs, I suspect— opened by itself."

"What did you do?"

"Naturally, I was frightened. Even my dog was scared stiff. Then I saw the nun. I chased her, but she vanished around the corner."

"Are there any others who have seen either the monk or the nun?" I asked.

"Mrs. Stackey, the Manager, she knows—lots of people kept complaining about all the goings-on. It only happens in that part of the house that is situated over the kitchen, on the first floor. The person who had my room before me told me she could not stand it there. One night, her door burst wide open just as it did for me. I lived in a haunted room all right."

Ghostly monk, or ghostly nun—if they appear only in November where do they spend the rest of the year?

Perhaps Douglas Johnson can find out, but the Old Manor Hotel was not long for this world, and the new building might very well send the ghosts packing without benefit of the Ghost Hunter.

One of the obvious places one might look for ghosts is in the Bloody Tower of London. As we passed by the sprawling fortress on our way back from Bexley, I decided to have a go at it.

First I asked for permission to visit the Tower at a time when visitors would not interfere with my research. The Governor of the Tower, Colonel Butler, refused.

It is very much regretted it is not possible to grant you facilities for a private visit to H.M. Tower of London as requested.

At this time of the year there were approximately 12,000 visitors daily to the Tower, and after the Tower is closed at 6:30 P.M. it would not be possible to reopen any of the buildings or permit visitors to enter the Tower.

In addition regulations do not permit any part of the Tower being used for commercial purposes.

By now I had a sneaking suspicion that Her Majesty's palaces were particularly closed to me for reasons other than those stated—obviously, where there is smoke, there is fire. The Royal preserves were indeed haunted and uncovering the evidence was undesirable. But then I have as yet to get permission to enter the Lincoln room of the White House, which is haunted also. I will keep trying, of course, and perhaps in a few years' time the official attitude towards parapsychology will have changed sufficiently to welcome a dignified investigation.

That the Tower ghosts were more than a legend can be seen by scanning two of the many accounts of ghostly encounters there. In 1864, one Major General J. G. Dundas of the 60th Rifles was quartered in the Tower. Looking out the window from his quarters, he noticed a guard below in the courtyard in front of the chamber where unlucky Queen Anne Boleyn spent her last moments on earth. The guard behaved strangely—he seemed to challenge "something" which, to the General, looked like a whitish female figure gliding towards the soldier. He charged right through the form, and then fainted. Only the General's testimony and corroboration saved the soldier from a long prison sentence at the court-martial which took place as a consequence of his fainting while on duty. Those were stern times, remember.

As recently as February, 1957, a Welsh Guardsman on duty at the Tower reported seeing a ghost on the upper battlements of the Salt Tower on the anniversary of the execution of Lady Jane Grey, who died four hundred years ago after a reign of only nine days. In the Church of St. Peter ad Vincula, within the Tower compound, there have been reports of presences in the pews, like "a second shadow." Only a trance medium could ascertain the truthfulness of these reports. Perhaps I can smuggle one in next time I'm in London. The Queen need never know.

THERE IS NOTHING LIKE A SCOTTISH GHOST

W HEN IT COMES TO flavor and personality, there's nothing quite like a Scottish ghost, or for that matter, like the people who see 'em. Our visit to the country of Burns was short this time, but long enough to know how much we wanted to return.

We landed on a misty morning at Prestwick Airport, and immediately set out for the town of Ayr, where we bedded down in the Station Hotel, one of the lesser delights of western Scotland. Immediately upon our arrival, Jack Weir of the BBC came to interview us, and I knew I was in a land where ghost hunting was a respected pursuit. Jamison Clarke, the television commentator, came along with him and we talked at length about a television show I would do from Edinburgh; Mr. Clarke would be in Glasgow at the same time. Nothing like a little magic via split-screen and other twentieth-century miracles!

But we had not come to Ayr just to be miserable at the Station Hotel or talk to these delightful Scots. Our aim that afternoon was Culzean Castle, pronounced Coleen, unless you were a Sassanach or, worse, a Yankee. We rented a chauffeur-driven car, for they drive on the left side here, and set out for Culzean along the coastal hills of western Scotland.

Shortly afterwards we entered the formal gardens and rode along a gently descending road towards the cliff on which Culzean Castle rises sheer from the sea on the Ayrshire coast.

Built by Robert Adam in the latter part of the eighteenth century, the castle had been associated with the Kennedy family, the Earls of Cassillis and the Marquises of Ailsa, whose portraits are seen all over the house. These days, it is administered by the National Trust for Scotland as a museum. Its main tower rises majestically four stories from the cliff, and one of the top floors contains an apartment given to General Eisenhower as a gesture of gratitude from Britain. He stayed there with his family from time to time.

We were cordially welcomed by the administrator of Culzean, Commander John Hickley.

"I'm afraid we don't keep a tame ghost in this castle," he said apologetically, as Mrs. Hickley served us tea.

I assured him that we enjoyed the visit just the same. Neither the Commander nor Mrs. Hickley had seen a ghost in this comparatively modern castle, nor had any of the help complained about any unusual visitors. But a British visitor to Culzean by the name of Margaret Penney was somewhat luckier—if seeing a ghost is luck.

According to an Associated Press report of August 9, 1962, Mrs. Penney was going through the castle just like any other tourist when she encountered the ghost.

"She came down a corridor when I was visiting Culzean Castle recently," said Mrs. Penney, "and said to me—'It rains today.'"

Mrs. Penney said the ghost was dark-haired and very beautiful.

"She appeared to be in evening dress though it was only about five o'clock in the afternoon when I encountered her.

"Anyway, I squeezed myself against the corridor to let her pass and told her, 'Not much room for passing when you're as plump as me.' "

Mrs. Penney said the girl looked at her very sadly and answered, "I do not require any room nowadays."

Mrs. Penney said her entire right side then went cold.

"Suddenly I realized that she had walked through my side."

Was she one of the Kennedy ladies who had come to a sad end in the lonely house on the Fyrth of Clyde? Until I bring a medium to Culzean at some future date, we can only guess.

Another nearby haunted castle drew my interest because its current occupants were British nobility from Baltimore, Maryland. Sir Adrian and Lady Naomi Dunbar inherited the ramshackle estate and castle of Mochrum Park by virtue of being the nearest cousin to the last British baronet, who died in 1953.

The Americans found the house a shambles and the income of the estate far from grand. Nevertheless, they still lived in it, having restored some of it, and they were making a go of their newly found position in life.

When the new owners arrived late in 1953 to take over their new home, the villagers at Kirkcowan, Wigtownshire, were wondering how the Americans would take to the ghost. This was the "White Lady" of Mochrum Park, allegedly the shade of Lady Jacobina Dunbar, who married the sixth baronet back in 1789, and whose portrait was found in the debris of the old house a few years before 1953.

The National Gallery of Scotland in Edinburgh now owns this valuable painting by Raeburn. Servants of the tenth baronet, Sir James Dunbar, who died in early 1953, always complained that the ghost portrait would always be found askew, no matter how often they straightened it out, as if someone were trying to call attention to something!

Elgin Fraser, chauffeur of the Dunbars for many years, twice saw the "white lady" standing at the foot of his bed.

Perhaps the saving of the valuable painting, which was in danger of being destroyed by the customary dry rot, had assuaged the fury of the ghost. No further disturbances have been reported, and when I asked the American-born Lady Dunbar about the ghost, she said, with a broad Baltimore accent, "Nonsense. It's all just imagination."

A fine thing for a ghost to be called—imaginary! Especially by an American.

When we reached Edinburgh, the *Weekly Scotsman*'s Donald MacDonald was already waiting for us to tell our story to the Scottish people. Then, too, the Kenneth MacRaes came to tell us of their experiences with Highland ghosts—hauntings we shall follow up on next time we're in Scotland. And a fellow author, MacDonald Robertson, offered us his index-card file on ghosts of Scotland. Unfortunately, only a few of these cases were of sufficiently recent origin to be looked into with any reasonable degree of verification, but Mr. Robertson's enthusiasm for the good cause made up for it.

That evening, we drove out to Roslin, a suburb of Edinburgh, to visit a famed Scottish medium, Anne Donaldson. She gave us a pretty good sitting, although most of the material obtained was of a private or personal nature.

The next day we set out early for the Border Country between Scotland and England, traditionally a wild area with a long association of war and strife. Hours of driving over sometimes unlit, unmarked roads, with only sheep populating the rolling hills, finally brought us to Hermitage Castle, an ancient medieval fortress associated with the de Soulis family, and dating back to the thirteenth century. It was here also that the Earl of Bothwell, wounded in a border raid, was visited by Mary Queen of Scots, his lover, in 1566.

Rising squarely in a commanding position on the border, this fortress boasts of a dungeon into which numerous enemies were thrust to starve to death. Their remains were never removed. This barbaric custom was general usage in the Middle Ages, and Hermitage is by no means unique in this respect.

Our reasons for visiting this famous ruin were not entirely sight-seeing. One of the early owners of the castle, Lord Soulis, was a black magician and committed a number of documented atrocities until he was caught by his enemies and dispatched in a most frightful manner. Ever since his ghost has been said to return on the anniversary of this deed to haunt the walls and ruined chambers, especially the ancient kitchen downstairs.

J. R. Wilson, now the custodian of the castle, readily played the bagpipes for us to set the mood, but he had never seen or heard a ghost.

"The only thing I know," he said, "is that some dogs will not go into the castle. A lady was here a while ago, and her dog just absolutely refused to go near it, set up a howl and refused to budge."

But there were other dogs which did, in fact, go inside the castle walls. Those, presumably, were the dogs which didn't believe in ghosts.

Back of Holyrood Palace, Edinburgh, residence of Mary Queen of Scots and other Scottish monarchs, stands a little house of modest appearance going by the quaint name of Croft-en-Reigh. This house was once owned by James, Earl of Moray, half brother of Mary, and Regent of Scotland in her absence. The house had been subdivided into three apartments, one of which belongs to a Mrs.

Clyne. But several years ago this was the official residence of the warden of Holyrood Palace. The warden was the chief guide who had charge of all tourist traffic. David Graham, the onetime warden, had now retired to his house in nearby Portobello, but fourteen years ago he had a most unusual experience in this little house.

"There were twelve of us assembled for a séance, I recall," he said, "and we had Helen Duncan, who is now dead, as our medium. There we were, seated quietly in the top floor of Croft-en-Reigh, waiting for developments."

They did not have to wait long. A figure materialized before their astonished eyes and was recognized instantly: Mary Queen of Scots herself, who had been to this house many times in moments of great emotional turmoil. Within a moment, she was gone.

On several occasions, Mr. Graham recalls, he saw the ghost of a short man in sixteenth-century clothes. "I am French," the man insisted. Graham thought nothing of it until he accidentally discovered that the house was built by an architect named French!

GHOSTS AND
GEMÜTLICHKEIT

WHAT GHOSTS ARE, YOU know by now, and those of my readers who are unfamiliar with the term *gemütlichkeit* ought to be told that it is a German word meaning "pleasant, go-easy way of life." When we flew into Hamburg, we did not expect *gemütlichkeit,* which is mostly found in southern countries like Switzerland and Austria anyway. But we found a genuine interest in psychic matters among radio and television people, although the vast masses of Germans were quite unaware of the seriousness with which Sixth-Sense experiences were studied in the Anglo-Saxon world. A small, keenly intelligent minority is, of course, trying to establish research on a respectable basis. Hans Bender and his parapsychological laboratory at Freiburg were unique, though. In Hamburg, we met with Erich Maria Koerner, author and translator of books on extrasensory perception, and Milo Renelt, a medium, called "the seer of Hamburg." But, simply because people were reluctant to talk, we could not find any leads to haunted houses, of which there must be many.

When we arrived in Vienna, Austria, things were a little better. For one thing, my dear friend Turhan Bey had kept me abreast of existing research, and the very day of our arrival in the Danube city, we went to see Countess Zoë Wassilko-Serecki, the president of the Austrian society for psychical research. She brought us up to date on the situation in Austria, where the press was openly hostile and derisive of any serious efforts to report para-psychological studies. An American of Austrian descent myself, I found the use of the local tongue most helpful when I called on the television and radio people the next day. I quickly found out that radio would have nothing to do with me, since a local magician had convinced the responsible producers that all psychic experiences were hokum and could be reproduced by him at will. Somewhat more of an open mind awaited me at the newly created television headquarters of Austrian TV, which was about ten years behind ours, but full of good will and operating under great handicaps of low budgets and pressures. Finally, a reporter named Kaiser agreed to accompany Catherine and me on a ghost hunt and to do a straight reporting job, without bias or distortion. I must say he kept his word.

On August 20, 1964, Kaiser and a cameraman picked us up at our hotel and we drove to the Imperial Castle, which was a sprawling array of buildings in the very heart of Vienna. There we went on foot into the portion known as Amalienburg, the oldest part of the castle. All I had to go on was a slim report that a ghost had been observed in that area.

Right off the bat, Kaiser turned to the police officer at the gate and asked him if he knew of any ghosts.

"Ghosts?" the officer asked, somewhat perplexed, and scratched his head. "None that I know of." He suggested we pay the *Burghauptmann,* or governor, a visit.

The governor was a fortyish gentleman with the unusual name of Neunteufel, which means Nine Devils. Far from being hellish, however, he invited us into his office and listened respectfully, as Kaiser explained me to him. Considering that we were in arch-

Catholic Vienna, in the inner offices of a high government official, I admired his courage. But then Kaiser had admitted to me, privately, that he had experienced an incident of telepathy he could not dismiss. His open-mindedness was not a drafty head but sincere.

"Well," the governor finally said, "I am so sorry, but I've only been in this post for five years. I know nothing whatever about ghosts. But there is an old employee here who might be able to help you."

My heart had begun to falter and I saw myself being ridiculed on television. "Please, boys," I said inaudibly, addressing my Friends Upstairs, "help us a little."

Mr. Neunteufel dialed and asked to speak to a Mr. Sunday. There was a pause. "Oh, I see," he then said. "You mean Mr. Sunday isn't in on Friday?" Black Friday, I thought! But then the governor's face brightened. Mr. Sunday would be over in a moment.

The man turned out to be a quiet, soft-spoken clerk in his later years. He had worked here practically all his adult life. "Yes," he nodded. "There is indeed a ghost here; but not in the Amalienburg. Come, I'll show you where."

You could have heard a pin drop, or, for that matter, a ghost walk, when he had spoken. Kaiser gave me a look of mixed admiration and puzzlement. He and his cameraman were already on their feet. With the governor at our side, we followed Sunday up and down a number of stairs, along corridors, through musty halls, and again up a staircase into a back portion of the castle.

"I've never been here myself," the governor apologized to me, as we walked. "In fact, I didn't even know this part existed," he added.

What the hell! I thought. It's a big house.

Now we stood in front of a *Marterl,* a peculiarly Austrian type of Blessed Virgin altar built into the wall and protected by a metal screen. To the left were the stairs we had come up on, and to our right was another, smaller stairway, closed off by a wooden door.

"Where are we?" Kaiser asked.

"This is the private apartment of Baroness Vecera," Sunday said.

Baroness Vecera was the sweetheart of Crown Prince Rudolph, central characters of the famed Meyerling tragedy, resulting in a major national scandal that rocked the Austria of the 1880's.

"The Crown Prince arranged for this flat," Sunday explained, "so he could see his lady friend quietly and privately. These stairs are not marked on the plans of the building."

"No wonder!" The governor sighed with relief.

Part of the castle had evidently been rented out to private citizens in recent years, since the Republic had toppled the monarchy, and the officials of the castle had paid scant attention to that wing since then.

"Has anyone seen a ghost here?" I inquired.

Sunday nodded. "A *Jaeger* reported seeing a white woman here some years ago, under the Empire." A *Jaeger* is a soldier belonging to a Tyrolean or other Alpine regiment. "Then there is the guardist Beran," Sunday continued, "who saw this white woman right here, by the altar of the Virgin Mary. As a matter of fact, many servants have seen her, too."

"When did all this start—I mean, how far back has she been seen?" I asked.

"Not too far back," Sunday answered, "about eighty years or so."

Since the death of Rudolph and Vecera, then, I thought. Of course! This was their home, the only refuge where they could meet in secrecy. There are among historians growing voices that say the suicide of Meyerling wasn't a suicide at all, but an execution.

Would the restless ghost of Baroness Vecera demand satisfaction or was the specter her remorseful form, praying by the shrine, seeking forgiveness for the tragedy she had caused?

Sunday now took us farther down the narrowing corridor into what must have been the oldest part of the castle. The thick walls and tiny slit windows suggested a fortress rather than a showplace of the Habsburgs.

"Not long ago," he said, "a patient of Dr. Schaefer, who had his offices here, saw a Capuchin monk walk down the corridor."

"What would a monk be doing here?" I demanded.

"In the early days, the Emperors kept a small number of monks here for their personal needs. There was a Capuchin monastery built into the castle at this very spot."

We waited for a while, but no Capuchin showed up. They were probably all too busy down in the Imperial Crypt, where the Capuchin Fathers do a thriving tourist business letting visitors look at the gaudy Imperial coffins for fifty cents a head.

I looked at Kaiser, and there was a thoughtful expression on his face.

We returned to the TV studio and filmed some footage, showing me with photographs of haunted houses. Then a reporter took down my dialogue, and the following day, as is their custom, the daily newsreel commentator read the story of our ghost hunt to some seven million Austrians who had never before been told of psychic research.

The chain of events is sometimes composed of many links. A friend of a friend in New York introduced me to Herta Fisher, a medium and student of the occult, who, in turn, suggested that I contact Edith Riedl when in Vienna.

Mrs. Riedl offered to take us to the two haunted castles I wanted to visit in southern Austria. In fact, even before I arrived in Vienna, she was able to help me. The *Volksblatt*, a local newspaper, had published a highly distorted report of my activities two weeks before our arrival. Mrs. Riedl sent me the clipping for such action as I might see fit to take.

I picked up the phone and dialed the *Volksblatt*.

"The 'responsible editor,' please," I said, in German. Austrian newspapers employ "responsible editors," usually minor clerks, who must take the blame whenever the newspaper publishes anything libelous.

"Hello," said a pleasantly soft voice on the other end of the line.

"Hello, yourself," I replied. "Did you not publish a piece about Hans Holzer, the Ghost Hunter, recently?"

"*Ja, ja,*" the voice said. "We did."

"Well," I said in dulcet tones, "I am he, and I'm suing you for five million schillings."

There was a gasp at the other end. "Wait!" the voice pleaded. "Let us talk this over."

The following afternoon, Turhan Bey drove us to the editorial offices of the newspaper, awaiting our return in a nearby cafe. I had a three-o'clock appointment with the publisher. At three fifteen I reminded the receptionist that time was of the essence. When nothing further had happened five minutes later, I sent in my card with a note: "Sorry can't wait—am on my way to my lawyer, from whom you will hear further."

Faster than you can say "S. O. B.," the publisher came running. I repaired to his offices, where I was joined by his editor and a man named Hannes Walter, a reporter.

It was agreed that I could indeed sue for libel. But they were willing to print another piece, far more thorough and bereft of any libelous matter. Would I agree?

I always believe in giving felons a second chance. When I read the piece a few weeks later, I realized I should have sued instead. Mainly the brain child of Herr Walter, it was still full of innuendoes, although it did report my activities with some degree of accuracy. Austrian TV was only ten years old, but its press goes back several hundred years—yet the only fair treatment I received in public was on the home screens. As was the case in many countries, newspapermen frequently underestimate the intelligence of their readers. That was part of the reason so many TV sets have been sold.

Mrs. Riedl turned out to be a cultured lady in her late fifties or early sixties, capable of speaking several languages, and full of intellectual curiosity. Of noble Hungarian ancestry, she was married to one of the owners of the Manners chocolate factory, and lives in a sprawling villa in the suburb of Dornbach.

At first, she was to drive us to the Burgenland Province in her car, but, when Turhan Bey offered to come along, we switched to his larger car. The four of us made a marvelous team as we discovered mutual bonds in many areas. I wanted to know more about Edith Riedl's mediumship, and asked her to tell me all about herself.

We were rolling towards the south, that part of Austria annexed in 1919 which had been a Hungarian province for many centuries, although the people of the area always spoke both German and Hungarian. Soon we left the sprawling metropolis of Vienna behind us and streaked down the southern highway towards the mountains around Wiener Neustadt, an industrial city of some importance. Here we veered off onto a less-traveled road and began our descent into the Burgenland, or Land of Castles.

"Tell me, Mrs. Riedl," I asked, "when did you first notice anything unusual about yourself—I mean, being psychic?"

Speaking in good English interlarded with an occasional German or French word, the lively little lady talked freely about herself. "I was only three years old when I had my first experience," she replied. "I was in my room when I saw, outside my window, smoke billowing, as if from a fire. This, of course, was only an impression—there was no smoke.

" 'We'll get a war!' I cried, and ran to my mother. Imagine a small child talking about war. I certainly did not know the meaning of the word I was using!"

"Amazing," Turhan Bey said, and I agreed. I had never before heard of psychic experiences at such an early age.

"Thirty years later, the house was hit by a bomb, and smoke rose indeed at the spot where I had seen it as a child, and the house burned down."

"When was the next time you experienced anything unusual along psychic lines?" I asked. The countryside was getting more and more rustic and we encountered fewer cars now.

"I was seventeen years old. A cousin of mine served with the Hungarian Hussar Regiments, and we were engaged to be married. The First World War was already on, but he did not serve at the front. He was stationed deep inside the country, near Heidenschaft.

" 'I don't mind fighting at the front,' he often told me. 'I'm not afraid of the enemy. The only thing I'm afraid of, somehow, is fog.' "

"Fog?" I said. "Strange for a Hussar officer in Hungary to worry about fog. You don't have too much fog down here, do you?"

"No, I couldn't understand why fog could be something for him to fear. Well, Christmas came, and I sent him a card, showing an angel. Without thinking much about it, I wrote the word 'Peace' into the halo of the angel, and sent the card off to my fiancé.

"Later, I regretted this—after all, one should wish a soldier victory, not peace—I wanted the card back, because the whole idea bothered me. I got the card back all right—with a notation by a strange hand across it, reading, 'Died in service, December 22nd.'

"I couldn't understand how he could have died in the war at Heidenschaft, where there was no enemy within many hundred miles. I felt terrible. I wanted to die, too. I went to my room and put out the lights; I wanted to go to bed early. I was not yet asleep—in fact, still wide awake—when I saw a kind of light near me, and within this luminous case I recognized a rock, a tree, and at the bottom of the tree, a crumbled mass of something I did not have the courage to look at closely. I knew at this moment that I could either join him in death, or live on. Being very young, my life force triumphed. As I decided to stick to the world of the living, the vision slowly lost color and faded away. But I still wondered how he could have died where he was stationed. The vision immediately returned, but my power of observation was weakening; perhaps the excitement was too much for me. At any rate, I could not make it out clearly.

"The next morning, I reported the incident to my parents. Mother and Father looked at each other. 'It is better to tell her,' Mother said, but my father shook his head. A year passed by, but I had never forgotten my fiancé.

"One day I helped my father sort some papers in his study. As I helped him go through his desk, my eyes fell on a letter with a black border. I had the feeling it had to do with Francis, my fiancé. I asked my father if I could take it, and my father, preoccupied with his own affairs, nodded in affirmation.

"I immediately went to my own room and opened the black-bordered letter. It was from one of Francis' friends, and he told the family how my fiancé had died. He was flying a small plane on a reconnaissance mission towards the Italian front, but he was stopped short by sudden fog. In the dense fog, he underestimated his altitude and hit a rock. The plane broke into pieces and his body was later found at the foot of a tree. Just as I had seen in my vision!"

"I believe you mentioned to me some startling experiences with premonitions—your ability to warn of impending disaster," I said.

"It happens quite often," Mrs. Riedl replied. "During the last war, for instance, on one occasion when my children were away at Laa on Theyer, in school, I went to visit them by school bus along with many children and a few mothers. I was seated behind the driver, when there was one of those sudden thunderstorms we have in the area. Suddenly, I heard myself shout to the driver, 'Stop, stop at once!'

"He stopped and turned around. 'Are you out of your mind? What is it?' he demanded. Before he had finished talking, a huge tree fell onto the road hitting the spot where the bus would have been if I hadn't stopped it.

"On another occasion, after the last war, my daughter and I were invited to go to Mistelbach, out in the country, to a wedding. At that time it was not possible to use your own car, trains weren't running yet, and transportation was quite primitive.

"There were two groups of people: one was our wedding party, the other was a funeral party also going in that direction. Transportation was by bus. Our numbers were called, and we were about to board the bus, when I cried out to my daughter, 'Come back, this isn't our bus.'

"Our entire group turned back and I was asked why I had recalled them, when our numbers had obviously been called.

"I could not tell them. I never know why I do these things. All I know is I must do it.

"Meanwhile the other party, those going to that funeral, boarded the bus, taking our place. I said, 'The bus is supposed to return to take us next.'"

"Did it?" I asked.

"The bus was supposed to come back in half an hour. Three hours went by and no bus. Then the news came—there had been an accident. We were saved by my warning, but the funeral party were badly hurt."

"How often have you had these warning flashes?"

"Maybe twenty times during the last five years."

"You also have the ability to sense where objects might be safe, as well as people, isn't that right?"

"Yes," Mrs. Riedl nodded. "As you know my husband has a valuable collection of rare books. When war broke out, he decided to send the most valuable ones to a safe place in the country. But as soon as the books had been unloaded there, I had to order the driver to take them back again. I felt the place was far from safe. We went to a parish house and tried to hide them there, but again something warned me against the location. Finally, we did unload the books at another parish house. The priest had already received some books belonging to a Vienna book seller and invited me to add ours to this pile. But I politely refused. Instead, I went around until I found what my Inner Voice told me was the only safe place in the house: the washroom!"

"How did the priest take that?"

"Well, he didn't like it. He remonstrated with me, but to no avail. As it turned out, the house was consumed by fire, except the washroom, and our books were safe at the end of the war!"

"Have you accepted this gift of yours as something that is part of you?"

"Certainly. Just think how much good it has brought me already."

By now we had reached the border country where today's Hungary meets Austria, and we had to be careful not to pierce the Iron Curtain accidentally by taking the wrong road. The land was green and fertile and the road ran between pleasant-looking hills sometimes crowned by ancient castles or fortresses, a striking demonstration of how the country got its name—Land of Castles.

Our destination was Forchtenstein, a yellow-colored compound of imposing buildings sitting atop a massive hill that rises straight out of the surrounding landscape. As we wound our way up the hill we could see its towers beckoning to us.

Shortly after, we drove up at the imposing castle and Turhan parked the car. This was one of the biggest of Esterhazy castles, of which there were many, since that family was wealthy and powerful in Hungary and southeastern Austria for many centuries, and though the Communists have taken the Esterhazy lands in Hungary, the family still controls huge estates in Austria, and was likely to continue to do so. Forchtenstein was run as a museum. Its fortifications, long, vaulted galleries and rooms, its magnificent collection of paintings and enough medieval and seventeenth-century arms to equip a small army make it a major tourist attraction in this part of Central Europe. Although it was started in the fourteenth century, it really reached importance only in the time of the Turkish wars, when the Crescent and Star were very near indeed.

During that time also the Court of Justice for the entire land was held here and executions took place in the courtyard.

We passed over the front ditch, over a wooden bridge, into the outer courtyard.

"There are noises and all sorts of goings-on in this castle," Mrs. Riedl explained.

"There is a well, four hundred and twenty feet deep, dug out by Turkish prisoners of war. When the well was completed, the prisoners were thrown into it. I am sure some of them are still around."

"How do you know?"

"Many people have heard sighing in the vicinity of the well."

Turhan Bey, who was half Turkish, half Austrian, smiled. "I am here as ambassador of peace," he said.

"Also chain rattling," Mrs. Riedl continued.

"Did you ever feel anything unusual here?"

"I was here once before," Mrs. Riedl replied, "and whenever I could be by myself, away from the others in the group being shown around, I felt a presence. Someone wanted to tell me something, perhaps to plead with me for help. But the guide drove us on, and I could not find out who it was."

If there is one thing I dislike intensely, it is guided tours of anything. I went to the local guide and asked him for a private tour. He insisted I buy a dozen tickets, which was the smallest number of people he could take around. We started out at once, four humans, and eight ghosts. At least I paid for eight ghosts.

We walked into the inner courtyard now, where a stuffed crocodile hung high under the entrance arch, which reminded us of the days when the Esterhazys were huntsmen all over the world.

"This is supposed to scare away evil spirits," Mrs. Riedl remarked.

"They must have had a bad conscience, I guess," I said grimly. The Hungarians certainly equaled the Turks in brutality in those days.

We walked past the monument to Paul Esterhazy, ornamented with bas-reliefs showing Turkish prisoners of war in chains, and into the castle itself. Our guide led us up the stairs onto the roof which was overgrown with shrubbery and grass.

Suddenly, Mrs. Riedl grabbed my arm. "Over there, I feel I am drawn to that spot. Somebody suffered terribly here."

We retraced our steps and followed to where she pointed. The ground was broken here, and showed a small opening, leading down into the castle.

"What is underneath?" I asked our guide.

"The dungeon," he replied. He didn't believe in ghosts. Only in tourists.

Quickly we went down into the tower. At the gate leading into the deep dungeon itself, we halted our steps. Mrs. Riedl was trembling with deep emotion now.

"Somebody grabbed my skirts up there," she said, and pointed to the roof we had just left, "as if trying to call attention to itself."

I looked down into the dimly lit dungeon. A clammy feeling befell all of us. It was here that the lord of the castle threw his enemies to die of starvation. One time he was absent from the castle, leaving its administration to his wife, Rosalie. She mistreated some of his guests and on his return he had her thrown into this dungeon to die herself.

Her ghost was said to haunt the castle, although her husband, taken with either remorse or fear of the ghost, built a chapel dedicated to Rosalie, on a nearby hill.

"What do you feel here?" I asked Mrs. Riedl.

"A woman plunged down here from a very high place. I feel her very strongly."

"What does she want?"

Mrs. Riedl kept still for a moment, then answered in a trembling voice, "I think she wants us to pray for her."

With the guide pointing the way, we walked up another flight of stairs into the private chapel of the Esterhazys. To a man with twelve tickets there were no closed doors.

Mrs. Riedl quickly grabbed the railing of the gallery and started to pray fervently. Underneath, in the chapel itself, the lights of many candles flickered.

After a moment or two, Edith Riedl straightened up. "I think she feels relieved now," she said.

We continued our inspection of the building. "This is the execution chamber," the guide said casually, and pointed out the execution chair and sword. Then the guide, whose name was Leitner, took us to the prisoners' well, showing us its enormous depth by dropping a lighted flare into it. It took the flare several seconds to hit bottom. "Five thousand Turks built it in thirteen years' time," he said.

Mrs. Riedl stepped closer to the opening of the well, then shrank back. "Terrible," she mumbled. "I can't go near it."

I wondered how many of the murdered Turks were still earthbound in this deep shaft.

Outside, there was sunshine and one of those very pleasant late-summer afternoons for which southern Austria is famous.

We passed the chapel dedicated to Rosalie, but in our hearts we knew that it had not done much good. Quite possibly our visit had done more for the tormented spirit of the ancient *Burgfrau* than the self-glorifying building atop the hill.

We consulted the maps, for our next destination, Bernstein, lay some thirty miles or more to the west. We drove through the backwoods of the land, quiet little villages with nary a TV aerial in sight, and railroad tracks that hadn't seen a train in years. It was getting cooler and darker and still no sign of Bernstein!

I began to wonder if we had not taken a wrong turn somewhere when all of a sudden we saw the castle emerge from behind a turn in the road.

Not as imposing as Forchtenstein, Bernstein impresses one nevertheless by its elegance and Renaissance-like appearance within a small but cultured park. There was a mine of semiprecious stones called *smaragd* nearby, and the downstairs houses a shop where these stones were on display. This was a kind of wild emerald, not as valuable as a real one, of course, but very pretty with its dark green color and tones.

Bernstein castle goes back to the thirteenth century and had changed hands continuously between Austrian and Hungarian nobles. Since 1892 it had belonged to the Counts Almassy, Hungarian "magnates" or aristocrats.

We arrived at a most inappropriate time. The Count had a number of paying guests which helped defray the expenses of maintaining the large house, and it was close to dinnertime. Nevertheless, we were able to charm him into taking us to the haunted corridor.

On November 11, 1937, Count Almassy, a tall, erect man now in his late sixties, was sitting in his library when one of his guests asked for a certain book. The library can be reached only by walking down a rather narrow, long corridor connecting it with the front portion of the building.

"I left the library, walked down the passage with a torch [flashlight]—I don't like to turn on the main lights at night—well, when I came to this passage, I saw by the light of my torch a female figure kneeling in front of a wooden Madonna that stands at that spot. It was placed there in nineteen fourteen by my mother when both my brothers and I were away in the war. Of course I had often heard talk of a 'White Lady of Bernstein,' so I realized at once that I was seeing a ghost. My first impression was that she looked like a figure cast in plaster of Paris with hard lines. She wore a Hungarian noble-woman's dress of the fifteenth century, with a woman's headgear and a big emerald-green stone on her forehead which threw a dim, green light around her. She had her hands folded under her left cheek."

"What did you do when you saw her?" I asked.

"I had time to switch on the light in the passage," the Count replied, "so that I had her between two lights, that of my torch and the electric light overhead. There was no possible mistake, I saw her clearly. Then just as suddenly, she vanished."

"What is the tradition about this ghost, Count Almassy?" I asked.

"Well, she is supposed to be an Italian woman, Catherine Freschobaldi—of a Florentine family which still exists, in fact—mentioned in Dante's *Inferno*. She married a Hungarian nobleman, Count Ujlocky, of a very old Hungarian family. Her husband was the last King of Bosnia. The family died out. He was very jealous, with-out any reason, and so he killed her, according to one version, by stabbing her; according to another, by walling her in. That is the story."

"Has anyone else seen the White Lady of Bernstein?"

"Many people. When I was a boy, I remember every year some-one or other saw her. When I was in the army, between nineteen ten and nineteen thirteen, she was seen many, many times. In nineteen twenty-one she was seen again when there were Hungarian occupa-tion troops garrisoned at Bernstein during the short-lived Austro-Hungarian campaign of that year—and the ghostly lady chased them away! Then, of course, in nineteen thirty-seven, as I told you, and that was the last time I saw her."

"I believe also that a friend of yours saw her in Africa in the Cameroons? How does this fit in?"

Count Almassy laughed. "Well, that's another story, that one. An Army friend of mine—I really did not know him too well, I met him in nineteen sixteen, and he left Austria in nineteen thirty-seven and bought a farm in the Cameroons. He became a wealthy man. In nineteen forty-six he experienced a strange incident.

"An apparition very much like the White Lady of Bernstein (although he knew nothing whatever about our ghost) appeared to him and spoke to him in Italian.

"In nineteen fifty-four he came to see me to check on the story this ghost had told him. The ghost claimed to be the famous White Lady and he decided to come to Austria to see if there was such a ghost."

"Remarkable," I said. "I can only assume that the apparition in the Cameroons was a thought projection, unless, of course, your ghost is no longer bound to this castle."

The Count thought for a moment. "I do hope so," he finally said. "This is a drafty old castle and Africa is so much warmer."

HAUNTED
SWITZERLAND

WHO WOULD EVER connect Switzerland, that epitome of material good living, with the world of specters? But the facts were, that ghosts have been seen or heard even there. Oh, the Swiss were reluctant all right to talk about them. They don't need any further tourist attractions. But I found out, anyway.

There is, for instance, a certain house in Berne, the capital, housing the Luxembourg embassy, that hadn't been very quiet for years. Then there was the "Green Lady" that spooks at Oron Castle near Fribourg on the border between the German and French parts of Switzerland. And at Lucerne, there is or was a well-documented poltergeist in a suburb called Emmerbruecke.

As a matter of fact, it seems to me that the Germanic countries tend to have more poltergeists than ghosts proper—perhaps something related to the national character—while the Anglo-Saxon spectral world is more attuned to silent sufferings.

That which creates the ghost phenomenon anywhere, the maltreatment of a human being resulting in tragic death, is, of course, just as common in Switzerland as in other countries. True, the Swiss have been at peace since Napoleon's time, around 1800, but there were violent struggles in the Middle Ages and many a castle in the lovely Swiss mountains and valleys was the scene of death and destruction and misdeeds.

I contacted the President of the Swiss Society for Psychic Research, Dr. Hans Naegeli-Osjord, a psychiatrist by profession, who was kind enough to open his files to me. There was a house at the outskirts of Zurich with a fine record of being haunted. Since I was already in Zurich, would I mind looking into it? He would join me there later that evening, after his office hours.

It was nine o'clock when I started out to motor up the steep hill behind Zurich to the house on Hoenger Street. Twice, my driver missed it, but my inner sense of direction finally told me that the large, square country house, set back a bit from the main road and looming so forbiddingly in the summer night, must be the house we were aiming for. It was, and I never saw a taxi driver disappear so fast as this one after he had left me at the entrance gate.

The house dates back to the seventeenth century. It had been repaired from time to time and had become an elegant country house of the kind one does not expect in democratic Switzerland, but sees frequently in the English countryside. Owned by Colonel and Mrs. Reger, it was a quiet island above the bustling traffic of Zurich.

I should explain that Mrs. Reger's name was spelled differently, but I want to protect her privacy since her husband was a high officer in the army and ghosts and General Staff just don't mix in Switzerland.

It was pitch-dark now outside, except for a forlorn lantern above the entrance gate. I walked up three or four steps and rang a bell, which I heard sounding way inside the house. Then there were footsteps, and the door opened. Mrs. Reger had been expecting me downstairs, although her own quarters in the big house were the upper two floors.

A woman in her forties or thereabouts, she was slightly stout, with the deep-set eyes of a medium, and a voice capable of emotional involvement. Quickly she led me up the wooden stairs to the next floor and thence into an apartment filled with antiques and fine furniture.

"What are some of the manifestations in this house?" I asked as soon as we had seated ourselves in comfortable chairs.

"The house has three floors," Mrs. Reger explained in German, "and above the third floor, there is an attic. In this attic there is a certain window, opening towards the main road, which does not want to be closed."

"The window doesn't want to stay closed?" I asked somewhat taken aback. I never knew of windows with wills of their own.

Mrs. Reger nodded gravely. "We've closed that window any number of times—yet when we pass by again, it stands open, even though nobody has been up there to open it. For a while we kept accusing each other of doing it, but everybody denied having been up there at the time."

I followed Mrs. Reger up to the attic, a musty, dank place underneath the ancient wooden beams of the roof heavy with an atmosphere of doom and despair, somehow, it seemed to me. The window was open again. I tried it and it closed without difficulty. There was no question of accidental opening.

Mrs. Reger beckoned to me to follow her down the stairs again and we entered a smallish room, well lighted, which had for years served as a maid's room. I queried Mrs. Reger about the room.

"Many domestics have slept and lived in this room over the years. One in particular, a girl named Liesl Nadoma, age sixteen, was going to bed one night, when she suddenly saw a man standing between the bed and the wall. He wore a kind of chauffeur's cap, she said, and held a candle in his hand. Naturally the girl panicked. She cried out and ran to my room to tell me about the intruder."

"Did you find anyone in her room?"

"No, there was no one there. No one could have escaped so quickly down the stairs either. But a year and a half later, another servant girl who slept in the room also saw this apparition. She too emphasized the peculiar cap he wore."

Across the hallway from this room we entered another small room used as a guest room for the Regers' occasional overnight visitors. This room had a long record of hauntings. Nobody had seen a ghost here, but many have complained of being very unhappy and extremely nervous somehow, while staying in the guest room. "Nobody ever slept well here," Mrs. Reger added.

"Come up to the next floor," she said, and we ascended the stairs to the third floor once more. At the rear of the house we entered a room, also used as a maid's room over a period of years.

"Here a servant girl named Elizabeth used to sleep," Mrs. Reger commented. "She was nineteen years old at the time she saw the ghost. This same man appeared to her and she said he wore a beret."

Whatever the strange headgear the ghost wore, it seemed to have been sufficiently odd in our times to attract the attention of several observers!

Mrs. Reger's eight-year-old son also had his share of frightening experiences in the house. He was sleeping in a small room in the attic one night, but he could not really find rest. Finally, his mother took him to her own bedroom downstairs. But the boy's troubles were far from over.

"Suddenly he saw a man emerge from between the window curtains," Mrs. Reger said, "and he described him as wearing this peculiar kind of cap. Now my son knew nothing whatever of the stories told by the servant girls, since naturally we keep such things from a youngster as we don't want to frighten him. Two nights later, the same apparition sat on his bed."

Other servants reported seeing the ghost in the basement of the house, describing him as a man of about thirty-five, and always wearing that Swiss *daeschli kappe*, or brimmed cap.

I questioned Mrs. Reger about the background of the house. It developed that it had been a military hospital during the seventeenth century and wounded soldiers were brought here and presumably died here as well. There were still battles being fought then in Switzerland, between cantons or with outsiders, and the cap described by the observers does indeed fit the period.

"Did anyone else have any unusual experiences here?" I asked.

"Well, there was a sewing woman who came to work here," Mrs. Reger replied, "and she went to what is now my bedroom. Before she could open the door herself, she saw a hand do so for her. There was no one inside the room. She also reported seeing a gray-haired, older man coming up the stairs and disappearing into nothingness before her eyes."

Were there two ghosts roaming the corridors of the Reger house? A busy house it was indeed. At this point, the doorbell rang, and Mrs. Reger admitted the President of the Swiss Society for Psychic Research, Dr. Naegeli-Osjord, a lively man in his late forties or early fifties. We returned to the large sitting room on the second floor.

"Dr. Naegeli," I asked, "you've investigated this house yourself. Have you ever had any uncanny experiences here?"

"Yes," the doctor replied, "one day I was sitting in the dining room, composing the obituary of a member of our Society who had just died. I wrote, 'He was a skeptic,' but Mrs. Reger corrected me, saying the man was a believer in psychic matters, and I secretly wished there were some way of checking it."

"What happened then?"

"At this very moment, a clock here which had not been running for thirty years suddenly started to run of its own volition. It ran for about two minutes, then stopped again. What makes this the more remarkable is the fact that we had a pact. Long before he died, he and I agreed that he would try to communicate with us after death if there was that possibility."

"He evidently did," I said, and the doctor nodded.

I thanked my hostess and the doctor, and started to return to Zurich. As I walked down the wooden stairs I could not help wondering if the ghost with the brimmed cap had ever found peace. But Mrs. Reger is mediumistic, so that any message the ghost would have wanted to transmit would surely have come to her at one time or another, yet Mrs. Reger never did get such an impression. Perhaps the unhappy soldier really did not know why he was being drawn to the house, having died without the power of reasoning?

"One more question," I said, as the heavy oaken door opened for me and the cool night air started to seep in. "What are you using that haunted room upstairs for now?"

"Oh, that room," Mrs. Reger replied lightly. "It's the offices of the Swiss Society for Psychic Research."

"That's really making it easy for your ghost, isn't it?" I said.

Mrs. Reger laughed a little uncertainly and looked back over her shoulder.

DIARY OF A POLTERGEIST

O NE GENERALLY THINKS of the Swiss as sober, practical people not given to daydreaming or mysticism. Especially the Germanic Swiss. Nevertheless it was near Zurich that I found one of the most amazing cases in modern psychic research, amazing because an up-to-the-minute diary was kept by the farmer to whom all this happened.

Paul Leuthold was a man in his late forties with a pleasant personality and reasonably good educational background, perhaps better read than most farmers in other countries but, certainly, far from sophistication or knowledgeability in areas of philosophy or the occult. He had a wife and two children—a son, now in his seventeenth year, and a daughter, a few years younger.

Life on the Leuthold farm—a modest-sized establishment consisting of a house, stables, acreage and perhaps two dozen cattle housed in stables directly across from the farmhouse on a narrow street in the little village of Maschwanden—was normal and routine year after year. That is, until the year 1960 rolled around. In the cold, moist fall of 1960, the Leuthold family and their homestead became the center of a poltergeist case unique in the annals of Swiss psychic research.

The "cast of characters" at the time consisted of Paul Leuthold, forty-eight; Mrs. Leuthold, forty-seven; daughter Elizabeth, ten; son Paul, thirteen; and a maid named Elfi, age eighteen, who was somewhat mentally handicapped, a factor not to be overlooked in cases of this kind. There was also an Italian handy man named Angelo, who was at the farm only a part of the time during which the uncanny happenings took place.

Next door to the Leuthold homestead stands the house of the Eichenberger family. Mr. Eichenberger, fifty, was an active spiritualist, a rarity in Switzerland. His wife, forty-five, is a simple woman without any interest in the subject, and there were four children ranging in age from three to nine years at the time.

At first, the strange events only puzzled the Leuthold family, and they did not suspect that anything unusual was happening. But when no human agency could be found responsible for the moving of objects, disappearances and reappearances and other obviously mischievous actions in and around the house and stables, it dawned on Leuthold that he was the victim of a poltergeist and he began to take notes.

Between November 12, 1960, and August 20, 1961, no less than 104 separate entries were made by him in his "diary of a poltergeist." They were brief, to the point, and without any attempt at a rational explanation. That he left for others to ponder over. His first entry dates from November 12, 1960:

November 12, 6 p.m. The large metal milk can has moved 3 yards to the west. At the same time, stones are thrown against the window—no one there.

November 13, 6 p.m. The milk container with 18 liter milk in it has disappeared. We find it again at a far corner of the stables.

November 14, 6 p.m. Neighbor Eichenberger's umbrella stand disappears and the scraper, usually at the staircase, is found outside against the wall.

Same day, half an hour later. Two boots disappear from the stables and are later found in the feeding area behind the potato rack. Mrs. Eichenberger, the neighbor, brings our pig bucket which she found in the cellar next to their umbrella stand! My wife had fed the pigs barely ten minutes before and left the pig bucket in the stables. How did it get to the cellar?

Every day now, something disappears, moves from its accustomed spot and reappears at a strange place. Such things as milking accessories, very necessary in the daily work of a farmer, were not where they should be and this interrupts the normal life on the farm.

Two bicycles were suddenly without air in their tires. Another inconvenience, since the Swiss use bikes extensively. Most of these events take place around 6:00 or 7:00 P.M. Leuthold examined all possibilities of pranksters. His own family and household were always accounted for at the critical times. The village is small and strangers lurking about could not escape attention, certainly not that often.

As I carefully examined the written notes of poltergeistic or other uncanny activities in the Leuthold house, I realized that it was certainly worth looking into. Consequently, I telephoned the farmer and we arranged for a visit the following afternoon. The Swiss television network had evinced great interest in my work, although they had never heard of the Maschwanden case, or, for that matter, of any other psychic investigation. It took an American to bring the entire area to their attention and, reluctantly, Jacob Fischer, the production head, agreed to send a crew with me.

"But we won't pay for this, you understand," he added with careful Swiss frugality.

The next afternoon, my wife and I joined two television news reporters, one handling the camera and the other the sound equipment, in a station wagon. We rode along the outskirts of Zurich, over a couple of hills and out into the open country to the west of the city. It took us more than an hour to get to Maschwanden, a village very few people, especially Americans, ever visit. When we reached the Leuthold farmhouse, we were expected. While the television people started to set up their equipment, I lost no time asking Paul Leuthold about the most memorable incident in the haunting of his house.

"My wife and I were inside the house. Suddenly, there was a knock at the door which sounded as if it was made by a hard object. My wife was in the kitchen. She left her work and went to look outside. There was no one outside. Shortly after, there was another knock. The maid was downstairs in her room and she didn't see anyone either. My wife went back to her work. Soon there was a third set of knocks. This time, she was alerted and kept close to the door. As soon as she heard the knocking, she jumped outside."

"Did she see anything or anyone?" I asked.

"She saw a piece of wood, about a yard in length, hitting the ground from a height of about a foot."

"You mean a piece of wood moving through the air by itself?"

"Yes. The wooden stick was there in the air, all by itself. Nobody could have thrown it and run away. It was plain daylight, too."

I examined the wooden stick. It was a heavy piece of wood, weighing perhaps half a pound.

"How did the whole thing get started, Mr. Leuthold?" I asked, and he brought his diary and showed me an entry:

November 18, 5:15 p.m. The cover of the milk can is found inside the barn, on the grassy floor. Fifteen minutes earlier I had left it in place in the stable.

"The next day," he added, "the cover was again found in the ash can."

"Charming," I said. "May I see the book?" The entries followed each other in the orderly, clinical manner of a medical history. Only, the patient was invisible.

November 19, 5 a.m. I plug in the motor of the cider press and leave it to do my milking chores. Suddenly, there is a single boot in the middle of the barn. The milking pail floats in the water trough. I decide to check on the cider press. I hear the motor sputtering as I reach the cellar. I find the plug pulled out and the cable pulled back about four yards.

That day was a particularly busy one for the ghost. At 7:30 A.M., Leuthold finished his first meal and returned to the stables.

I turn the light on and fetch a container full of un-thrashed corn, which I place inside the barn, in front of the door leading to the stables. Elfi, the maid, is busy washing milking equipment at a considerable distance in the feed kitchen. I leave for a moment to go to the bathroom, when I return, I find the light turned out and the container of unthrashed corn gone. I find it upside down, in the middle of the barn, and next to it, a broom, which had not been there before either.

But that wasn't the end of it by a long shot, that busy morning. Half an hour later, Mrs. Leuthold appeared in the barn and asked where his watch was.

"Where it always is," Leuthold replied, somewhat cross, "on the window latch where I always hang it when I clean the cattle."

Not so, his wife replied, and dangled the watch and chain before his eyes. She had just found them in front of the stables on top of a milk can.

That very evening one of their cows was due to give birth. Consequently it was necessary to have all the help available present for the occasion. But the poltergeist was among them.

9 p.m. The following are present to help with the birth: schoolteacher Strickler, Max Studer junior, Werner Siedler, my wife, Elfi the maid, my son Paul and myself are in the stables. The spout of the milking machine disappears under our eyes! We search and finally find it tucked away in the aluminum shelf that holds the rubber nipples. My wife sends Elfi to lock the house while we are all over here. The maid returns, the key is gone. Later we find it on the window sill outside. We had left it in the lock on the *inside.*

By midnight it was all over. The calf had come and the Leutholds went to bed. But the uncanny phenomena did not cease. From the direction of the pigsty there was a loud whistling sound. It changed direction from time to time. There were people in front of the house still up, who heard it too. Elfi, the maid, complained about the noises. The moment she was out of the house, the whistling stops. By 2:00 A.M., all was finally quiet.

I asked Mr. Leuthold to show me the ash can in which the milk bottle cover was found and the potato bin where it showed up next. The lid of the potato bin weighed perhaps twenty pounds. Anyone placing the aluminum cover of the milk can inside it must have had considerable strength. Two people had to pull it to open it.

All was quiet now for a few days. Then the mysterious events started up again.

December 1, 6:30 p.m. I open the door to the stables to do my milking chores. Everything is normal. My wife arrives a few moments later and opens the same door. This time a hay fork is leaning against it from the outside. "Where is the plate for the cat?" my wife wants to know. "Next to the milk can, as always," I reply. It isn't. My wife finds the plate on top of the refuse. The light goes on and off by itself.

Flickering lights going on and off by their own volition are old stuff with hauntings. In an earlier case of mine, the Rockland County Ghost case, I reported similar happenings which drove to distraction a certain Broadway composer then guesting at the Danton Walker home.

Evidently, the Swiss ghost had discovered the usefulness of the lights in the stables, for a series of incidents involving the electric installations now followed.

December 2, 5:15 a.m. The light goes out by itself for a short time. The plate for the cat disappears again and is discovered on top of the refuse, like yesterday. I put it back on the refuse. Suddenly, the light goes on by itself in the barn. There is no one there who could have turned it on.

That day turned out rather significantly for the Leutholds, since it brought the first visual phenomena to their tranquil midst. The incident with the knocks at the door and the subsequent discovery by Mrs. Leuthold of the stick of wood suspended in the air, described earlier, took place that day around 10:15 A.M.

Saturdays were usually quiet periods in the small towns and villages of Switzerland. But not this time. Leuthold's diary continues:

December 3, 7:35 a.m. Suddenly the light in the barn goes on. I go to check on it and notice that the light is also on in the hayloft. I turn out both lights and go to the stables. Just then, I clearly hear knocking in the hayloft. I go up to look, but there is nobody there. Since it is getting lighter outside, I turn off the light in the stables, but suddenly it is on again. I am busy distributing the fertilizer. I go inside, turn the light off again. Shortly afterwards it is burning once more. Werner Frei, a tractor driver, was passing by at that time. He saw the light. There was, of course, nobody about who could have done it.

December 4, 8 a.m. The lights go on by themselves in the barn. Elfi is in front of the stables and asks if everything is quiet. It is now 8:30. I reply, in jest, "The ghost is gone." Within seconds, the light is on again in the stables, although no one could have gotten in to do it.

At one time, four lights were burning simultaneously although no human agency could be held accountable for it. For weeks on end the Leutholds were harassed by the poltergeist's game of turning the lights on.

"Finally I said one day," Leuthold explained, "it is strange that the lights should only go on, but never off by themselves. I had hardly finished when I stood in total darkness in the stables—the light had been turned off."

"As if the ghost were listening?" I said.

Leuthold nodded and smiled somewhat sheepishly. "But it really got worse later in the week," he said, and showed me the entry for the eighth of December.

December 8, 7:40 a.m. Elfi goes to feed the chickens, but the pot containing the chicken feed is gone. She finally finds it in front of the barn door. Six pumpkins, used for decorative purposes, are scattered around the yard. The rabbit hutch is open and two rabbits are running around outside. The feed tray for the rabbits has disappeared. It is later discovered by my wife on a cart in the carriage house.

Evidently, the ghost had it in for the domestic animals as well as the people. The following day, matters got even worse.

December 9, 7:30 a.m. The pot with the chicken feed is gone again. The plate for the cat is again on top of the refuse heap. Elfi prepares new chicken feed in another pot, puts it down for a moment on the stairs and goes into the kitchen. When she gets back just seconds later, the new chicken feed is also gone. She comes to tell me about it. I go back with her and find the chicken feed hidden behind the stairs, covered with a burlap bag.

The Leutholds were beginning to get furious. Mrs. Leuthold decided to trap the furtive ghost. She put the chicken-feed pot onto the window sill near the house door, and tied a nylon string to it, with a small bell at the other end, putting it down in the corridor leading away from the entrance door. That way they thought they would hear any movements the pot might make.

By 9:30 A.M. the pot had moved twice in both directions, yet no human agency could be discovered!

That very afternoon the poltergeist played a new kind of trick on them. When Mrs. Leuthold entered the barn around 2:00 P.M., she found all sorts of boots scattered around, and in one of them four receipts for cattle, which Mr. Leuthold distinctly remembered to have placed high on a shelf that very morning. The ghost stepped up his activities in the following days, it seems. Not content with moving objects when nobody was looking, he now moved them in the presence of people.

December 10, 9:30 a.m. The light goes on by itself in the hayloft. The missing pot for chicken feed is finally found near the door of the old stables. 6:30 P.M. the light goes on in the barn, nobody is there. I put it out just as Elfi enters and tells me the milking brush is gone. We look everywhere, without success. Just then I notice the umbrella which is usually found in front of the house door hanging from the window sill of the pigsty! Elfi takes it down and replaces it next to the entrance door of the house, and we continue our search for the milking brush. Suddenly, the umbrella lies in front of us on the ground near the old stables! Three times the lights in the barn go on and I have to put them out. There is, of course, nobody in there at the time.

Whatever happened to the missing milking brush, you'll wonder. The next morning, a Sunday too, Mrs. Leuthold was doing her chore of feeding the pigs. In one of the feed bags she felt something hard and firm, that did not feel like pig's feed. You guessed it. It was the milking brush. The Leutholds were glad to have their brush back, but their joy was marred by the disappearance of the chicken-feed pot. If it wasn't the pigs, it was the chickens the ghost had it in for!

"I remember that morning well," Mr. Leuthold said grimly. "I was standing in the stables around quarter to eight, when the light went out and on again and a moment later something knocked loudly in the hayloft, while at the same moment the light went on in the barn! I didn't know where to run first to check."

Those who suspected the somewhat simple maid, Elfi, to be causing these pranks did not realize that she was certainly not consciously contributing to them. She herself was the victim along with others in the house.

On the twelfth of December, for instance, she put the milk cart into a corner of the barn where it usually stood. A few minutes later, however, she found it in front of the chicken house.

That same day, Paul Leuthold again came to grips with the ghost. "It was nine fifteen in the morning and I walked up the stairs.

Suddenly the window banged shut in the fruit-storage room ahead of me. There was no draft, no movement of air whatsoever."

"Your wife mentioned something about the disappearing apple sauce," I said. "This sounds intriguing. What happened?"

"On December thirteenth," Leuthold replied, refreshing his memory from his diary, "my wife put a dish of hot apple sauce on the window sill next to the house door, to cool it off. I came home from the fields around four thirty in the afternoon and to my amazement saw a dish of apple sauce on the sill of the old stable, across the yard from the house. I went to the kitchen and asked Elfi where they had put the apple sauce. 'Why, on the kitchen window, of course.' Silently I showed her where it now was. Shaking her head, she took it and put it back on the kitchen window sill. A few minutes later, we checked to see if it was still there. It was, but had moved about a foot away from the spot where we had placed it."

That, however, was only the beginning. All day long "things" kept happening. Parts of the milking machine disappeared and reappeared in odd places. Lights went on and off seemingly without human hands touching the switches. These switches incidentally are large, black porcelain light switches mounted at shoulder height on the walls of the buildings, and there is no other way of turning lights on or off individually.

At 7:45 P.M., dinnertime, the entire family and servants were in the main room of the house. The barns and other buildings were securely locked. Suddenly, the lights in the barn and chicken house went on by themselves. The following morning, auditory phenomena joined the long list of uncanny happenings.

December 14, 6:50 a.m. As I leave the chicken house I clearly hear a bell, striking and lingering on for about half a minute, coming from the direction of the other barn. But, of course, there was no bell there.

"This is going too far," Mrs. Leuthold remarked to her husband. "We've got to do something about this."

She took the chicken-feed pot and placed it again on the stairs from where it had disappeared some days before. Then she tied a nylon string to the pot, with a small bell on the other end; the string she placed inside the corridor leading to the door and almost but not quite closed the door. In this manner the string could be moved freely should anyone pull on it.

The family then ate their breakfast. After ten minutes, they checked on the string. It had been pulled outside by at least a foot and was cut or torn about two inches from the pot. The pot itself stood one step below the one on which Mrs. Leuthold had placed it!

Once in a while the ghost was obliging: that same day, around 8:00 A.M., Elfi, the maid, took a lumber bucket to fetch some wood. As she crossed by the rabbit hutch, lights went on in the cellar, the hayloft and the chicken house. Quickly Elfi put the bucket down to investigate. When she returned to pick it up again, it was gone. It was standing in front of the wood pile, some distance away—where it was needed!

Daughter Elizabeth also had her share of experiences, Leuthold reports:

December 14, 5:30 p.m. Elizabeth is busy upstairs in the house. She hears something hit the ground outside. Immediately she runs downstairs to find the six ornamental pumpkins scattered around the yard, all the way to the pigsty. When she left the house again an hour later, she found that somehow the carpet beater and brush had found their way from inside the house to be hung on the outside of the door!

And so it went. Every day something else moved about. The chicken-feed pot, or the boots, or the milk can. The lights kept going on and off merrily. Something or someone knocks at the door, yet there is never anyone outside. Nobody can knock and run out of sight—the yard between house and barn and the village street can easily be checked for human visitors. The milk cart disappears and reappears. The washroom window is taken off its hinges and thrown on the floor. The manure rake moves from the front of the barn to the inside of the washroom. The pigsty gate is opened by unseen hands and the pigs promenade around the chicken house. Lights keep going on and off. Even Christmas did not halt the goings-on.

December 24, 3 p.m. My cousin Ernest Gautschi and I are talking in the stables, when suddenly the light goes on—in the middle of the afternoon. 5:30 P.M. I enter the barn to give the cows their hay, when I notice the lights go on by themselves in the old barn. I go back immediately and find the dog howling pitifully at the light switch! I went on to the house to see if anyone was outside, but nobody left even for a moment. My son, Paul, returns with me to the barn. It was he who had left the dog tied up outside half an hour earlier. Now he is tied up inside the barn, and the barn door is locked tight. How did the dog get inside?

Evidently, the poltergeist had now begun to turn his attentions towards the dog.

December 25, 7:30 a.m. The dog is found locked into the stables. Yet, half an hour ago Elfi left him roaming freely outside after giving him his food.

February 2, 5 a.m. I went to the stables and the dog, which slept in the barn, followed me into the stables. He became noisy and one of the calves seemed to get frightened, so I said to the dog, "Go outside at once!" As I am turning around to open the door back into the barn for him to let him out, I see him already outside the barn. Who opened the door for him? I didn't.

The children also got their attention from the obnoxious spirit. That same day, February 2, Leuthold reported in his diary:

February 2, 6:15 p.m. The three sleds, which normally are stacked in the corner of the barn, are found across the manure trough.

The Leutholds took their unseen "visitor" in stride, always hoping it would go away as it had come. Their spiritualist neighbor insisted that "Leo the Ghost," as they had dubbed it, was somehow connected with Elfi, a notion the Leutholds rejected instantly, since they were in an excellent position to vouch for the maid's honesty and non-involvement. The phenomena continued unabated, however.

March 14, 6 a.m. The window in the dining room is taken from its hinges and found in a flower pot in front of the house. 7:30 A.M. My slipper disappears from the barn and reappears in another part of the stables beneath a shoe shelf.

March 29, 7:30 a.m. The dog lies in the yard. A few minutes later he is locked into the old stables. Everybody in the house is questioned and accounted for. Nobody could have done it. 7 P.M. Elfi and I empty the skimmed milk into four pails which we then place next to the door to the pigsty. At 9 P.M. we find the four pails directly in front of the door.

Elfi got married in April and presumably her "uncommitted" vital energies were no longer free to be used in poltergeist activities. But the Maschwanden ghost did not obey the standard rules laid down by psychic researchers. The disturbances went on, Elfi or no Elfi.

August 9, morning. As I clean my boots, I find below the inner sole a small tie pin which I had missed for three months.

August 10, 5:30 p.m. A pitchfork is left stuck in a bag of mineral salt. It took two men to pull it out. Half an hour before the same fork was still in the barn.

August 19, 4:45 a.m. Angelo, the Italian worker, misses one of his boots. He finds it 3 yards distant inside the barn and a heavy pitchfork on top of it.

Similar events took place for another few weeks, then it gradually became quiet again around the Leuthold farm.

I looked around the house, the stables, the barn. I talked to all members of the family, except the Italian, who had only shared their lives briefly, and Elfi, who had left long ago for wedded bliss.

I asked, "Did anyone die violently in the house?"

Paul Leuthold, Sr., thought for a moment. "About ten years ago we had an Italian working for us. His pride was a motorcycle, but he could not afford insurance. One day he decided to return to Italy with some friends for a vacation. To get an early start, they would leave around three in the morning. The night before my mother warned him, 'Be careful, and don't get home with your head under your arm.' He replied, shrugging, 'If I am dead, it doesn't matter either.'

"He started an hour late the next morning. When he got to the St. Gotthard, his motorcycle started to kick up. The other fellows went on ahead and promised to wait for him at the height of the mountain. He went to a garage and had his machine fixed, determined not to miss his colleagues. He would have been better off had he stayed behind, for a short time later a piece of rock fell down onto the road and killed him instantly."

"And you think it may be his ghost that is causing all this?" I asked.

"No, I don't," Leuthold assured me. "I'm only wondering who is doing it."

I gathered that Leuthold had some suspicions about his neighbors. Could an active spiritualist "cause" such phenomena to happen? Not a spiritualist, I assured him, but maybe a black magician.

Nobody had died violently in the house or farm. But then, an older house of which we know nothing may have stood on the spot. The Leuthold children are now beyond the age of puberty where their untapped energies might have contributed the power to make the phenomena occur.

My guess is that both Elfi and the children supplied that energy. When Elfi left, and only the children were available, the phenomena gradually faded away. They have not returned since. They are not likely to, unless, of course, another unwitting supplier of such energy moves into the house. The discarnate personality behind the disturbances may still be lurking about, untamed, waiting for another chance. If this happens, Mr. Leuthold can bet that the Ghost Hunter will be on hand, too!

THE GHOSTS AT
JUMEL MANSION

HARDLY HAD WE RETURNED to our home in New York, when my friend Elizabeth Byrd telephoned to inquire if I had gotten that grave opened yet.

I hadn't, but I should really let you in at the beginning. You see, it all started with an article in the *New York Journal-American* on January 11, 1964, by Joan Hanauer, in which the ghostly goings on at Jumel Mansion, New York, were brought to public attention.

> Youngsters on a field trip from P.S. 164, Edgecombe Avenue and 164th Street, say a tall, gray-haired, elderly woman stepped out onto the balcony last Wednesday and told them to be quiet.
>
> The description fits Mme. Jumel.
>
> Could it have happened?
>
> Mrs. Emma Bingay Campbell, curator of the Mansion at 160th Street and Edgecombe, says no.
>
> "I don't believe in ghosts," she said, "but it was very strange. The house was locked and empty.
>
> "We know that. There could not have been a woman there.

"But several of the children insist they saw and heard her.

"It was shortly before 11 A.M., opening time for the house which dates back to 1765.

"When I came over to the children to explain they must wait for John Duffy, the second gardener, to unlock the doors at 11," Mrs. Campbell said, "one of the girls wanted to know why the tall woman who had come out on the balcony to reprimand them for boisterousness couldn't let them in.

"There couldn't have been any such woman—or anyone else—in the house.

"The woman the children described resembled Mme. Jumel, who some thought murdered her husband in the house in 1832, then married Aaron Burr the following year.

"But the children couldn't know that, or what she looked like.

"They also couldn't know that the balcony on which the apparition appeared separated Mme. Jumel's and Burr's bedrooms."

Elizabeth Byrd was then working on a story about Manhattan ghosts for a magazine and we decided to follow up this case together. First we contacted the public-school authorities and obtained permission to talk to the children. The school is for black children, who turned out to be bright, clever, or not so clever, just as other children of their age group might be anywhere else. The teacher assembled the entire group she had originally taken to the Jumel Mansion and we questioned them, separately and together. Their story was unchanged. The woman appeared on the balcony, suddenly, and she told them to be quiet.

"How did she disappear?" I wanted to know.

One youngster thought for a moment, then said hesitantly, "She sort of glided back into the house."

"Did you see the balcony doors open?" I asked the girl.

"No, sir," she replied firmly.

"Then did she glide through the door?"

"She did."

The dress they described the ghost as wearing does exist—but it is put away carefully upstairs in the Mansion and was not on display, nor is this common knowledge, especially among eleven-year-old schoolgirls.

There was a cooking class in progress when we arrived and the girls cheerfully offered us samples of their art. We declined for the moment, and went on to see the Curator of the Mansion, Mrs. Campbell. This energetic lady takes care of the Mansion for the Daughters of the American Revolution in whose charge the City of New York had placed the museum.

"Is this the first report of a haunting here?" I wanted to know.

Mrs. Campbell shook her head. "Here," she said, and took down from one of the shelves in her office a heavy book. "William Henry Shelton's work, *The Jumel Mansion,* pages two hundred and seven and two hundred and eight report earlier ghosts observed here."

"Have you ever seen or heard anything?"

"No, not yet, but others have. There was that German nurse who lived here in eighteen sixty-five—she heard strange noises even then. Footsteps have been heard by many visitors here when there was no one about. The ghost of Mme. Jumel appeared to a retired guard at the door of this room."

"How would you like me to investigate the matter?" I offered, and a date was set immediately. First, however, I thought it wise to familiarize myself with the physical layout of the historic house. I was immediately struck by its imposing appearance. John Kent Tilton wrote:

Located on the highest elevation of Manhattan is one of the most famous old historic houses in the nation, the Morris-Jumel Mansion. The locality was originally called Harlem Heights by the Dutch in the days of New Amsterdam and was then changed to Mount Morris during the English ownership, before receiving the present name of Washington Heights.

The plot of land upon which the old mansion is situated was originally deeded in 1700 to a Dutch farmer named Jan Kiersen, from part of the "half morgen of land of the common woods" of New Harlem.

Lieutenant Colonel Roger Morris purchased the estate in 1765. The new owner was born in England in 1728 and came to America at the age of eighteen with a commission of Captaincy in the British army.

It was here that the Morris family, with their four children, spent their summers, living the domestic life typical of a British squire and family until the outbreak of the Revolution.

Colonel Morris fled to England at the beginning of hostilities, where he remained for two and one-half years.

As early in the war as August, 1776, Mount Morris was taken over by the American troops and General Heath and staff were quartered there. After the disastrous Battle of Long Island, General Washington retreated to Harlem Heights and made the place his headquarters. After Washington decided to abandon this location, the British moved in and the Morris Mansion housed General Sir Henry Clinton and his officers and, at intervals, the Hessians, during the seven years the British occupied New York.

During the following quarter of a century it was sold and resold several times and witnessed many changes in its varied career. Renamed Calumet Hall, it served for a time as a Tavern and was a stopping place for the stage coaches en route to Albany. It was the home of an unknown farmer when President Washington paid a visit to his old headquarters and entertained at dinner, among others, his cabinet members, John Adams, Alexander Hamilton, Henry Knox and their wives.

The locality was one that Stephen Jumel with his sprightly and ambitious wife delighted driving out to on a summer's day from their home on Whitehall Street. Mme. Jumel became entranced with the nearby old Morris Mansion and persuaded her husband to purchase it for their home in 1810, for the sum of $10,000, which included 35 acres of land still remaining of the original tract.

The old house was fast falling into decay when Mme. Jumel energetically went about renovating and refurnishing it and when completed it was one of the most beautiful homes in the country. The Jumels restored the mansion in the style of the early nineteenth century, when the Federal influence was in fashion.

Mme. Jumel first married, some say by trickery, the rich Frenchman, Stephen Jumel. He had at one time owned a large plantation in Santo Domingo from whence he was obliged to flee at the time of the insurrection. Arriving in the United States a comparatively poor man, he soon amassed a new fortune as a wine merchant and at his death in 1832, his wife became one of the richest women in America. A year later she married Aaron Burr, former Vice President of the United States. This second marriage, however, was of short duration and ended in divorce. Mme. Jumel died at the age of 93 in 1865.

The Morris-Jumel Mansion is of the Mid-Georgian

period of architecture. The front façade had four columns, two stories in height, with a pediment at the top.

The exterior is painted white. One of the post-colonial features added by the Jumels is the imposing front entrance doorway, with flanking sidelights and elliptical fanlight.

In the interior, the wide Central Hall with arches, is furnished with late 18th and early 19th century pieces. At the left of the entrance is the Small Parlor or Tea Room where the marriage ceremony of the Widow Jumel and Aaron Burr was performed in 1833 when the bride was fifty-eight and the groom twenty years her senior.

Across the hall is the stately Georgian dining room where many persons of fame assembled for elaborate dinner parties.

At the rear of the hall is the large octagonal drawing room.

The broad stairway leads to the spacious hall on the upper floor which is furnished with personal belongings of the Jumels. There is a group portrait of Mme. Jumel and the young son and daughter of her adopted daughter, Mary Eliza, who married Nelson Chase.

The northwest bedroom contains furniture owned by the Jumels, including a carved four-poster bed.

In the old days the rooms on the third floor were probably used as extra guest chambers, since the servants' quarters were then located in the basement with the kitchen.

On January 19, 1964, a small group of people assembled in Betsy Jumel's old sitting room upstairs. Present were a few members of the New York Historical Society and the Daughters of the American Revolution, *Journal-American* writer Nat Adams, and a late-comer, Harry Altschuler of the *World-Telegram*. I was accompanied by Ethel Meyers, who had not been told where we were going that winter afternoon, and Jessyca Russell Gaver, who was serving as my secretary and doing a magazine article on our work at the same time.

We had barely arrived when Ethel went in and out of the Jumel bedroom, as if someone were forcing her to do so. As she approached the room across the hall, her shoulder sagged and one arm hung loose as if her side had been injured!

"I feel funny on my left side," Ethel finally said, and her voice had already taken on some of the coloring of someone else's voice.

We went back to the bedroom which is normally closed to the public. One side is occupied by a huge carved four-poster, once the property of Napoleon I, and there are small chairs of the period in various spots throughout the room. In one corner, there is a large mirror.

"The issue is confused," Ethel said, and sounded confused herself. "There is more than one disturbed person here. I almost feel as though three people were involved. There has been sickness and a change of heart. Someone got a raw deal."

Suddenly, Ethel turned to one of the men who had sat down on Napoleon's bed. "Someone wants you to get up from that bed," she said, and evinced difficulty in speaking. As if bitten by a tarantula, the young man shot up from the bed. No ghost was going to goose *him*.

Ethel again struggled to her feet, despite my restraining touch on her arm. "I've got to go back to that other room again," she mumbled, and off she went, with me trailing after her. She walked almost as if she were being taken over by an outside force. In front of the picture of Mme. Jumel, she suddenly fell to her knees.

"I never can go forward here . . . I fall whenever I'm near there." She pointed at the large picture above her, and almost shouted, "My name isn't on that picture. I want my name there!"

Mrs. Campbell, the Curator, took me aside in agitation. "That's very strange she should say that," she remarked. "You see, her name really used to be on that picture a long time ago. But that picture wasn't in this spot when Betsy Jumel was alive."

I thanked her and led Ethel Meyers back to her chair in the other room.

"Henry . . . and a Johann . . . around here . . . ," she mumbled as she started to go into a deep trance. Hoarse sounds emanated from her lips. At first they were unintelligible. Gradually I was able to make them out. Halfway into trance, she moved over to the bed and lay down on it. I placed my chair next to her head. The others strained to hear and there was an eerie silence about the room, interrupted only by the soft words of the entranced medium.

"You think me dead . . ." a harsh, male voice now said.

"No, I've come to talk to you, to help you," I replied.

"Go away," the ghostly voice said, "go away!"

"Are you a man or woman?" I asked.

A bitter laughter was the reply.

"Man . . . ha!" the voice finally said.

"What is your name?"

"Everybody knows who I am."

"I don't. What is your name?" I repeated.

"Let me sleep."

"Is anything troubling you?"

There was a moment of silence, then the voice was a bit softer. "Who are *you*?"

"I'm a friend, come to help you."

"Nobody talks to me. They think I'm dead."

"What exactly happened to you?"

"They took me away," the voice said in plaintive tones. "I am not dead yet. Why did they take me away?"

Now the body of the medium shook as if in great agitation,

while I spoke soothing words to calm the atmosphere. Suddenly, the ghost speaking through the medium was gone, and in his place was the crisp, matter-of-fact voice of Albert, Ethel's control. I asked Albert to tell us through the entranced medium who the ghost was.

"I don't hear a name, but I see a sturdy body and round face. He complains he was pronounced dead when he in fact wasn't. I believe he is the owner of the house and it bears his name. There are many jealousies in this house. There is an artist who is also under suspicion."

"Is there a woman here?"

"One thwarted of what she desired and who wants to throw herself out the window."

"Why?" I asked.

"Thwarted in love and under suspicion."

Later, I asked Mrs. Campbell about this. She thought for a moment, then confirmed the following facts: A young servant girl, involved with one of the family, tried to commit suicide by jumping out the window.

I questioned Albert further. "Is there a restless woman in this house?"

"That is right. The one in the picture. Her conscience disturbs her."

"About what?"

The medium now grabbed her side, as if in pain. "I am being threatened," Albert said now, "I feel the revelation would disturb."

"But how can I release her unless I know what is holding her here?"

"It has to do with the death of her husband. That he was strangled in his coffin."

I tried to question him further, but he cut us short. The medium had to be released now.

Soon, Ethel Meyers was back to her own self. She remembered

very little of the trance, but her impressions of a clairvoyant nature continued for a while. I queried her about the person on the bed.

"I get the initial J," she replied and rubbed her side.

I turned to Mrs. Campbell. "What about the story of Mme. Jumel's guilty conscience?"

"Well," the Curator replied, "after her husband's death, she refused to live in this house for some time. She always felt guilty about it."

We were standing in a corner where the medium could not hear us. "Stephen Jumel bled to death from a wound he had gotten in a carriage accident. Mme. Jumel allegedly tore off his bandage and let him die. That much we know."

Mrs. Campbell naturally is a specialist on Betsy Jumel and her life and she knows many intimate details unknown to the general public or even to researchers not particularly interested in the house and its background.

It was five thirty in the afternoon and we left the house, which must be closed for the night after that hour.

The next morning two newspaper accounts appeared. One, fairly accurate, in the *Journal*, and a silly one in the *Telegram*, by a man who stood outside the room of the investigation and heard very little, if anything.

Several weeks went by and my ghost-hunting activities took me all over the country. Then I received a telephone call from Mrs. Campbell.

"Did you know that May twenty-second is the anniversary of Stephen Jumel's death?" I didn't and I wagered her nobody else did, except maybe herself and the late Mr. Jumel. She allowed as to that and suggested we have another go at the case on that date. I have always felt that anniversaries are good times to solve murder cases so I readily agreed.

This time, *The New York Times*, in the person of reporter Grace

Glueck, was invited, and I am indebted to her for the notes she took of the proceedings that warm May afternoon.

Present also were the General Manager of King Features, Frank McLearn; Clark Kinnaird, literary critic of the *Journal;* John Allen and Bob O'Brien of *Reader's Digest;* Emeline Paige, the editor of *The Villager;* writers Elizabeth Byrd and Beverly Balin; Ed Joyce of CBS, and several members of the New York Historical Society, presumably there as observers ready to rewrite history as needed— since the famous Aaron Burr might be involved!

Ethel Meyers was told nothing about the significance of the date, nor had I discussed with her the results of the first séance.

Again we assembled in the upstairs bedroom and Ed Joyce set up his tape recorder in front of Napoleon's bed, while Ethel sat on the bed itself and I next to her on a chair. To my left, the young lady from the *Times* took her seat. All in all there must have been twenty-five anxious persons in the room, straining to hear all that was said and keeping a respectful silence when asked to. Within a few minutes, Ethel was in deep trance, and a male voice spoke through her vocal cords.

"Who are you?" I asked as I usually do when an unknown person comes "through" a medium.

"*Je suis Stephen*" the voice said.

"Do you speak English?"

In answer the medium clutched at her body and groaned, "Doctor! Doctor! Where is the Doctor?"

"What is hurting you?" I asked.

The voice was firm and defiant now. "I'm alive, I'm alive . . . don't take me away."

"Did you have an accident? What happened to you?"

"She tricked me."

"Who tricked you?"

"I can't breathe . . . where is she? She tricked me. Look at her!"

"Don't worry about her," I said, "she's dead."

"But I'm alive!" the entranced voice continued.

"In a sense, you are. But you've also passed over."

"No—they put me in the grave when I was not yet dead."

"How did you get hurt?" I wanted to know.

The ghost gave a bitter snort. "What matter—I'm dead. You said so."

"I didn't say you were 'dead,' " I replied.

The voice became furious again. "She took it, she took it—that woman. She took my life. Go away."

"I'm your friend."

"I haven't any friends . . . that Aaron . . ."

"Aaron? Was he involved in your death?"

"That strumpet . . . hold him! They buried me alive, I tell you."

"When did this happen?"

"It was cold. She made me a fool, a fool!"

"How did she do that?"

"All the time I loved her, she tricked me."

"I want to help you."

"I'm bleeding."

"How did this happen?"

"Pitchfork . . . wagon . . . hay . . ."

"Was it an accident, yes or no?"

"I fell on it."

"You fell on the pitchfork?"

"Look at the blood bath . . . on Napoleon's bed."

"What about that pitchfork?" I insisted.

"There was a boy in the hay, and he pushed me off."

"Did you know this boy?"

"Yes . . . give me *her*. She wanted to be a lady. I saw it. I wasn't so foolish I didn't see it."

"What happened when you got home?"

"She told me I was going to die."

"Did you have a doctor?"

"Yes."

"Wasn't the wound bandaged?"

"They took me out alive. I was a live man he put in the grave. I want to be free from that grave!"

"Do you want me to set you free?"

"God bless you!"

"It is your hatred that keeps you here. You must forgive."

"She did it to me."

I then pleaded with the ghost to join his own family, and let go of his memories. "Do you realize how much time has gone on since? A hundred years!"

"Hundred years!"

The medium, still entranced, buried her head in her hands: "I'm mad!"

"Go from this house and don't return."

"Mary, Mary . . . !"

Mary was the name of Jumel's daughter, a fact not known to the medium at the time.

"Go and join Mary!" I commanded, and asked that Albert, the control, help the unhappy one find the way.

Just as soon as Jumel's ghost had left us, someone else slipped into the medium's body, or so it seemed, for she sat up and peered at us with a suspicious expression: "Who are you?"

"I'm a friend, come to help," I replied.

"I didn't ask for you."

"My name is Holzer and I have come to seek you out. If you have a name worth mentioning, please tell us."

"Get out or I'll call the police! This is my house."

There was real anger now on the medium's entranced face.

I kept asking for identification. Finally, the disdainful lips opened and in cold tones, the voice said, "I am the wife of the Vice President of the United States! Leave my house!"

I checked with Mrs. Campbell and found that Betsy Jumel did so identify herself frequently. On one occasion, driving through crowded New York streets long after her divorce from Aaron Burr, she shouted, "Make way for the wife of the Vice President of the United States!"

"Didn't you marry someone else before that?" I asked. "How did your husband die?"

"Bastard!" A hiss followed.

"You've been dead a hundred years, Madam," I said pleasantly.

"You are made like the billow in the captain's cabin," she replied, somewhat cryptically. Later I checked this out. A sea captain was one of her favorite lovers while married to Jumel.

"Did you murder your husband?" I inquired and drew back a little—just in case.

"You belong in the scullery with my maids," she replied disdainfully, but I repeated the accusation, adding that her husband had claimed she had killed him.

"I will call for help," she countered.

"There is no help. The police are on your trail!" I suggested.

"I am the wife of the Vice President of the United States!"

"I will help you if you tell me what you did. Did you cause his death?"

"The rats that crawl . . . they bit me. Where am I?"

"You're between two worlds. Do you wish to be helped?"

"Where is Joseph?"

"You must leave this house. Your husband has forgiven you. . . ."

"I adored him!"

"Go away, and you will see Stephen Jumel again."

"Only the crest on the carriage! That's all I did. He was a great man."

I had the feeling she wasn't at all keen on Monsieur Jumel. But that happens, even to ghosts.

I finally gave up trying to get her to go and join Jumel and tried another way . . .

"Go and join the Vice President of the United States. He awaits you." To my surprise, this didn't work either.

"He is evil, evil," she said.

Perplexed, I asked, "Whom do you wish to join?"

"Mary."

"Then call out her name and she'll join you and take you with her."

"No crime, no crime."

"You've been forgiven. Mary will take you away from here."

I asked Albert, the control, to come and help us get things moving, but evidently Madame had a change of heart: "This is my house. I'll stay here."

"This is no longer your house. You must go!"

The struggle continued. She called for Christopher, but wouldn't tell me who Christopher was.

"He's the only one I ever trusted," she volunteered, finally.

"It's not too late," I repeated. "You can join your loved ones."

"Good-by."

I called for Albert, who quickly took control. "She's no longer in the right mind," he said, as soon as he had firm control of the medium's vocal cords. "You may have to talk with her again."

"Is she guilty of Jumel's death?"

"Yes. It was arranged."

"Who was the boy who pushed him?"

"A trusty in the house. She told him to."

"What about Stephen Jumel?"

"He is in a better frame of mind."

"Is there anything else we did not bring out? Who is this Christopher she mentioned?"

"A sea captain. She buried him in Providence."

Mrs. Campbell later confirmed the important role the sea captain played in Betsy's life. There was also another man named Brown.

"Did Aaron Burr help bury Jumel?"

"That is true. Burr believed Mme. Jumel had more finances than she actually had."

"What about the doctor who buried him alive? Is his name known?"

"Couldn't stop the bleeding."

"Was Aaron Burr in on the crime?"

"He is very much aware that he is guilty. He still possesses his full mental faculties."

I then asked the control to help keep the peace in the house and to bring the medium back to her own body.

A few minutes later, Ethel Meyers was herself again, remembering nothing of the ordeal she had gone through the past hour, and none the worse for it.

Jumel died in 1832 and, as far as I could find, the first ghostly reports date back to 1865. The question was: Could his remains disclose any clues as to the manner in which he died? If he suffocated in his coffin, would not the position of his bones so indicate?

I queried two physicians who disagreed in the matter. One thought that nothing would be left by now; the other thought it was worth looking into.

I thought so, too. However, my application to reopen the grave of Stephen Jumel, down in the old Catholic cemetery on Mott Street, got the official run-around. The District Attorney's office sent me to Dr. Halpern, the Chief Medical Examiner, who told me it would be of no use to check. When I insisted, I was referred to the church offices of Old St. Patrick's which had nominal jurisdiction over the plot.

Have you ever tried to reopen a grave in the City of New York? It's easier to dig a new one, believe me!

NEW YORK IS FULL
OF GHOSTS

G HOSTS WALK THE STREETS of Manhattan or the parkways of its suburbs with the same regularity as they do in lonely Midwestern farmhouses or English manors. Subways and noisy buses seem to have no ill effect on the specters, who have other business on their etheric minds, it seems.

What is more prosaic than a brownstone house on West Eighty-seventh Street? Several years ago, Mrs. William DeGeldern moved to an old house on that block, along with her husband, their young child, and her mother-in-law, Mrs. Worm. The house was built in 1894 and consists of five floors connected by heavy wooden stairs in the elegant manner of that time. It had been the property of one family until 1925, when it passed into the hands of an artist, followed by a Mr. Judd, who in turn was followed by the DeGeldern family. To the best of the DeGelderns' knowledge, nobody had reported anything unusual about the house before. Mrs. Worm had had some psychic experiences in Europe, but her daughter-in-law was completely untouched by the hand of the Sixth Sense.

On moving in, during the summer of 1962, Mrs. DeGeldern, working busily, had her back towards the entrance door downstairs.

It was twilight, around the end of the afternoon, when she suddenly felt someone watching her. It was that indefinable feeling that you're not alone.

"What did you do?" I asked, as we sat in front of the downstairs fireplace.

"I looked around and I saw a young girl standing up on the staircase leading to the first floor and watching me very seriously. She seemed about sixteen years of age, had blonde hair in braids and wore a blue dress—nothing current, you understand, but something women might have worn in the last century."

"What did you do then?"

"She was standing there, motionless, with her hand on the wooden rail. I got up and walked towards her. But as I got real close to her she just faded away before my eyes."

"Did you ever seen anything, Mrs. Worm?" I asked the elder lady.

"Not see, but I've felt a presence a number of times. And last Christmas, while we were having dinner in the dining room downstairs, I felt a hand on my shoulder, as if someone were trying to get my attention! Many times I feel someone brush by me without talking—still, I can feel the rush of air."

"And you, sir?" I turned to the husband. "Have you ever seen anything unusual?"

"No, nothing," he replied casually, "but I do hear noises—strange noises I cannot readily explain."

The way things are nowadays in New York, the West Side is no place for a young girl ghost, but there you are.

Mrs. Rose Margolies was then living in Florida, but some years earlier she made her home on Snyder Avenue, in Brooklyn. This was a section primarily consisting of small homes. The time had come to have the apartment, which was part of a small house, done over and the landlord was in the process of having Mrs. Margolies' ceiling fixed. But as happens so often, the workmen doing the job left some gaping holes in the ceiling. Mrs. Margolies was rather unhappy and disappointed, especially as the landlord had personally promised her that the job would be done properly. There she sat, contemplating the holes in her living room ceiling.

"Then what happened?" I asked the peppery lady, who remembers the incident well.

"Towards evening I heard a knock on the door. I said come in, and heard nothing at first. But then I heard my landlord's voice—only it sounded odd, as if he were far, far away. I got up to let him in, but before I reached the door I saw a black shadow come right through it—a shadow in the shape of a man. It lasted only a second, then I had reached the door and opened it. My landlord walked in. He told me the men would return the next morning to finish the ceiling."

"Was there anything unusual about that?" I inquired.

"There was. Again he seemed a million miles away from me. After he left, I sat there thinking about it. Later that evening the superintendent came to call on me. He had sad news. The landlord had had a stroke that afternoon and had died instantly."

In 1964, I had the pleasure of meeting a Miss Boyd down on Charles Street in the Greenwich Village section of Manhattan. Miss Boyd was a ghost. But let me explain. Barrie Gaunt was an English designer of fashions and an actor but recently arrived in our midst. Although he was very English, he knew nothing about ghosts. He moved into a small ground-floor apartment on Charles Street a few weeks before and ghosts were the farthest thing from his mind.

Our mutual friend, writer Elizabeth Byrd, tipped me off that all was not as it should be with the old house and asked if I would please have a go at it.

It was Halloween night, 1964, when Catherine and I descended on the haunted apartment in the company of Sybil Leek, the English lady-witch, who also was a good trance medium. The fire was licking the logs in the fireplace, the wind was howling outside in the back yard, and the setting could not have been more appropriate for a ghost hunt if Cecil B. DeMille had arranged it.

"The first time I heard about the place being haunted was in mid-September," Elizabeth Byrd explained, "when Barrie Gaunt had a house guest visiting here. She was a Mexican lady named Adriana de Sola and had come to stay here for ten days. But on the third or fourth night she was awakened in bed by a rather violent push on her arm. At the same time she felt herself compelled to burst into tears, and she wept profusely, although she is not given to weeping at all. She felt an enormous grief here.

"Somebody had been badly hurt here and she felt it. A few nights later, she was awakened again by a push as if someone were trying to rouse her. Again, she had to cry uncontrollably.

"However, she decided not to tell her host about it. He had been here only a short time and she did not wish to upset him."

"What about you, Barrie?" I asked. "When did you notice anything unusual about your place?"

Barrie Gaunt was a quiet man in his middle or late twenties, and not easily given to hysterics.

"I arrived home around one o'clock one night and I heard this crying—my friend Miss De Sola weeping away. Since she left, things have happened to me also. One night I could not sleep. I woke up sure there was someone else in the place watching me. I saw a peculiar sort of mist, but I shrugged it off and went back to sleep. Another time I felt sure there was a presence in the room. I discussed it with Miss Byrd and she finally told me about Adriana's experiences here."

"Something happened just a few hours ago, didn't it?" I

inquired. Elizabeth Byrd had told me we should come right away.

"Last night I woke up at ten to four, sure I was not alone. Up to the time I came here, I had always slept well without waking up in the middle of the night. But lately I can't get any sleep here."

Neither Barrie Gaunt nor Elizabeth Byrd had any knowledge of the background of the house. Barrie had gotten the apartment from a friend, and made no inquiries whatever.

I then asked Sybil Leek, who had come dressed in her witches' best, complete with purple stockings and cape, to sit on the bed near the spot where Barrie had seen the misty cloud.

"Somebody's kept chickens here," Sybil said, gradually slipping into trance.

"There is a woman here with us all the time," she added with a faltering voice not quite her own any longer. "Her name's Boyd! B-o-y-d."

I like a medium who spells things out for you. But then Sybil is very British.

"Chickens, chickens—I don't know why there are these chickens here."

"What does this Miss Boyd look like?"

"She is wearing a cotton pink dress, high neck, long sleeves."

"What does she want?"

"She wants to be here."

"Why?"

"Because she lived here. Her home. Died here. Not in this room, though. There are chickens in this room. She is looking for something. Something she lost here. I think a Spanish girl did not like her. There was some foreign person here with her. Austa. A-us-ta. Ay-u-sta."

I asked Miss Boyd not to disturb the living with her pushes and tears, then turned to Sybil Leek again and asked what Miss Boyd was looking for in this room.

"It's a paper," Sybil, entranced, replied after a moment's hesitation. "It's got something to do with this house."

"How long ago did all this happen?"

"Eighteen eighty-six."

"Did she own this house?"

"No."

"Who owned the house?"

"A-NU-SSI. A-nu-ssi."

The medium seemed to repeat a name she was hearing.

I asked, "Did this person have a first name?"

"She called him Mr. Anussi, she says," the medium replied.

"Why is she so unhappy?"

"Wants the paper."

"Go in peace," I said, "never to be drawn back here by your unhappy memories. Your loved ones await you on the Other Side of the Veil. Go in peace."

Confident that we had dispatched Miss Boyd to the nether world, we brought Sybil Leek out of trance and went out into the cold October night, as All Hallow's Eve faded into the mist of morning.

But Miss Boyd wasn't going to be satisfied that quickly. A few nights later, Barrie awakened when he saw in the middle of the room a rainbow-like light for which there was no explanation.

About that time, a call from radio station WINS, asking me if I knew of any good haunt on which they could come along with me, brought back Barrie Gaunt's apartment. Again I summoned Sybil Leek—by telephone, not magic—and we assembled at the Charles Street place. By we, I mean Elizabeth Byrd, Mr. Gaunt, Sybil and Westinghouse's Squire Rushnell of Boston, Stan Bernard and Mrs. Bernard, Paul Rohrer, M.C. and producer of "Contact" and myself. It was a Sunday night in December, 1964, and again a fire was burning lustily in the old fireplace.

I questioned Barrie Gaunt about the misty shape he had

observed in the apartment. He admitted that he had experienced a
similar misty cloud when he was fourteen years old, at the very
moment when his father died.

Between these two sessions Elizabeth Byrd had gone down to
the Hall of Records, the place where the City of New York keeps the
records of all buildings and parcels of land within its boundaries.
After going through several volumes of material along the lines suggested by me, she found that the house on Charles Street had
indeed belonged to the Boyd family for many years! In 1827 Samuel
Boyd appears as the owner of the parcel of land on which the house
stands, in 1850 John T. Boyd is named, and in 1861 the house
passed into the hands of the latter's heirs.

"We did not get a first name for Miss Boyd in the séance,"
Elizabeth Byrd said, "but there is no doubt that the house was in the
Boyd family in the year mentioned, eighteen eighty-six, and in those
days many people kept chickens in their back yard. In eighteen
eighty-six, a lawyer named William Boyd was living here. The
records bear this out. A Mary Boyd was living right next door. As far
as the landlord Anussi is concerned, there was a Moeslin [pro-
nounced Muslin] connected with this house. He and his wife Emma
rented it to Mary Boyd in eighteen eighty-six."

"Fascinating," said Sybil, to whom all this was, of course, news.

Since our last séance, Barrie had had some more unusual experiences. Several times when he and Miss Byrd were talking on the
telephone, both distinctly heard a deep breathing sound above
Barrie Gaunt's voice, as if another person were breathing close to
him. "I heard heavy breathing," Elizabeth confirmed, "but I simply
thought Barrie was coming down with a cold." He wasn't though.

It was time to put Sybil into trance, to see what Miss Boyd had
to say to us today.

Within a few moments, Sybil's own personality was gone, and,
in her stead, I was speaking to a stranger.

"Go away!" the strange voice said. "This is my house!"

"What is your name?"

"Boyd. Miss Boyd."

"Your first name?"

"Mary Elizabeth Boyd." This without a moment's hesitation.

"How can we help you?"

The voice was almost crying. "Find the paper. My house."

"Who wrote the paper?"

"My father."

"What is your father's name?"

"Billy. Billy Boyd."

"Where was the paper left?"

"I don't know! Musli took the house. Did not like us. Father owed him a lot of money."

"Where did Musli live?"

"Here."

"What did he do for a living?"

"He bought things—houses, land."

"Your father's profession?"

"Lot of papers. Business."

"Where was his office?"

"In this street. Number 37."

Next door, I thought. How convenient! But people did have their offices near their homes, even then, at times.

"Father signed. They don't need my house . . ."

"Did you have any sisters or brothers?"

"They're all dead. Jane—Jane died."

"Was she married?"

"Yes."

"Her husband's name?"

"Stephen Muslin."

"Then he was related to you?"

"My house," she cried, and I calmed her down.

"Then the man who took your house was your brother-in-law. What was his profession?"

"Bought land."

"Who is the Spanish woman you talked about?"

Derisive laughter. "Stayed here."

"Who brought her here?"

"Musli."

"Who was she?"

"A friend."

"Her name?"

"Alexi."

"What profession did she have?"

Derisive laughter was my answer. Words were not needed.

"If we found the paper, what would you do?"

"Live here."

I then explained that much time had gone by, that the papers had been found and the house was again rightfully hers. I did this to rest her distorted mind. "Go and join your father, who is waiting for you," I suggested. "Eighty years have gone by."

I then brought Sybil Leek out of trance. She was fine, albeit a bit tired. Eighty years can be a long journey. She remembered nothing.

Immediately, I pointed out a small but significant factor: In discussing her research, Elizabeth Byrd had mentioned only a *Mary Boyd*. Yet, in trance, Miss Boyd, speaking through Sybil Leek, identified herself as *Mary Elizabeth Boyd*. The records, we discovered, had her down as *Mary E. Boyd*. But neither Sybil nor, for that matter, I, had any way of knowing this prior to the second séance!

"William Boyd lived on Block 611—that is this house," Elizabeth Byrd said, "and Mary Boyd had Number 612, next door! So she must have been moved out of here sometime around eighteen eighty-six—her wanting to get back into her father's house makes sense."

Then she added, "About that Spanish lady—" and I suddenly remembered the intruder the ghost described with a sneer. "There is a court case on record between William Boyd and one Isabella Haviland. Could she be that woman? At any rate, in eighteen eighty-seven, Isabella was in firm possession of this house. This is a matter of record."

When we left the house, we recommended Miss Boyd to Barrie Gaunt, but I had a feeling this was merely a polite gesture. Miss Boyd had left her chickens far behind and had joined her father, Billy, in the world where land grants mean very little.

WHAT DOES IT ALL MEAN?

S INCE YOU ARE READING this epilogue, you have come a long way to this point—all the way from the front of the book. What does it all mean, this account of true experiences of many people very much like yourself, and some not at all like yourself?

I am convinced it means that there is, indeed, another world where life continues to function on a mental basis. I am convinced there is evidence that warrants scientific acceptance of a nonphysical component in human personality, one that transcends the grave.

If I can make you wonder about these tenets, I have done my job. Not on faith, on belief, or because it is the thing to do—but because you accept my evidence as compelling, and it does something to you, and for you. It changes your perspective. Life is everlasting. Moral values continue beyond physical death. The life of all human beings, and all animals, and all plants must be respected. Our deeds do not die with us. We are always aware of them, for better or worse. Why not, then, make this sum total of our physical sojourn on earth as good, as moral, as beautiful as we are able to? If there is one thing you can actually take with you, it is *that*.

Where do I fit in?

If the Boys Upstairs will have it, I will bring the good word to all who wish to listen and judge for themselves. To tell a good story and let the facts speak for themselves is far more effective than the most hard-hitting sales technique.

The mass media, books, newspapers, television and radio are my tools.

If you have an item to contribute to my files, by all means write to me.

If you're in trouble with the Unseen, let me know. Perhaps I can help you.

Remember also, there is only a short distance from Here to There.

HANS HOLZER

ro|''